MIRAGE-LAND

WILBUR S. SHEPPERSON SERIES IN HISTORY AND HUMANITIES

MIRAGE-LAND

IMAGES OF NEVADA

BY WILBUR S. SHEPPERSON

With Ann Harvey   Foreword by Ann Ronald

University of Nevada Press   Reno / Las Vegas / London

Wilbur S. Shepperson Series in History
and Humanities No. 32 (formerly Nevada Studies in
History and Political Science)
Series Editor: Jerome E. Edwards

 This book was funded in part by a generous
grant from the Nevada Humanities Committee, an affiliate of the National Endowment
for the Humanities.

The paper used in this book meets the requirements of
American National Standard for Information Sciences—
Permanence of Paper for Printed Library Materials, ANSI
Z39.48-1984. The binding is sewn for strength and dura-
bility.

Library of Congress Cataloging-in-Publication Data
Shepperson, Wilbur S. (Wilbur Stanley)
Mirage-land : images of Nevada / by Wilbur S. Shepperson
with Ann Harvey ; foreword by Ann Ronald.
p.   cm.—(Wilbur S. Shepperson series in history and
humanities ; no. 32)
Includes bibliographical references and index.
ISBN 0-87417-191-1 (alk. paper)
1. Nevada—Description and travel.   I. Harvey, Ann, 1951–
II. Title.   III. Series.
F841.S54 1992
979.3—dc20   91-34066 CIP

To Peg
The golden key for almost fifty years
and to Clare and Chelsea

CONTENTS

FOREWORD

Idah Meacham Strobridge, often called "Nevada's first woman of letters" because she was the state's first female who consciously wrote for the press, published a 1904 collection of vignettes called *In Miners' Mirage-Land*. In its pages she set a tone for writers who were to describe the paradoxical reaches of her state. In its title she pointed out what images of Nevada so frequently suggest—a "mirage-land," a place where nothing is quite what it seems.

Wilbur S. Shepperson's examination of such mirages—imaginary, literary, historical, real—is the subject of his latest study, *Mirage-Land: Images of Nevada*. In the pages of this book the reader will discover ways in which a variety of men and women have envisioned the Silver State, as well as ways they have communicated their visions to others. The reader also will find Shepperson's shrewd assessment of how such images of Nevada have influenced perceptions and skewed interpretations of the state.

Strobridge opened *In Miners' Mirage-Land* with a sentence which defines the mirage as "that Lorelei of the Desert." A paragraph later she alluded again to the "Siren of the Dry Lakes" and observed that many poor travelers have been "led far astray by following the ever-calling, ever-retreating enchantress." Then she summed up her introductory words by envisioning the mirage as "a tantalizing glimpse of Paradise in the great awful desolation of those Desert days."

With this paradoxical expression of emptiness and promise, Strobridge both suggested the puzzle and expressed the analogy that

Shepperson finds characteristic of the multifarious images of Nevada. As he explains, the aridity and the relative absence of human landmarks have always been juxtaposed against such colorful magnets as minerals and tourism. And observers have always been quick to point out the irony of a barren land with an entrepreneurial facade. Because of this perceived tension between desert and dream, the language of the state's image makers has oscillated from the illusive to the real and back again. Strobridge said as much when she testified to the silence of the desert and then spoke of the transforming power of the mirage. In *Mirage-Land: Images of Nevada*, Shepperson brings forth the voices which break that silence, the words of men and women who for a hundred and fifty years have articulated the language of the Nevada mirage.

By nature and by training, a historian looks at trends from a chronological perspective. Thus *Mirage-Land* begins with the first explorers, surveyors, and pioneers who trekked back and forth across the Great Basin. Its pages then turn to the miners whose claims pockmarked the terrain and whose exploitations brought infamy to a brand-new state. "Nevada coin thy golden crags," wrote Emerson in his "Boston Hymn." Nevadans and outsiders alike did just that.

Booms and busts fluctuated, as did Nevada's population. Emigrants came; some stayed, some left, and many wrote home about their experiences. Agriculture, irrigation, and water diversion experiments were tested at both ends of the state—the north's Newlands Project and the south's more spectacular success, Hoover Dam—while reporters broadcast the results. Meanwhile, long after the mining camps began to disappear, a reputation for instant gratification and overnight success hung on. Nevada became a twentieth-century home for prize fights, for gambling, for divorces, for glitz and glamour and get-rich-quick fun. Reno blossomed. Then Las Vegas took over where Reno stopped, attracting millions of visitors who now expand and elaborate and stretch the mirage.

Shepperson explains the process of mirage building by introducing the reader to details from a variety of sources—journals, diaries, old newspapers, government reports, essays, magazines, novels, and even chamber of commerce promotional brochures. The well-known accents of John C. Frémont and Mark Twain and Dan De Quille mingle with such little-known voices as those of Louise M. Palmer

and Henry T. Williams and George Wharton James. Some sound
derogatory, like the storyteller who wrote that "no portion of the
earth is more lacquered with paltry, unimportant ugliness," or the
Idaho legislator who called Las Vegas the "cesspool of the world."
Others offered kinder assessments—seeing in Nevada a "wild, majestic stormy beauty" and describing Reno as "a full-blown desert flower
brilliant as a poppy." So mixed were the assessments that even the
poets made antithetical observations.

> The Goddess of Gold flew o'er the earth
> And pitied the desert bare;
> A kiss she pressed on the desert's breast
> And the wealth of a world was there!

Shepperson gives the reader more than a string of quotations
about a pitiful desert kissed with the wealth of the world, however. He
also interprets the ways in which the voices of the mirage have been
swayed by history and hopes. His analysis of Nevada images from the
decades between the two world wars, for example, is both perceptive
and thought-provoking. The fact that those twentieth-century images
were dominated by a consumer culture and a pragmatic present leads
him to conclude, "Rather than developing a traditional mythology and
an organized will, the state became iconoclastic and singularly individualistic." Yet self-aggrandizement did not lead to self-destruction.
As Shepperson metaphorically sums up in the last line of Chapter V,
the result was quite the opposite. With the characteristic optimism of
the entrepreneur, "Nevada found itself 'on a roll'."

So the author of a book about the images of Nevada can, himself,
use the language of mirage-land. In so doing, he reveals just one of the
many reasons why he is the appropriate man to conduct this study.

Wilbur Shepperson knows the state better than most. He
moved to Reno in 1951 as an assistant professor of history
at the university. With a B.S. from Northeast Missouri State College, an M.A. from the University of Denver, and a brand-new Ph.D.
from Western Reserve University, he was ready to pursue an academic
career in Nevada, a professional commitment that has lasted more
than forty years. He brought with him a profound interest in the ways
in which newcomers have responded to the American scene.

During his first decade in Reno he published two books—*British-Emigration to North America* (University of Minnesota Press, 1957) and *Samuel Roberts: A Welsh Colonizer in Civil War Tennessee* (University of Tennessee Press, 1961). He also produced two monographs for the fledgling University of Nevada Press—*The Promotion of British Emigration by Agents for American Lands, 1840–1860* (1954) and *Six Who Returned: America Viewed by British Repatriates* (1961). The former, the first publication to bear the imprint of a press that was still to be formally founded, actually was printed with history department funds. The latter was brought out the year the press officially came into existence.

After these more global studies Shepperson moved closer to the Nevada landscape, beginning to fuse his findings about emigrants' perceptions with his growing attachment to his adopted state. In 1966 he published *Retreat to Nevada: A Socialist Colony of World War I.* Four years later, *Restless Strangers: Nevada's Immigrants and Their Interpreters* appeared. Each was a direct result of the author's new discoveries about what outsiders had said.

To list all of Shepperson's reviews, articles, monographs, and books on this subject and on others would require pages. What is important here is not to itemize his bibliography but to indicate instead the direction in which his mind was moving. Quite clearly he was beginning to amass a quantity of materials written by people about their Nevada experiences. A sabbatical leave in 1963–64, a leave of absence in 1966, and another year as a Fulbright scholar at the University of Liverpool not only enabled him to do research both locally and abroad, but gave him opportunities to find diverse firsthand sources.[1] When Shepperson was unable to incorporate every detail of those materials in *Retreat to Nevada* and *Restless Strangers*, he began thinking of other ways to capitalize on his notes.

Meanwhile, he found himself playing an increasingly important role in the intellectual life of the state. He served as chair of the history department at the university. After working hard to help establish

1. Some of Shepperson's notes were taken in the days before copy machines and word processors, and several of his transcriptions—twenty years later—are difficult to decipher. As a result, documentation for *Mirage-Land: Images of Nevada* may occasionally be incomplete, even though the author and the University of Nevada Press would have liked to extend full credit to those quoted in the pages of this book.

the University of Nevada Press, he joined the editorial board and founded the History and Political Science Series that recently was re-named in his honor. He worked with the Nevada Historical Society, as a member both of its editorial board and its board of trustees.[2] Along with Robert Whittemore and Laurance Hyde he helped create the Nevada Humanities Committee, and in 1990 he reported that he had not missed an official committee meeting since 1971.

With a firm commitment to the land grant mission that weds effective teaching with quality research and dedicated public service, Shepperson also became a role model for faculty and community leaders throughout the state. Friends and colleagues have long recog-nized the scope of his work. For nearly a decade he has held the Grace A. Griffen endowed chair at the University of Nevada, Reno. In 1991, a further honor was bestowed when he was elected to the Nevada Writers Hall of Fame. Taken together, these diverse accom-plishments suggest what is perhaps Wilbur Shepperson's most signifi-cant achievement.

John Irsfeld, of the University of Nevada, Las Vegas, says that Shepperson's "greatest contribution to our time and place has been in his capacity as a relentless unifying agent in a state historically split." Certainly it is Shepperson who so clearly has perceived the state as a single entity—north and south, urban and rural, cowboy and cul-ture, gold and glitz. Because of his own commitment to statewide unity, and because he articulates this belief as the operative principle for every board and committee on which he serves, he has been most influential in bringing together disparate people and their discordant ideas. *Mirage-Land* exemplifies that vision, too, for in these pages he documents the scholarly version of his personal allegiance to the one-

---

2. In the midst of writing this sentence, I walked over to a bookcase in my office and pulled, at random, a *Nevada Historical Society Quarterly* off a shelf. I was trying to find out Shep's exact role at the Historical Society and thought a copy of their journal might tell me. I have a twenty-year supply of the *Quarterly*, perhaps eighty issues. For no good reason whatsoever, I opened one published in Fall 1980. What was the lead article? "Portraits from an Antique West," written by Wilbur S. Shepperson. What was its topic? An examination of four memoirs, each from Nevada and the nearby Sierra range, each written between 1860 and 1920, each providing the scholar with additional information about the ways in which men and women perceived the region. A more systematic investigation of Shep's personal bibliography would surely reveal many such items. "Portraits from the Antique West" is just one of many seeds that germinated into *Mirage-Land*.

ness of the Silver State. That is, the point of view of *Mirage-Land* is uncompromisingly holistic.

While the exemplary voices themselves may express paradox, self-contradiction, antithesis, even confusion, Shepperson arranges his examples in a way that shows the reader an aggregate vision. For him, Nevada history and Nevada humanity together embrace the length of Highway 395, the width of Interstates 80 and 15, and the breadth of a good many gravel roads in between. Essentially Shepperson sees few meaningful differences between the Comstock of the 1860s, other mining camps, sheep and cattle operations, Reno of the 1930s, and the present-day Las Vegas. Because each has waxed and waned through a separate chronology of decay and progress, progress and decay, each has attracted a share of both detractors and supporters. Each, by its very nature, has called forth its share of the mirage.

Various historic combinations—barren landscape and mining riches, neon glitter and gambling bonanzas—led first to a confusion between what is real and what is illusion, then to a disjuncture between perception and truth. Now the historian steps in and sets the record straight. The paradox itself is a mirage; the mirage, a unifying concept. Shepperson explains this with characteristic clarity and grace in *Mirage-Land: Images of Nevada*. Not only the synthesis of more than forty years of reading and thinking, *Mirage-Land* is also a synthesis of its author's own perceptions of his own adopted home.

Many years ago Shepperson was sitting in a distant library, reading a Cornish newspaper called *The West Briton*. In the July 19, 1894, edition he found a quaint little narrative titled "A Visit to the Comstock." Written by an anonymous Cornish girl, the piece repeats the tension that has led inevitably to the Nevada mirage. She saw "a most weird appearance, surrounded as it is by high mountains, bleak and bold, which are covered with nothing but rocks and sage brush, and whose summits are often capped with snow, even during the summer," yet she acknowledged the problem of fairly drawing the panorama. Prefacing her essay was a poem which voiced the admonition of *Mirage-Land*.

> Paint me, Washoe, as you see it,
> Tinting with a truthful touch;

Line it with a faithful pencil,
Do not colour overmuch.

Too many Nevada observers have been guilty of precisely this fault. When they looked at the physical landscape of the desert and then at the psychological terrain, they did indeed color overmuch. They resorted to hyperbole and to the bizarre exaggeration so characteristic of what has been written about the Silver State. Nevada, of course, invites the excess adjective, as Michael Cohen explained when describing John Muir's Nevada prose. "The Great Basin was a realm of extremes, of extreme cold and extreme heat, of drought and cloudburst, of hopeful prayer and blank despair, of great wealth and great waste. In this place, paradox reigned." To portray that paradox Muir, like so many other writers who sought to image the region, used words outrageously colorful, language necessarily extreme.

But coloring overmuch gave Nevada a single image that Shepperson can pinpoint, led to a rather specific sense of place that can be defined. It is the extreme paradox itself—the colorful turn of phrase—that finally describes the state best, a land "fiery hot and deadly weary" but with "greener fields ahead and a host of pretty butterflies." Throughout this book the examples themselves are colorful. In the end, however, *Mirage-Land* draws a clear-sighted, wholly-integrated, black-and-white picture of the Nevada scene, the Silver State mirage.

Ann Ronald
Reno, August 1991

PREFACE

This work at times may seem to reflect the negative at the
expense of the positive, the critical at the expense of the
judicious, the theatrical at the expense of the prudent. It is
often the unusual which makes news and the dramatic which is recorded and remembered. Images evolve from both fact and fantasy,
they are both long lasting and fleeting. They are also basic to promotion and advertising as well as to the economy and politics. They
often find a place deep within the human psyche. The intemperate
and spontaneous condemnation of Nevada by Secretary of Interior
Harold Ickes, by President Harry Truman, by Chief Justice Warren
Burger, and others suggests that image is as profound and impreg-
nable as racism.

Throughout the nineteenth century Nevada was seen as a geographically borderline region where a reasonable observer could declare "Survival is more instinctive than principle or art." It was a place
where the people's "fundamental interactions are practical, indeed
immediate, and devoid of reflective long-term considerations."

Until the last half of the twentieth century Nevada's image was
probably forged as much by the absence of agriculture and greenery
as by the decaying towns and mines, or the prominence of saloons
and gambling. The aridness of the land and the absence of memen-
toes and man's handiwork deeply disturbed the middle-class visitors
from east of the 100th meridian. The old reassuring landmarks so
common in the East were rarely found. Seldom were there giant old

trees controlling the sun on the courthouse lawn; seldom was there a prominent water tower with its spidery steel legs; seldom a clattering bridge riding high at the bend in the river; seldom a Catholic church with a majestic steeple piercing the sky; seldom an equestrian statue to an old pioneer or an Indian chief dominating the center of town; and after 1920, seldom a gray-brown monument bearing the chiseled names of those who had died for democracy.

Over the decades, relatively few observers have been guilty of softness, vagueness, or quiet indulgence while they created a Nevada image. Most reporters claimed to stand for the dry light against the flickering neon. There were the ruthless comments made by those contemptuous of the personal and sensual institutions for which the state was famous. There were the declared pragmatists holding a low estimate of Nevada's capacity for goodness and showing in themselves a strong strain of nihilism. There were the inept whose turgid and discordant accounts left the odor of a stagnant marsh. There were the shocked and surprised who declared themselves defeated and de-hydrated by the aridity of both climate and culture. There were the pseudo intellectuals who coined impenetrable neologisms, their writing often a barrier instead of an avenue to rational understanding. And finally there was the clear majority, observers who were friendly, or at least balanced, when reporting on society and customs. Indeed, a segment of the friendly majority attempted to justify Nevada institutions by placing the state under the appealing mystique of the Old West. However, Nevada could not be explained by forcing it under the tattered umbrella of "frontier traditions." In every generation Nevada, more than most states, underwent dramatic shifts and changes both in attitude and in direction.

Mirage-Land attempts to encompass most of the major shifts and nuances of image making. It is designed to be historical and informative but also to be enjoyed. Enjoyed not because some of the epitaphs leveled at the state are amusing or deadly and not because one hoped to find a comprehensive body of myth or legend forged around clean John Wayne heroes, but enjoyed because of colorful outside attitudes and a series of running quotes which have lost nothing with time or in transcription. Enjoyed because contemporary reporters have come to sense Nevada's heterodoxy; a desolate frontier with overwhelming constraints of environment and few natural resources being slowly transformed into a much sought after playland and world center; a resort which has grown from a barren vacuum into a human magnet and where expansive urban vistas spring from the arid desert. Enjoyed because America's great outback, with neither climatic security, economic stability, nor a traditional ideology, could defy a hundred predictions and develop a sense of place, a new wealth, and even a viable social philosophy.

Acknowledgments

It is a pleasure to recall the exciting little finds used in this book. Many were made over the past thirty years while I was pursuing other research projects in the United States and Great Britain. During the past fifteen months of more concentrated effort, the Nevada Historical Society has provided both personal and professional assistance. Lee Mortensen and Phillip I. Earl not only officially responded to my sometimes bizarre inquiries, they also made available their personal knowledge and research. Farida Mahan of the Nevada Humanities Committee tolerated my shifts and changes and prepared a legible manuscript; and Judith Winzeler, executive director of the Nevada Humanities Committee, supplied the spirit as well as the detailed support which made the project possible. I have freely used the insights and the commentary on Las Vegas fiction and on rural Nevada provided by Professors John H. Irsfeld and Charles R. Greenhaw. Jerome Edwards, William Rowley, and the personnel of the University of Nevada Press have provided counsel, suggestions, information, and a welcome exchange of views.

Ann Harvey, my research assistant for some years, has not only collected many of the statistics but has consulted scores of journals and newspapers and pursued myriad elusive details. When medical problems slowed progress, she graciously agreed to write Chapter VI. I am deeply indebted.

W.S.S.

August 1, 1991

OVERVIEW

Image is always poised between magic and history.

Nevada, more than most regions of the West, has experienced the ups and downs of a turbulent economy and a checkered history. During the 150 years since John Charles Frémont led his exploring party across its wintry landscape, the state has been the subject of almost obsessive interpretation, inspection, and interrogation. Long before divorce, gambling, and prostitution became public fascinations, it was contemptuously labeled "The tagend of Creation," "The rubbish of Noah's Flood," "Dying Nevada," "The State Without Qualities," and "America's Great Mistake." And when it "stooped" to host the Corbett-Fitzsimmons prizefight of 1897, a San Francisco newspaper carried the pointed caption, "Filth on the Skirts of Columbia."

Stories of progress and decay, success and failure are all bound together in the newspapers and magazines, in the books and memoirs chronicling the state's often unflattering history. Inscribed in diaries by early migrants are tales of fatigue and sickness, childbirth and tragic death. Explorers, mountain men, surveyors, and others graphically recorded their reactions to a hostile climate and geography where life literally depended upon the whims of nature. During the Comstock era the exponents of the school of frontier humor often turned disaster into bizarre comedy by using exaggeration, overstatement, profanity, and irreverence. And finally there were passing sophisticates and intellectuals who readily supplied the Eastern and British demands for vivid accounts of the Wild West. *Mirage-Land* will attempt to reflect both the exuberance and the disdain of the many writers, journalists, reporters, critics, humorists, politicians, and others who have emphasized the beauty or scorned the sterility of Nevada.

Even the most mendacious criticisms must entertain some sort of relation with the truth. Even if it manipulates and distorts, criticism still needs both fact and originality to attract readers. Therefore, the untwisting of journalistic exaggeration, if skillfully effected, should yield a number of insights. Early observers argued that Nevada was visceral, not spiritual; accepting, not demanding. While claiming to move at its own internal tempo, in reality it seemed a classic reflector of outside influences. In times of depression and collapse of mining in both the nineteenth and twentieth centuries, a few writers and newspaper editors tried to establish a mining myth or a geographical mystique similar to that built around the magnolias and cotton fields of the Old South. But it proved physically and emotionally impossible to equate once noisy and fleeting boom camps or even the desert landscape with the more deep-seated "lost cause" traditions of the moldering southland.

Perhaps four rather random examples will help to suggest the difficulties and pitfalls that confront anyone in search of a Nevada image. First there is the danger of assuming that writers are consistent or even take seriously what they propose. During the summer of 1859 Horace Greeley, the famous publisher of the *New York Tribune*, adopted his own slogan, "Go West young man, go West," and traveled across the United States to California. After crossing Nevada in a slow and most uncomfortable mail wagon, he declared, in an oft-repeated quote, "the Humboldt, all things considered, is the meanest river of its length on earth . . . Here . . . famine sits enthroned, and waves his scepter." Over the years several paragraphs of Greeley's tirade have been used to suggest his contempt for the western Great Basin. Only four pages later in his *Overland Journey*, however, he offered an almost lavish hope for the agrarian future of the region. "Great dams over the Carson will render the irrigation of these broad, arid plains on its banks perfectly feasible. . . . The vegetable food of one million people can easily be grown here." And some five years later in articles in the *Tribune* Greeley returned to his journey and almost apologized to the rising Nevada Territory for his earlier hasty outbursts. He expressed only hope and praise for the new "pearl of the West." Nevada could finance the Civil War, pay the national debt, and provide employment for a generation of eastern youth.[1]

A second problem in determining image is to find what is genuine and what is the promotional handiwork of corporate, state, or local agencies. Throughout much of the twentieth century, Nevada had been likened to Hollywood stars, "I don't care what you say about me, just spell the name right." In short, some elements within the state have believed that almost any publicity is good publicity. A classic period of promotion was the first decade of the century when Nevada enjoyed unparalleled attention from the publishing media of the West. The *Land of Sunshine, The Californian, Sunset,* and in a more formal sense *The Overland Monthly* and *The Mining World* gave the state's activities detailed attention. San Francisco newspapers ran special editions exclusively devoted to Nevada with titles like *Manhattan,* a magazine entitled *Tonopah* was launched in the Bay Area, and provincial California papers featured regular columns on Nevada industry and growth. Unfortunately, most of the stories were prepared by banks, mining promoters, reclamation officials, and the Reno Chamber of Commerce and were seldom designed to provide a balanced picture. During the same period famous reporters who frequented the state were wined and dined in an effort to predispose them kindly toward their subject, and few writers or journalists were allowed to travel or write anonymously.

There was also the perennial image of Nevada as the scrawny youth who never grew up, or as the bad boy who needed a steady hand. This image was fostered by California newspapers. Starting in mid-nineteenth century with the founding of Genoa, elements within the California press adopted the "mining territory beyond the Sierra" and assumed the paternalistic stance of promoter and regional mentor. Until well into the twentieth century two or three San Francisco publications and one or two Sacramento papers consistently extended their coverage to Nevada. The *Sacramento Bee* was one of the papers devoted to the Nevada scene. A systematic random sample of articles in the *Bee* between July 1 and December 31, 1931, showed that an average of seven substantial stories about Nevada were being published each day, for a total of approximately 1,073 articles in a six-month period. In addition, the *Bee* carried birth, death, and marriage notices along with advertisements, classified ads, letters to the editor, and numerous other social listings. Simultaneously it employed special correspondents to ferret out sensational stories dealing with Nevada corruption and wrong-doing. It could heap undeserved praise and scathing criticism on the state in a single issue. In short, any researcher quickly discovers that the amount of material designed and published by newspapers and journals about the state is not only overwhelming, it is also often puzzling and contradictory.[2]

The Cowboy Poetry Gathering held annually in Elko suggests another difficulty encountered when trying to sample the many images of Nevada. In 1989 the four-day affair attracted some 7,000 cowboys and friends and was reported in at least 250 American newspapers, excluding the Nevada press. The coverage was broad-based geographically with almost a third of the articles appearing in newspapers east of the Mississippi River. Twenty-one articles discussing Nevada's festival were presented by the Texas press, nineteen in the Illinois press, and thirteen in the Florida press. Fourteen American magazines and numerous tabloids carried stories about the gathering; thirty-one live or taped television and/or radio broadcasts featured the Nevada exposition, including ABC's "Good Morning America," NBC's "Tonight Show," and CBS's "Sunday Morning," with Charles Kuralt. Many Canadian radio stations made Nevada the idiomatic center of cowboy lore with titles like "Get Along, Little Doggerels" and "Writing the Range." Over the years the British, West German, Italian, and Japanese media reproduced much of the program for showing in their home countries. *The Atlantic* praised the state for conducting "The Cowboy's Cultural Event of the Year," and The International Events Group that monitors corporate sponsorship from the Olympics to the New York Philharmonic declared, "The Cowboy Poetry Gathering in Elko, Nevada is authentic through and through . . . the event represents all of the right reasons for starting a festival. Just when we were at our most cynical, we read next month's program [1990] and were reminded once again of the possibilities inherent in festivals." Clearly the image of the state is still in the making and continues to reflect dramatic shifts in public opinion.[3]

Throughout the nineteenth century, travelers and critics, while disparate in their personal comments, tended to agree in their overall evaluation of the land. Perhaps geography has always been the overarching force in Nevada. In 1844 Frémont found the region more like the Middle East or the heartland of Asia than North America. He returned to the theme of an Asian landscape at least three times in his journals and over the following half century travelers borrowed the characterizations and likened Nevada to a score of distant, exotic, but always arid places.

While crossing the state, the Englishman Richard Burton was reminded of the Suez country. General Lew Wallace, who often reflected upon biblical scenes, rode along the Humboldt River in a plush railroad car and wrote at length on "how much this is like the River Jordan." Others likened Nevada to Palestine's Jericho, or central China, or Turkestan, or central Australia. Nevada was often associated with various areas of Arabia, western India, Tunisia, Algeria, and Granada, Castile, or ancient León in Spain. A few thought Nevada similar to regions around the Caspian Sea, the Black Sea, or the Dead Sea. The term "Great American Sahara" became standard usage for those who pulled the shades in their Pullman cars as they crossed the "desolate basin." Two or three railroad watering stops became oases and wadis.

Other observers were less generous. As a young journalist for the *Springfield* [Massachusetts] *Republican*, Samuel Bowles was rapidly developing into a major force within the Republican party and one of its more knowledgeable spokesmen on the West. He published *Across the Continent* in 1865 and along with leading politicians visited John Wesley Powell in the Rocky Mountains during the summer of 1868. Through Bowles the *Springfield Republican* was to become New England's leading western advocate. Bowles was not impressed with Nevada's potential, however. The newspaper recorded the thoughts of a New Englander who declared that man had arrived in Nevada before God had finished His work, and that nature was as yet incomplete. Another easterner reversed the scenario by explaining that Mother Earth and all hope had died, "leaving the dead embers of a burnt-out land as witness to the awful despair of nature."[4]

Perceptive lovers of the arid West, like the struggling rural businesswoman Idah Meacham Strobridge, could write as late as 1904 in *In Miners' Mirage-Land* that the Nevada mirage was the "Lorelei of the Desert." Nevada was a land that lured hopeful emigrants to wreck and destruction in the wide sagebrush valleys. Those who survived the mirage found that, "To love [the desert] is to hold out one's wrists for the shackles to be snapped thereon."[5] Such emotionally charged and somewhat contradictory love-hate wonderment at Nevada's geography, its flora and fauna, and its people had already been reflected by the young John Muir during his "wild man of the mountains" period. In 1878 he traveled over 1,800 miles throughout the state, writing articles at camps in eastern Nevada. Muir's "Nevada's Dead Towns," composed in the Ward-Pioche area and published in the *San Francisco Evening Bulletin* in January 1879, revealed the author's pensive description of a place "already strewn with ruins," where civilization seemed to have perished, although "tradition [was only] ten years old."[6]

By the turn of the century, however, space and wilderness were ceasing to be an evil. The "glorious wasteland" theme was being implemented by artists, writers, and other friendly observers; typical was Richard Lillard, who wrote in the thirties but romantically depicted an earlier Nevada.[7]

> It is the "sagebrush country" that Mary Austin found as distinctive a type of landscape as the moors of England and the Campagna of Italy. It is the desert of John C. Van Dyke, Mary Austin, J. B. Priestley, and many another who has experienced the golden fire of a Nevada sunrise, the varying shadows and colors and outlines of each hour of the day, the sunsets with their pink summits and knife-edged ridges of amethyst, their iridescent clouds, and the afterglow that reminded William Morris of Italian skies. And at night the stars shimmer and dazzle the crests of the desert ranges so that they seem half sisters to the towering Rockies, half sisters to the icy, lifeless mountains of the moon. This is a subworld in which any human being is a trifling interloper, a land that is "geology by day and astronomy at night."

With the widely heralded Newlands Reclamation Act of 1902, there grew an exaggerated image of Nevada as an agrarian paradise. Technology and the federal government were to build a new Midwest in the Far West. Later in the century the arid Sahara epitaph quickly faded as movie stars, millionaires, and agri-industrialists purchased and developed ranches. And by the last decades of the twentieth century, space and desert life along with parks, recreational areas, and the pursuit of nature had turned Nevada's geographic image from a fearful negative into an attractive positive.

The reclamation steps taken in Nevada were, until late in the twentieth century, accepted as inviolate. The image of conquering the desert, of reservoirs and irrigation, of dams and canals, of railroads and wagon roads, financed in whole or in part by the federal government, did not face the heavy rapids of relativism until the emergence of the ecological revolution. From the outside, Nevada was seen as a thoroughly utilitarian state. Even John C. Van Dyke's love of nature without changing it and, two generations later, Edward Abbey's wish to turn back the clock and to destroy man's dams and hydroelectric systems were slow to be taken seriously in Nevada.

Indeed, during the first decade and a half of the twentieth century, the mining and agricultural revival infused new vitality into Nevada life. The state became a magnet for investment, emigration, and a growing tourism. By the 1920s, however, American magazines were most attracted by divorce and gambling. They yearly provided a large shelf of routinely lame and repetitious articles with occasional gritty or cynical tales of political corruption and underworld viciousness. Obviously a majority of the reporting was for economic gain; racy Nevada stories became commonplace for journalists dispatched to the state for the purpose of increasing circulation back home. Many freelance scribblers were merely vain or ambitious and wished to see their characterizations in print. Local newspapers throughout the country were generally pleased to publish a brief account of a local citizen's motor tour across the deserts to visit "a second Sodom" or "a dusty Gomorrah." A few writers had a desire to humiliate; with furtive malice or a thirst for revenge they sought out and emphasized the darker side of Reno or Las Vegas. Some sensitive visitors were genuinely shocked by the open and vulgar "profits from sin," but few turned prophet or became representative of a crusading faith.

Sometimes one person, through his life-style, his writings, and his personal aplomb, can define or encompass a widely expressed position. Basil Woon was such a person, such a model and image maker for Reno during the period between the world wars. He paralleled and typified two score Nevada observers of the period. While far from probing or profound, he was symbolic of the many writers who traveled widely, sought celebrity contact, claimed affinity with foreign cultures, wrote extensively and with ease, and drifted in and out of Nevada.[8]

Woon first arrived in Reno in 1910, at age 17, to witness the

Johnson-Jeffries prizefight. With all facilities crowded by the nearly 25,000 visitors, he easily found employment as a bartender and waiter. Woon had arrived in Canada from England when only 16. Immediately drawn to the mining camps near Nome, Alaska, he founded a newspaper; he soon became seriously ill and in 1910 "followed the train" to Reno. By 1911 he was in Mexico as a correspondent for United Press, returning to the United States to publish his first book when only 19. Soon thereafter he became an aviator. Woon joined the army early in World War I and as a member of the Signal Corps was shot down over Verdun. Remaining in France after the war, he became part of the "lost generation." By 1927 he was in Cuba as director of publicity for the government, but by 1930 he had become a rather successful screenwriter in Hollywood. The trip to Nevada in 1932 resulted in *Incredible Land*, a book tailored to the fast-paced, chatty promotional style of his *Frantic Atlantic*, *The Paris That's Not in the Guidebooks*, *When It's Cocktail Time in Cuba*, and other European and Caribbean travel accounts.

Part Five of *Incredible Land*, "The Road to Reno," included chapters entitled "The Divorce Highway," "How to Become Unmarried," "Gigolos in Chaps," and "The Man who is Nevada," an ode to power broker George Wingfield. As a versatile, sophisticated booster, Woon found Reno "larger, cleaner, busier, but the old free-and-easy atmosphere [of 1910] was still there." As a "magnetic place" it had been transformed from "Western frontier" to "socially élite" by a wealthy leisure class. After visiting the towns and ghost towns from Virginia City and Dayton to Rhyolite and Hornsilver, he visited Nevada's foremost southern city and wrote a chapter entitled "The Last Frontier: Las Vegas." Although in 1933 it was still a "raw frontier town," Woon dramatically predicted, "One day the tourist world will find Las Vegas, Nevada, and then indeed the old West will have passed."

In 1950, after working for the British Broadcasting Corporation in London, finishing his forty-fifth screenplay in Hollywood, and receiving his third divorce, Woon decided to settle in Reno. He assumed management of a guest ranch, wrote several books and pamphlets, and became a correspondent for a Paris news service. Woon promoted local casinos, presented a weekly radio broadcast, and wrote a column for the *Nevada State Journal*; he died in June 1974.

Basil Woon paralleled and typified scores of magazine and fiction writers of the day. He impressed his readers by using celebrities he had known, and he spoke glibly of night clubs he had frequented. Like so many of the other reporters on Nevada, he sought image, not content. He was more interested in reflexes than in validity. Woon did not dwell on culture, values, or traditions, but on a room "filled with smartly gowned men and women." Like 90 percent of the reporters of the twenties and thirties, he was able to dismiss religion with, "The city is littered with churches of all sizes and denominations." And he handled personal and social problems with, "Tragedy and gayety march hand in hand" in Reno.

In short, Reno's image makers before mid-century had traveled widely, often knew America well, and wrote with ease, but they seldom wove folktales into myth or created meaning out of popular concern. Nor did they practice the old Swedish proverb with its dual admonition, "Grow where you are planted and care much for that for which you are." And yet differing from the blind man who touched the elephant only once, Woon and many of his literary compatriots traveled to Reno often and over the years said much about the little elephant.

Starting in the 1930s with the construction of Hoover Dam, southern Nevada began to draw the image makers of the state. As secretary of interior and head of the Public Works Administration under Franklin Roosevelt, Harold Ickes had long abhorred Las Vegas and had insisted that Boulder City be the administrative headquarters for federal activities in the area. Visiting the dam in February 1939, Ickes noted in his *Secret Diary* that Boulder City was "the neatest and most attractive-looking place in Nevada." But upon being driven into Las Vegas and losing $5.50 in a slot machine, the "righteous pilgrim" was deeply offended. "Three quarters of an hour was all the time we needed to get the savor of this rotten, little town, and we drove back to Boulder City." Las Vegas was "an ugly little town where gambling dens and saloons and prostitution run wide open day and night," and there was "nothing colorful or romantic about [the] intent-looking people."[9]

Following World War II, federal bureaucrats, reporters, and assorted politicians became very much aware of the image Ickes had portrayed. After the spectacular but unproductive Kefauver Committee investigation into organized crime in 1951–52, federal pressure and interference were muted during the Eisenhower years. In the meantime Thomas E. Dewey had denounced Nevada gambling during his last years as governor of New York. Legalized gambling had "brought nothing but poverty, crime and corruption, demoralization of moral and ethical standards and ultimately lower living standards, and . . . misery for all the people."[10]

Outside assessment of Nevada gambling has ranged from malevolent, to spiteful, to imaginative. In 1955 Harry S Truman projected all three positions while flying from Salt Lake City to San Francisco.

> We came to the great gambling and marriage destruction hell, known as Nevada. To look at it from the air it is just that—hell on earth. There are tiny green specks on the landscape where dice, roulette, light-o-loves, crooked poker and gambling thugs thrive. Such places should be abolished and so should Nevada. It never should have been made a State. A county in the great State of California would be too much of a civil existence for that dead and sinful territory. Think of that awful, sinful place having two Senators and a Congressman in Washington, and Alaska and Hawaii not represented. It is a travesty on our system and a disgrace to free government. . . . Well we finally passed the hell hole of iniquity. . . .[11]

Starting in 1961, both the attorney general, Robert F. Kennedy, and the Federal Bureau of Investigation, under J. Edgar Hoover, propelled Washington into an investigation of Nevada gambling in an unprecedented way. Kennedy explained in an article in *The Atlantic* in April 1962 that we do not know how much money is involved in gambling, but we do know that "the American people are spending more on gambling than on medical care or education; that, in so doing, they are putting up the money for the corruption of public officials and the vicious activities of the dope peddlers, loan sharks, bootleggers, white-slave traders, and slick confidence men."

Reporters like Fred J. Cook, quoted in *The Christian Century* of February 27, 1963, could reject the idea of a glamorous Las Vegas or the suggestion that there should be local autonomy. Rather, "The sinister truth is that Nevada's legalization of gambling was one of the greatest boons ever bestowed on the American underworld by a grateful government." After the Kennedy era, the *Chicago Sun-Times* and

Life reporter Sandy Smith carried on the fight by declaring the need for the federal government to pursue a dynamic role in Nevada law enforcement.[12]

By the seventies, however, the image of corruption had begun to fade. Howard Hughes, at the top of the Desert Inn, was eccentric, but not a Godfather. His aim for Las Vegas was to make the city's institutions "as respectable as the New York Stock Exchange" and to give Nevada gambling "the reputation of Lloyd's of London." He surrounded himself with "honest" Mormons. Billy Graham could take his "Crusade for Christ" to Las Vegas in 1978 and find not vice or corruption or the Mafia, but something similar to London's Soho. By the end of the eighties, with over sixty companies a year relocating in Las Vegas, with a projection that thirty million tourists a year would visit the city, with new Romanesque shopping plazas, with the Excalibur hotel opening with 4,032 rooms, with the most expensive hotel in the world, the Mirage, costing $630 million, with the University of Nevada, Las Vegas, projected to double to 35,000 students in the near future, President Maxson of the university reflected the Las Vegas image. When there is opportunity and the chemistry is right, "dynamic organizations just seem to explode. . . . And now is not the time to sit back and reflect. I'm a great believer that you never call time-out when you're on a roll. . . . You may be witnessing the last great city to develop in America."[13]

And yet always countering the more positive image of Nevada and Las Vegas are the instinctive and spontaneous outcries from individuals with the Ickes and Truman sentiments. For example, in early February 1983 Chief Justice Warren Burger announced that he would not speak before the American Bar Association in 1984 because it was to meet in an "unsavory and unsuitable" city. Nevada officials were outraged and local newspapers fueled a firestorm of criticism. The *Las Vegas Sun* of February 14, 1983, spoke of the "exaggerated pomposity" of "an uncontrollable, blustery braggart." Burger "clarified his statement" and one year later lauded Las Vegas for its hospitality as he spoke before the Bar Association.

Two weeks after Burger's visit, on March 1, 1984, Governor Richard Lamm of Colorado informed a group of Denver High School students that one of every eight women in Las Vegas was a prostitute. Two days later he apologized to Governor Richard Bryan but continued to argue that his statistics were accurate since they had been drawn from the *U.S. News and World Report* of March 9, 1981. On December 18, 1985, Johnny Carson asked the "Tonight Show" audience, "What's the difference between a parrot and a Nevada woman?" The reply was, "You can teach a parrot to say no." Again apologies were demanded, and throughout the holiday period many suggestions were offered on how to improve the Nevada image. In June 1991 federal officials guided the Teamsters Union Convention away from Las Vegas since they were engaged in rooting out the violence and mob control long associated with the organization. Even a few days in the city were seen as corrupting.

At another level, numerous contemporary movements and conflicts have continued to focus nationwide attention on the broader institutional issues of state versus federal control. During the late seventies and early eighties, Nevada led the Sagebrush Rebellion which was to allow states greater authority over federal lands within their boundaries. In the late seventies the first major opposition to a federal project occurred when citizens objected to the placing of the MX racetrack missile within the Great Basin. Starting in the mideighties Nevada became the center of a national controversy on the location of a high-level nuclear waste dump in the open spaces northwest of Las Vegas.

By the sixties, seventies, and eighties Las Vegas not only drew the attention of financial investors and federal investigators but also the attention of philosophical and literary critics. Of the many foreign evaluators of the city one of the most difficult and perplexing has been the French sociologist and writer Jean Baudrillard. In his witty *America* of 1988, Baudrillard found, by page two of his book, that "pompous Mormon symmetry" gave Salt Lake City a pride "equal and opposite to that of Las Vegas, that great whore on the other side of the desert." Nevada's cities were themselves little more than "mobile deserts" and yet there was a "mythic banality," a "dream quality," and a particular "grandeur" about the place.[14]

Only two pages later, Baudrillard, rather inconsistently, declared himself not in search of a social or cultural America "but the America of the empty, absolute freedom of the freeways, not the deep America of mores and mentalities, but the America of desert speed, of motels and mineral surfaces." He was inevitably drawn to Nevada. And there he found that "Death Valley and Las Vegas are inseparable. . . . There is a mysterious affinity between the sterility of wide open spaces and that of gambling. . . . If you approach this society with the nuances of moral, aesthetic, or critical judgement, you will miss its originality, which comes precisely from its defying judgement. . . . It would be wrong-headed to counterpose Death Valley, the sublime natural phenomenon, to Las Vegas, the abject cultural phenomenon. For the one is the hidden face of the other and they mirror each other across the desert, the one as acme of secrecy and silence, the other as acme of prostitution and theatricality."[15] Baudrillard was not only unable to understand the economy and dynamic of Las Vegas, he was unable to escape the lure of the desert, of gambling, and of Nevada. In *America*'s final paragraph, he returned to the subject. "Gambling itself is a desert form, inhuman, uncultured, initiatory, a challenge to the natural economy of value, a crazed activity on the fringes of exchange."[16]

Oscar Wilde once said of a friend's essay, "He broke his shins over his own wit." Despite sweeping philosophical judgments and a lively continental style, Baudrillard insisted on breaking his shins; he insisted on being brash, even arrogant. His images of Las Vegas, while impertinent, like those of Tom Wolfe two decades earlier, were never touched with amusing generosity or influenced by a sense of humanity. Wolfe's *Kandy-Kolored Tangerine-Flake Streamline Baby* remains a meaningful image after almost thirty years; Baudrillard has already been withdrawn from the bookstores.

Leaping beyond philosophical treatises and promotional brochures, travel guides and picture books, magazines and newspapers, one arrives at fiction, the very heart of image making. One of the traditional and more permanent images of Las Vegas was highlighted in Tom Wolfe's essay *Streamline Baby* of 1965. The image of the blue-haired old lady wearing a work glove to protect her hand against blisters while she played one-armed bandits has survived the decades, although most one-armed bandits are now electronic and require little human effort to play. Wolfe's Las Vegas was an air-conditioned, clockless, smoke-and-alcohol-infested world of perpetual night, inhabited by retirees and degenerates wasting their days trying to beat, with their own systems, a larger, unbeatable system. It was the Las

Vegas of the Rat Pack, and a time when topless dancers were still titillating. It was a finned-auto America, a faded technicolor world of postwar exuberance and tentative excess. It now seems innocent, almost adolescent.[17]

But the innocence was being shed, and a new disconnectedness was emerging. In Hunter Thompson's *Fear and Loathing in Las Vegas: A Savage Journey to the Heart of the American Dream* (1971), both the author and Las Vegas appeared to be almost out of control. The second half of the book told of a savage journey which destroyed the very components that allow Las Vegas its existence—the visitors and the gamblers on the one hand, and the bartenders and comedians, the waitresses and dealers on the other. It described Las Vegas as a nexus, a kind of cultural battleground where all were out of control. Las Vegas was no longer innocent, the crimes were capital, the blood was real.

John Gregory Dunne's *Vegas: A Memoir of a Dark Season* turned the fear and loathing inward, but found Las Vegas the appropriate place to work out such emotions. Las Vegas was as much a dark season of the narrator's heart as it was a place on the map. And yet the city controlled the book. As a tawdry town, full of tawdry people prematurely burnt-out, there was "a sense that failed expectations are the mean, the norm." But the landscape he detailed was more inside Dunne than it was in the streets and alleys of the city itself. In short, Dunne, like thousands of other visitors, used Las Vegas as the locale for his personal or literary depression.

In *The Desert Rose* (1983), Larry McMurtry was less strident, less apparent than most of the other novelists. *Desert Rose* is set in Las Vegas but ends in Reno. Synthetic beauty and fast entertainment were the main images cast in an arid world. Las Vegas became a town where youth was worshipped by people not smart or sensitive or deep enough to get past the surface of things and where the town's lights were like its aspirations, more spectacular than the underlying reality. Mario Puzo, in *Fools Die* (1978), also presented a kinder image of the city and, like McMurtry, was aware of place and geography. In *Fools Die* Las Vegas was hot and bright in summer and cold and bright in winter. It was a gambler's town, full of women and whiskey and money and the wanting of all three by men. Las Vegas, therefore, became essentially like any other place. It became real and the image less a cartoon, less a caricature, less strident than that of Thompson or Dunne.

In John Findlay's *People of Chance* (not a novel) Las Vegas was the epitome of incorporated fantasy, the home of mass-produced leisure and peopled by individuals who defied constraints. Baudrillard noted that as the puritan obsession for judging others had been reversed, "people pass in the street without looking at one another," which was less "a mark of discretion and civility" than "a sign of indifference." Carrying the point farther, Neil Postman, in *Amusing Ourselves to Death*, argued that Nevadans talked a great deal but did not communicate. With Gucci bags, sunglasses, and hair dryers, they were pretty but they did "not exchange ideas; they exchanged images." The world was the stage and Las Vegas was the play.[18]

Far away from the expansive gambling floors, far from tuxedoed casino workers, far from attendants costumed as Roman vestals, out in the Nevada outback, were the ol' boys driving pickups and wearing caps.[19] Tom Robbins in an *Esquire* article entitled "The Real Valley of the Dolls" found the lives of rural Nevadans ordinary, but their costumes weird and their dreams as broken as those on the Las Vegas Strip. Robbins, however, emphasized yet another image of the state when he declared, "If something is so hazardous and destructive and ugly and spooky that we don't know what to do with it, we stick it in Nevada. The state is blotched with 'Danger Areas' . . . In Nevada, a fluffy little cloud can suddenly exterminate a whole flock of sheep. And Nevada is the place the Bomb calls home."[20]

Bill Barich, also writing for *Esquire*, pushed the "desert outback" image even further. He found it a zone where things "function bizarrely, or not at all." Nevada was a kind of reservoir of eccentricity, a place of wild extremes, the center of negative truth, a land that "tends to attract" the Charlie Mansons and not the Georgia O'Keefes. Out of its over four hundred ghost towns the state had not been able to create a single Williamsburg of the West.[21]

Several observers have written about the new Nevada. The "Newest Jewel in the Park Service's Crown" and "Our Youngest National Park" revealed Nevada as an appealing natural wonder. And during the late eighties Elko was declared, in a self-conscious article entitled "Dropping on the Rubies," "the most un-ski-townish ski town in America."[22] But fewer authors have sought the image of the "other"

Nevada, the Nevada beloved by biologists, geologists, and environ-
mentalists. A land where over a hundred years ago John Muir in *Steep
Trails* saw mountains as jewels in the sky; where John McPhee in
Basin and Range located the geological epicenter of the world; where
Stephen Trimble in *The Sagebrush Ocean* saw a lush, ravishing Ruby
Mountain chain. There has always been the land and the lonely men
and women who live upon it. Even in the 1870s Henry Mighels in
Sage Brush Leaves was revolted by the slaughter of forests and the destructive search for minerals. Idah Meacham Strobridge in *In Miners'
Mirage-Land* lived with the coarse reality of late-nineteenth-century
rural Nevada, yet created stories with heroism and vision. And Robert
Laxalt in *Sweet Promised Land* discovered strength and dignity in a
father growing old while on the dusty trail of sheep. The friendly critics argue that such images will endure after the facile pretensions of
a culture based on entertainment have dissolved back into the desert.

Images of Nevada can be threatening, mildly illusory, or potent
with fact. All three have become intertwined with local identity and
have provided the romance for visionaries. Some images reflect explo-
sive greed, some reveal a profound trust in progress and the future.
Images can help define our culture and the process of our becoming;
they can create both fiction and history. If they provide a feeling of
awe and grandeur and immensity as well as of hope, comedy, and
buffoonery, they are worth preserving.

Fortunately, the majority of Nevada's image makers took pleasure in the exuberance and the folly of mere human beings. They
were not ashamed to confront the ebullient and bitter or to record the
progress and the decay that has been the story of Nevada.

CHAPTER I

Who enters here leaves hope behind.

—William G. Johnson

Throughout most of the nineteenth century, observers said more about the landscape than about the people of Nevada. Of course, western writers, American frontiersmen, and reporters generally began with the land and with nature. The locale and the physical features were used to arch the story and tie readers not to a sense of place, but to a place of novelty and uncertainty. The heat, the cold, the sand, the wind, the barren mountains tended to set the stage before people or animals or plants were noticed. Indeed "the sweating inferno" or "the drone of the wind" seems to have dwarfed both the human beings and the stories being told.

A few critics remembered Martin Luther when he held that nature "was deformed by sin and remains deformed still." Americans had always resented the forces that had blocked their way west. The first white men to cross the pleasant Berkshires saw them as "a hideous howling wilderness." And at about the same time other white men found the Appalachians to be "warts and wens" and "impustulated boils." However, as man began to sink shafts into quartz mountains and reshape the earth for reclamation projects, the observers remembered Isaiah's prophecy, "Every valley shall be exalted and every mountain and hill shall be made low." Man, the conqueror, had finally arrived.

In 1991 an opening phrase in an exhibit catalogue for the Nevada Historical Society deftly summarized the reaction of travelers to the land that was to become Nevada. Words like desolate, sterile, barren, forbidding, harsh, arid, dull, and monotonous were among the many unflattering terms applied by the beaver hunters and emigrants, miners and transients as they made their way across the gray sagebrush waste. Few white observers lingered in a Great Basin that was so unpromising, and Nevada was for decades viewed as a barrier to be crossed, a formidable obstacle on the way to sun-kissed California. Few observing the unattractive terrain and the aridity could have believed that within fifty years parts of the area would be acclaimed as a virgin agricultural district. And perhaps none could have believed that a century later the desert would become a magnet for settlement.

The first discoverers were mountain men and trappers, explorers and army scouts. They were young, hearty, skillful, and knowledgeable in the ways of the frontier. While almost all of them found the Great Basin unpleasant and even uninhabitable, their diaries and journals, their reports and memoirs are controlled and pragmatic assessments of the region. In 1826 Jedediah Strong Smith of the Rocky Mountain Fur Company led a small party through southern Nevada on his trek to southern California. Returning by the route now followed by Highway 6, he almost died near Ely in June 1827. Smith found the entire region devoid of game and water, a country of waste and savage desolation.

Peter Skene Ogden's trapping expedition up the Unknown River (the Humboldt) from near Winnemucca to east of Elko in November and December 1828 found "idyllic weather" almost "as mild as September," but the country was barren and "desolate of everything" and on both sides of the Humboldt was "one continued swamp." The Joseph Walker contingent was the first party to travel from the Bear River across Nevada by way of the Humboldt; the party wintered in California and returned by a slightly altered route the following year. The 1833–34 expedition was fortunate to include Zenas Leonard, who later compiled *Narrative of the Adventures*. Leonard's first interest was with the various Indian parties encountered along the way; however, he also pictured many desperate hours when thirst became so intense "that whenever one of our cattle or horses would die the men would immediately catch the blood and greedily swallow it down."[1]

Nevada became an object of close scientific scrutiny with John Charles Frémont's first expedition into the Great Basin in 1844. According to Frémont, the West was to become American, California was to be linked to the East, and emigrants were to flow freely to the Pacific. Frémont wrote in June 1848 in his *Geographical Memoirs* to the senate of the United States that the Humboldt possessed qualities which "in the progress of events" would give it value and fame. It was the most direct east to west line in traveling to the Pacific. The terrain along its banks was level and unobstructed for nearly three hundred miles. As a "beautifully covered" valley it could supply "articles of wood, water and grass." The image of the Great Basin was already being made to fit the ambitions of man. Hubert Howe Bancroft could later declare that, "In the progress of westward-marching empire few streams on the North American continent have played a more important part than the Humboldt River of Nevada." Without beauty or utility for transport, it nevertheless opened the way through a wilderness of mountains and desert. In a romantic vein, after having read Frémont, Bancroft found the Great Basin "a basket of chips," a country "full of peculiarities" where the sun was "bold and brazen-faced" but generally "harmless and kind," where the atmosphere was Asiatic and the entire desert expanse was a "broad plain of evaporation."[2]

Perhaps the most careful and thoughtful observation of Nevada was undertaken by Captain James H. Simpson. Eleven years after Frémont's surprisingly positive report to the United States Senate, Simpson established a new pioneer road across central Nevada. As one of the last official explorers, Simpson, on assignment for the U.S. Army Topographical Corps, passed along the area now served by Highway 50. With a master's degree from Princeton and with both an engineering and a humanistic background, Simpson befriended Indians, assessed the economic possibilities of the country, and saw the desert in a new and revealing way. Unfortunately, Simpson's report did not condition the American public or establish popular attitudes. He was too late as an explorer, following Smith, Ogden, and Frémont, and too early as a geographer-surveyor, with Clarence King, John Wesley Powell, and George Wheeler yet to come.[3]

Simpson was the first "priest of Nature" to comment on Nevada. John Muir and John Van Dyke should have read his *Report of Explorations Across the Great Basin*. Looking west from a mountain peak near present-day Ely on May 20, 1859, he found "these distant views have, at least on my mind, a decidedly moral and religious effect." The mountains and valleys accustom "the mind to large conceptions, and

thus [give it] power and capacity." It requires "the mysterious property of nature to develop the whole man, including the mind, soul,
and body." It is nature and the contemplation of nature which can
help man to reach the plateau of which he is capable. Three weeks
later Simpson found Eagle Valley and Carson City a pleasing prospect
and the most "Eastern-States-like of any [area] I have seen. It reminds
me of a pastoral landscape of the lower Delaware, below Trenton."

Simpson and his party of sixty-four men and fourteen wagons was accompanied by H. V. A. von Beckh, who, along with J. J.
Young, drew and colored some of the most original watercolor views
of Nevada. "Crossing of Carson River," "Genoa," "Carson Lake," and
"Lake Bigler" along with scientific diagrams and sketches provided an
unusually positive frontier image of the soon to be created Nevada
Territory.

Other German painters and artistic craftsmen had already discovered the power of the Nevada landscape. Five years before von
Beckh did his drawings, F. W. von Egloffstein, a Prussian cartogra-
pher and artist, had accompanied the Lt. E. G. Beckwith expedition
across Nevada. Beckwith's *Report of Exploration for a Route for the
Pacific Railroad* appeared in 1855 and carried a German-inspired and
most picturesque image of the frontier. On top of the Ruby Dome
and overlooking the Franklin River valley to the east, in present Elko
County, von Egloffstein sketched in May 1854 a classic noble savage
on the rugged cliff with bow and arrows and a fox reclining at his side.
The artist and steel engraver C. Schumann created one of the most
romantic allegorical nature-god portraits of the American West. It is
generally assumed that culture arrived with women, churches, and
schools, but some of the most lucid and graphic images ever produced
of Nevada were those supplied by the explorers and their artists.

The explorers made genuine discoveries which they reported
back to the older centers of culture. They were experimental scientists, always linked to reality. They were interested in attempting to
understand and explain the wonders and peculiarities of the Great
Basin, and most worked in a crisp, dry aesthetic way. They knew the
cost but were born to their work. They knew that life in the Far West
taught perilous lessons in danger. And on the Humboldt they faced
"the monotony of each day's march [which seems] to increase with
the desolation which more and more abounds."

The explorers were followed by a wave of humanity less knowl-edgeable, less well trained, and less realistic about the adventure. Although Bernard De Voto categorized the heated frenzy over west-ern discovery as "street corner parley, barber shop gossip," by the forties the great folk movement to the Pacific was in full swing. Few were classic explorers, historic individuals, or ideological imperial-ists; rather they were trail blazers and frontiersmen who learned to survive through personal experience. Of course, the western trek was merely a steppingstone, a road to success. The caravans did not leave Independence for the Humboldt. Nevada has seldom been a first choice in man's search for opportunity and a stable future. At mid-nineteenth century the Great Basin was a vacuum between societies, a place to get through as rapidly as possible. No one looked beyond the immediate objective of "the crossing."

In 1845 Lansford Hastings prepared his *Emigrants' Guide to Ore-gon and California*, and in 1846 Jessie Applegate was promoting an-other trail which branched off to Noble's road after 1850. There was the Peter Lassen trail of 1848, the Mormon trail of 1848, the Hudspeth cut-off of 1849, and the Jim Beckwourth pass of the early fifties. A score of roads, trails, cut-offs, passes, and routes were all short cuts on the road to California. They were designed to get people across Nevada as rapidly and as painlessly as possible. All viewed Nevada as an affliction to be briefly endured, a challenge to be surmounted, a formidable natural foe.

When emigrants gathered on the overland road, the Humboldt River and the Sierra crossing were always the topic of conversa-tion. Throughout the forties and fifties such final barriers became the nemesis for thousands of the tired and discouraged and long-suffering. They were the last obstacles to the new western Eden. By the time the parties reached the Great Basin they had been on the trail for months. All were exhausted, animals were weak, wagons were well worn, and the area was hot, dusty, and with a depleted supply of water and grass. Anxiety and monotony were producing quarreling, fighting, and other destructive behavior.

Too many emigrants had an inadequate concept of human limits in a desert environment. Sturdy resolve turned to flickering hope, and weakness and poor planning within the migrant parties became evi-dent. Harold Curran in his 1982 account, *Fearful Crossing*, has pulled together the startling story and dazed human reactions of dozens of individuals. William G. Johnson recorded in 1849, "The valley of the shadow of death . . . who enters here, leaves hope behind." Another diarist claimed to have counted 934 graves on the Forty Mile Desert, the barren stretch between the end of the Humboldt River and the first contact with the Carson River. In 1850 John Steele wrote of the many itinerant single men who failed to survive the journey. "They were buried in shallow graves, the earth heaped above them, and a stake bearing the single word 'Unknown' placed at the head." One questioning epitaph read "whose was he and who were his." And another observer movingly noted that for the many unknown "the tears of affection will never fall."[4]

In 1852 R. H. P. Snodgrass wrote, "Coming down this stream we have seen the skulls of a number of persons who have been buried in '49-'50-'51 and have been dug up by the wolves, and their bones left to whiten the plains." An 1852 diarist explained that graves were dug in the middle of the road. "We filled the grave with stones and dirt, and when we rolled out drove over it. Perhaps we had cheated the wolf by so doing—perhaps not." Although wagons were abandoned and pack trains formed, it was generally too late to save the emaciated livestock. In 1849 Bennett C. Clark noted, "All along the desert from the very start, even the waysides was strewed with the dead bodies of oxen, mules and horses and the stench was horrible. All our traveling experience furnishes no parallel to this."

The famous "Ode to Humboldt" composed by Horace Belknap in 1850 quickly became the most publicized of the several poems growing out of the traumatic episode. It became a standard refrain for journalists and historians for over half a century.

> What mean these graves so fresh and new,
> Along your banks on either side?
> They've all been dug and filled by you,
> Thou guilty wretch, thou homicide.
>
> Now fare thee well, we here shake hands
> And part—I hope—to meet no more—
> I'd rather be in happier hands than
> Longer live upon your shore.

It has been argued that the West was America's Book of Genesis—a birth, a beginning, a coming of a new spirit of life. However, the trek across Nevada was more like the Book of Job—thirst, sickness, despair. Rather than acting out the myth of creation, thousands succumbed to natural and human calamity, to forces beyond their control. They were torn apart by their own feeble attempt to subdue the great desert emptiness. Despite the Comstock, Nevada was to maintain the Book of Job image for the remainder of the century.

Starting as early as 1841, small numbers of emigrants crossed the Great Basin on their way to California. By 1846 the movement had skyrocketed to about 1,000 and in 1850 it reached an estimated 42,500 persons. During the forties perhaps 12 to 15 percent of the total were women and something over 15 percent were children. The wagon trains of the gold rush era were not an unmitigated catastrophe for the environment but rather for the intruders. Despite exceptions, it was not man but the environment which dominated mid-century Nevada.[5]

Not quite all the migrants passed through the future Nevada; a few remained and a few returned from California to farm and trade in the fertile valleys watered by the eastern slopes of the Sierra. Other migrants had been sent from Salt Lake City to farm and help govern the distant fringe of the Utah territory. The most highly charged and widely publicized issue in the western Great Basin during the late fifties was the clash between Mormons and Gentiles and the recall of the Mormons to Salt Lake City. In late 1856 the territorial legislature of Utah ordered all county records to be removed to Salt Lake City and recalled most of the appointed officials. Although there had been some friction and hostility between the two groups of settlers, it was not until the U.S. government clashed with Brigham Young that the recall of all Mormons was issued in 1857.[6]

The departure of the faithful from the Carson area created a wave of rumors and stories and supplied a continual series of far-reaching and improbable newspaper accounts. The New York Tribune was confident that the exodus of Mormons would create an unfavorable economic decline in the Carson district. But conversely in October 1857 the Daily Alta California argued that it was an ideal time to move over the Sierra. The Mormons had paid their debts, fulfilled their contracts, sold their property, and 985 persons (350 were men) along with 710 head of stock and 148 wagons had left the valley. "Their leaving so suddenly has been sensibly felt by the traders," therefore "there never will be a better opportunity afforded those who wish to procure good stock and agricultural farms." Wild stories in the *Daily Evening Bulletin* of San Francisco suggested that all the Mormons might migrate north to British territory and Genoa might become the capital for a new territory to be called Columbia. Conversely, the *Sacramento Daily Union* quoted the *Salt Lake Mountaineer* and explained that the Carson area was an "unremunerative burden on Utah" and "a worthless unaccountable scab, which cannot find a place in any class of an honest vocabulary. So let her remain, dried up, buried and forgotten." The *New York Evening Post* also quoted the *Mountaineer*, "All those who have been instrumental in sending them [the U.S. Army] here may be politically and eternally damned."

The exodus left a strangely mixed image of the Carson district. With deft satiric strokes several newspapers savaged the Mormons and suggested that they were preparing for guerilla warfare and were well placed in the Great Basin to interrupt trade and traffic with California. The *Daily Evening Bulletin* was certain that all wagon trains moving across the plains were accompanied by spies. The Carson district had shown "heroic conduct in exposing the iniquities of Mormondom." But an equal number of articles pointed to the Mormons' ability with plants and animals and their success in forging homesteads out of the wilderness. The recall of the Saints had left a frightening vacuum in agricultural production, political stability, and law and order. As late as 1860 it was noted that there were only about a hundred small farms in all of western Nevada, at least a hundred fewer than when the Mormons had left in 1857.

Often a single newspaper correspondent provided an oversize image and could set a discordant tone in publicity about Nevada. David Thompson has highlighted one such colorful and opinionated scribbler in *The Tennessee Letters*. Richard N. Allen, generally using the pen name "Tennessee," wrote some 92 letters or articles from his temporary home in Genoa between September 1857 and August 1860. Although regularly published in the *Weekly Herald* of San Francisco, Allen also supplied material for other California papers using the pen name "Mountaineer." A fretful, acrimonious, basically solitary man, Allen hungered for attention and became involved in a series of jealousies, intrigues, and vendettas. He was admitted to the practice of law in 1869 but was shot and killed in Hamilton in 1870. Allen helped to give Nevada extensive coverage not only by what he wrote but also by what was written about him. A letter in the *Territorial Enterprise* of May 21, 1857, proclaimed him "a base and unscrupulous disseminator of falsehood" and "a sponge on Genoa." Nevertheless, Allen saw, assessed, and publicized just about everyone who passed through Genoa or who traveled on the emigrant trail.[7]

Allen disliked Mormons unless they were apostate, he approved of Captain Simpson's expedition across the state, he noted the English, Welsh, Danes, Irish, and other Europeans who were rushing into the area by 1860, and he claimed to have counted fifty-six wagonloads of emigrants passing through Genoa on one day, September 3, 1859. When Horace Greeley arrived at Genoa in July 1859, Allen's southern sympathies were deeply offended. Greeley became "the great freedom-shrieker, Kansas-howler, Freesoiler, Abolitionist, and *Tribune* man" who fomented discord throughout the American Union.

Despite Allen's diatribe, Greeley was the most famous person to have visited the area. As a vocal politician, articulate newspaperman, and eloquent speaker, his travels were carefully promoted. All images portrayed by him were certain to be widely and repeatedly publicized. Indeed they were to be a subject for research and conversation for 100 years; Richard Lillard's *Hank Monk and Horace Greeley*, of 1973, has provided the most recent insights into Greeley's experiences in the Sierra.[8]

Horace Greeley was regarded in the West as a friend of labor, a promoter of the transcontinental railroad, a believer in hard work, internal improvements, and personal enterprise. The story of his ride across the Great Basin in a mail wagon and his trip over the Sierra with Hank Monk became a topic for conversation on the Pacific Coast and was quickly relayed to the East by enterprising editors. The *Springfield Republican* in 1866 declared that Greeley's story of crossing the Sierra "is now a classic with all the drivers and all the travelers on the roads." Richard Lillard has suggested that no "frontier story, true or untrue, has reached a larger audience over a longer period of time."

Various aspects of the Greeley episode in the West have been declared "apocryphal," a "fanciful legend," or a "bromidal anecdote," and otherwise questioned. However, as early as 1851 the *Tribune* began to cover the happenings in the region east of the Sierra, and Greeley's declarations in *An Overland Journey* are clear and striking. After he crossed the Great Basin in 1859, he wrote, "If Uncle Sam should ever sell that tract for one cent per acre, he will swindle the purchaser outrageously." After traveling down the Humboldt for 225 miles he found that all the water of the tributary streams "would barely suffice to turn a grindstone. The desolation seems therefore irredeemable." And after finding the Humboldt the "meanest" river on earth, he described its water as "about the most detestable I ever tasted. I mainly chose to suffer thirst rather than drink it."[9]

But as Greeley entered Carson City and later Genoa he saw fertile gardens and had visions of dams and cattle feeding in the mountains by summer and in the verdant valleys in winter. "Everything that contributes to human or brute sustenance can be grown actually cheaper by the aid of irrigation than without it." Science and technology were to open up the West. Carson City would be the "emporium of the new gold region, and perhaps of the embryo state of Nevada."

Despite repeated use of his negative pronouncements while on the Humboldt, Greeley remained the total optimist. Far from being a confused critic bitter with his travels in Nevada, Greeley, as he mounted the Sierra, pled that the forest not be cut; and then with infectious enthusiasm and verbal exuberance he wrote, "I may never see this lovely valley again—it is hardly probable that I ever shall—but its beauty, its seclusion, its quiet, the brightness of its abundant rivulets, the grandeur of its inclosing mountains, the grace and emerald verdure of their vesture of pines, have graven themselves on my memory with a vividness and force which only he who has passed weary weeks on some great, shadeless, verdureless desert can fully realize."[10]

After devoting much *Tribune* space to Nevada's mines, statehood, and future during the early 1860s, on March 29, 1864, Greeley listed thirty-seven Comstock mines, their size and value. "It is interesting to know that we have within ourselves bullion sufficient not only to pay the interest on the debt—however large it may be—but with sufficient men and machinery the entire debt can be paid off during the present generation." On April 7 he wrote, "Five years ago next July, we traversed the region now known as Nevada Territory." He found the countryside as desolate as Mount Sinai, but healthy, and believed that with a railroad on its way "the child is born" who would see Nevada produce enough gold and silver for greenbacks to be at par.

Nevada exploration was less a process than a sequence of events, less a continuous movement than individual discoveries. The adventurers provided the first character, they gave the first attributes to the Great Basin, and they established the region in the popular imagination. The explorers listened and questioned and conversed with the earth. They found the area vague, expansive, intriguing: the landscape was alternately perplexing and strangely out of balance. The winds tousled the horses and nudged them along as squinting, wind-burned eyes saw only another wall of mountains leaning against the horizon. But the reports were factual, scientific, and controlled.

Aldo Leopold wrote in *A Sand County Almanac* that "geography, climate and circumstances" forced people into different adaptations and created different patterns of life, customs, and beliefs. Indeed, almost all the images of Nevada before 1860 were based on geography and climate. The first travelers and settlers, therefore, were primarily an exoteric, outwardly oriented group with a focus on pragmatism and action. The esoteric, with myth, legends, and folktales, was slow to mature. The overland trails of the forties and fifties channeled the action. If Americans were reluctant to accept prairies and mountains or wetlands and badlands, the era of appreciation for arid landscapes was yet a half century in the future. The emigrants, failing to understand the desert and the concepts of limits, often foolishly braved the unknown, ill-equipped and poorly led. They sought advice from braggarts and ruffians; they labeled the Humboldt the Humbug and the Hellboldt; the region became known in the American mind as one of the most inhospitable on the overland passage.

By the fifties, however, permanent settlement was undertaken in the valleys watered by the eastern Sierra. Both small parties of Mormons and observers like Captain Simpson and Horace Greeley saw the district as harsh but attractive. They were in tune with the sentiments later expressed by Wallace Stegner. In reflecting on his youth in the West, Stegner found the country "both hard and simple." But since the world was young and the population thin, it could provide "a hard living" and "a beautiful life."

CHAPTER II

No matter how fast the train went, the caboose

[nineteenth-century Nevada] was always at the end.

—Wilbur S. Shepperson

About 1860, Nevada evolved from the heroic age of exploration into a brief herculean age of mining. The movement of machinery and supplies over the rocky mountain passes and sandy desert trails, and the driving of shafts into quartz mountains quickly engulfed the new territory. The merchants of Mammon, whether they were capitalists or workers, professionals or prostitutes, rushed to the Comstock after its discovery in 1859, and for some two decades they fanned out across the land. The wealth and assumed wealth created a mixture of admiration and extravagance, of enthusiasm and curiosity. But most important, it engendered a cold pragmatism. Even Lincoln could rationalize to his cabinet, "It is easier to admit Nevada than to raise another million of soldiers." And Emerson could encompass both gold and freedom in his "Boston Hymn." "Nevada coin thy golden crags with Freedom's image and name."

Folklorists suggest that the landscape becomes infused with power from what occurred there—a Thoreau's Walden Pond, a Twain's Mississippi River, a Cather's Midwestern prairie, a Steinbeck's Monterey Bay. But despite their involved reactions to Nevada, J. Ross Browne, Mark Twain, and Dan De Quille did not create an image of place or endow the landscape with guardian spirits. Rather the impoverishment of place seems to be the message of these early writers. They admitted that Nevada was the product of human history as well as of wild nature, but the state was to absorb the mining boom without the enchantment of illusive myth or the richness of legend.

Yearly the prospectors claimed new bonanzas, but the results were often hollow exploits, fruitless efforts, and wasted energies. Part of the reporter's assessment of Nevada's first mining era had been to turn these many brief and usually bleak mining strikes into amusing and picturesque episodes. Yarns were spun, facts enlivened, and humorous tales invented to stretch historical events into published and nonpublished synthetic fragments of history. But Nevada gained little from these early tidbits of stereotyping. Rather, the state lacked the true artist or image maker to weave the many pieces into a folkloric tradition or to create the romantic saga which would have evolved into a sense of place.

Of the three or four young writers and image makers who were responsible for picturing Comstock Nevada, all emphasized the avaricious and befuddled and profane nature of the society. J. Ross Browne was the first and perhaps the most explicit and personally mature. Browne possessed substantial literary and artistic abilities and was able to mingle satire with relevant fact to produce an accurate yet extravagant narrative. He consistently demonstrated an amusing and stubborn integrity, but his wanderlust made economic success a virtual impossibility. A Peep at Washoe was prophetic in that it tended to cover if not all of the early complaints leveled at Nevada at least most of them. It introduced physical geography and the extreme aridity of climate, the peccadilloes of the society and the absence of culture, the camp sickness and crime, the dishonesty and unemployment, and the internal conflicts and forlorn, unrealistic hopes displayed by most of the migrants.[1]

Browne was a native of Ireland, a child of Kentucky, an employee of the U.S. Senate, a deck hand on a whaling ship, and, after a quick trip to California in 1849, something of a newspaper correspondent in Europe. He returned to California and in March 1860 joined the disorganized throng crossing through the Sierra to Virginia City. But within a few weeks he traveled to the East Coast and embarked for Europe where in a German villa "without note or memorandum" he wrote *Peep*. The work was published in *Harper's Monthly Magazine* in 1860–1861. At 39, Browne was widely experienced, literate, a world traveler who was capable of using description as fact uncolored by personal emotion.

Browne was to write several books, hold government posts, and travel extensively in Europe and Africa before becoming minister to

China in 1868. His *Peep* suggests a young, intense, and ambitious man at the top of his form. He laughs at himself and at the thousands of others crowding over the Sierra for "a fortune ready made." All California newspapers were so "full of Washoe," that even in his dreams he saw Nevada dollars with spider legs shrieking "Washoe! ho! ho!" Later he admitted that he should have learned from the counter-current of "weather-beaten and foot-sore pedestrians" all "toiling wearily homeward . . . all bearing the unmistakable impress of Washoe."

Browne investigated each of the Comstock communities and wrote, "a more barren-looking and forbidding spot could scarcely be found elsewhere on the face of the earth. The whole aspect of the country indicates that it must have been burned up in hot fires many years ago and reduced to a mass of cinders, or scraped up from all the desolate spots in the known world, and thrown over the Sierra Nevada Mountains in a confused mass to be out of the way." He had visited Jerusalem, Constantinople, cities of the Dead Sea, Seven Cities, and new cities, but nothing equalled Virginia City for "shanties," for tents made of "potato sacks," for "coyote holes in the mountain side forcibly seized and held by man," for "total chaos, lawlessness, poverty." The city was a "mud-hole," its climate "hurricanes and snow," its water "a dilution of arsenic, plumbago, and copperas," its timber "none." Carson City was a mere accident with an income derived from "waylaying strangers bound for Virginia" and "selling whiskey."

In attempting to provide a perception of Nevada life, Browne could be more than witty and flippant. When heavy spring snows closed the roads over the Sierra and food supplies were nearing exhaustion, he discovered the true Nevada. After days of anxiety and concern, a pack train "hove in sight" above Genoa. "Like a row of ants" it crept down the mountain. But upon arrival, the leading mule carried a barrel, not of beef, or pork, or bacon, but rather of "old Bourbon whiskey." With great expectations he turned to the second mule, which upon examination did not carry pig's feet, or mackerel, or chicken, but "brandy." The third mule did not bring molasses or lard or butter but "gin." And the fourth mule carried no lifesaving food or medicine, but rather "glass-ware." In short, Browne found a hedonistic, ephemeral, immature society; personal survival and immediate gratification gave it a transitory image.

In April 1860 Browne rushed back over the Sierra to Califor-

nia and within a few weeks departed for the East Coast; he quickly
sailed for Europe. But by 1863 he was again in California and again
crossed the Sierra, this time to "busy-scenes" and new "evidences of
prosperity." As a government agent working for the Treasury Department to ferret out fraud in western mining and as a promising travel
writer covering a broad array of regions from Mexico to Norway,
Arizona to Iceland, Palestine to Zanzibar, J. Ross Browne had become more circumspect. Although he found the Nevada mines filled
with confidence men and thimbleriggers, his *Washoe Revisited* and
Report on Mineral Resources of Nevada were restrained and positive.
He now joked about a "stray bullet" whizzing by his head and the reaction to his *Peep at Washoe*. "The road was lined with blood-thirsty
men armed with pistols, double-barreled shot-guns, clubs, pitchforks,
bowie-knives, and axes," all on the lookout for the man who had
"damaged their reputation by various slanders in the public prints."

Despite Browne's concerns when he returned to the Comstock
in 1863, his negative image of Washoe, rather like that of Mark Twain,
was already being transformed into a positive frontier motif and in
the future was to provide a basis for pride in the past. Indeed, something of a precedent was started; the more pointed and devastating
the criticism, the more rapidly it was transformed into words of praise
and offered as proof of the virility of the past and Nevada's direct ties
with the rugged West.

The most often quoted and literally the most successful tale-
teller and critic of the Comstock era was the young Mark Twain.
Twain remained in the Territory for less than three years and was
active as a columnist on the *Territorial Enterprise* for the short period
from September 1862 to May 1864. Differing from most reporters, he
had an opportunity to rethink his ideas and restructure most of his
prose, since *Roughing It*, which recounted his experiences in Nevada,
was not published until 1872. In early 1863, when attempting to discredit a fellow reporter, Twain labeled a column of the *Virginia City
Union* as "festering masses of misstatement." Such boisterous exaggeration made him into a local celebrity and earned him titles like
"The Humorist of Silver Land" and "The Humorist of Sage Brush," but
unfortunately he contributed little to the establishment of a literary
tradition in the state.[2]

Perhaps all sensitive migrants and travelers carried some type of personal defense and innate fear of the desert and the rowdy boom camps. Patricia Limerick has suggested that Samuel Clemens (to become Mark Twain in January 1863) refused to pretend that he was unafraid and thereby did not need to maintain "an unshaken dignity." Rather, he took "the stance of a strident, outraged child." This allowed him to employ his true gifts; he could abuse both nature and the infant society. Soon after his arrival in Nevada in August 1861, he discovered that distortion and habitual exaggeration were easy ways to disguise his feelings and yet simultaneously amuse and project his verbal talents. He also discovered that sensationalizing was popular and could become profitable.[3]

Twain's most often quoted comments declared Nevada not a good place for a humble God-fearing Christian, and "I did not long remain one." He wrote to his sister that if the devil was forced to go to Nevada he would look sadly around and become homesick for Hell. And to his mother, "The birds that fly over the land carry their provisions with them" since "nothing but that fag-end of vegetable creation, sage brush, ventures to grow." Nevada was the home of bald-headed men since the wind blew the hair off their heads while they looked skyward for their hats. And Governor Nye had sent his staff to survey for an imaginary railroad across the state to provide employment for the idle.

The "real" Mark Twain seems at times to have shown through the rhetorical humorist; he wanted to be accepted and very much wanted to be a success. Therefore, he declared, to remain in Nevada he must go "mad like the rest" and become infected with "silver fever." He became annoyed by the repeated references made to Horace Greeley's visit and famous ride over the Sierra and quipped that he had heard the Greeley story 481 times during 13 stage journeys. But he could become serious when evaluating the fearful toll taken by Nevada geography. In speaking of the "forty miles desert," he found it "was one prodigious graveyard. And the log-chains, wagon tires, and rotting wrecks of vehicles were almost as thick as the bones." Clearly "fearful suffering and privation" had befallen the emigrants. Mark Twain made Nevada into a seductive hoax; the unstructured society fit his needs as an aspiring humorist. He established Nevada as a place adventurers might wish to visit, but where few God-fearing people would wish to remain.

During the early sixties, a surprisingly eclectic group of humorist-adventurers was drawn to Virginia City, and later in the decade a barrage of scribbler-visitors stopped by on their way across the state. When Artemus Ward, after only a few months in California, decided to trek east to Salt Lake City, he found it convenient to lecture in Nevada during Christmas week of 1863. According to historian John J. Pullen, "a bittersweet friendship" was formed between Ward and Mark Twain, but for Ward's agent, the Englishman Edward Hingston, it was an unsweet and bitter experience. Faced with keeping his employer sober and with crossing Nevada in December, he wrote, "No nightingales will sing to me on the way, no locusts will chirrup in the grass, nor any bull-frogs grunt me salutations from the ponds, simply because the ponds are too alkaline for any reptile, not iron-plated to exist in; the grass don't grow, nor the grasshoppers either; and the nightingales don't sing, because they have no boughs to sit on to sing from, nothing to sing about, and finally, there are no nightingales."[4]

Most of the writers and lecturers associated with Virginia City were "birds of passage," but William Wright was to find a permanent home on the Comstock. Born in Ohio in 1829, writing his first articles in Iowa, crossing to California in 1857, Wright arrived in Nevada in early spring 1860. A year later, under the pen name Dan De Quille and with two partners, he embarked on *Washoe Rambles*, a prospecting and note-taking tour throughout western Nevada. His reactions were published in the *Golden Era* and repeated in *California Magazine* before they appeared in book form in 1863. De Quille was to become a fixture at the *Territorial Enterprise*. For over three decades he assembled mining and other informational materials and authored authoritative books about the state, but in 1861 he was a thoughtful, visiting prospector-writer. Differing from most, he analyzed himself along with the country; he sought to understand his own weaknesses in the face of the "Helldorado" that was the Nevada mining boom.

> As I lay on this knoll with the wind whirling the sand over me, and into my hair, ears, and eyes, sad thoughts of months and years spent in the chase of that Will-o-the-wisp, the "big thing," crowded themselves on my mind, and I was anything but "gay and festive." . . . I thought of the many long wild-goose-chases I had taken across deserts and over mountains. . . . How often

had I sworn to be deluded no more by this deceitful phantom.
But alas, for my resolution! . . . I fear that in spite of all the rail-
lery . . . I will continue to follow the fiend till his designs against
me are accomplished![5]

Nevada was the fiend that would "entice all to perdition," and
European as well as American writers were lured to the scene. The
English in particular found that their images of the West were eagerly
received, both in the United States and at home. The November 1866
journey across Nevada by Sir Charles Wentworth Dilke was published
as part of *A Record of Travel in English Speaking Countries*, which
quickly went through four editions. Later Dilke was elected to Par-
liament, rose to become a member of Gladstone's cabinet, and was
disgraced when charged with adultery; the lady was a friend's wife.
As a political radical and a social free-thinker who found "robustness"
and "emotional courage" on the frontier, Dilke later became editor of
Notes and Queries, proprietor of the Athenaeum, and an art collec-
tor. Neither as a lawyer nor as a literary or art critic was Dilke ever
content with ritual responses. Perhaps he should have remained in
Nevada.[6]

The twenty-three-year-old Dilke and an Irish miner crossed "the
roof . . . of the world," passed over "the Grand Plateau," and enjoyed
the land with "a passion." In Austin he dined at an Italian restaurant "with luxury." Despite many miners being "liquored up," every
man in Austin "walks as though he were defying lightning" and "the
royal gait, the imperial glance and frown, belong to every ranchman
in Nevada." "Every woman of the Far West is a duchess." Certainly
there were "border ruffians," the roads were terrible, and "not even the
Sahara so thoroughly deserves the name of 'desert.'" But he had faith
that Nevada would not undergo a "reformation," the society would
not turn pious. And yet Dilke acknowledged that most of the mines
had failed, heavy machinery and equipment were transported to the
state and never used, camps were started and never completed, stone
walls were erected where there were no fields, and all had been left to
slowly dissolve back to nature. Twelve years before John Muir declared
Nevada in decay, Dilke observed the economic and human failures.

No nineteenth-century writer more clearly caught the natural
image of Nevada than John Muir during his autumn 1878 wanderings. Recording his thoughts in the field and publishing his detailed

accounts in the *San Francisco Evening Bulletin* in late 1878 and 1879, Muir evaluated Nevada deserts, farms, forests, and towns.[7] He admitted that the state seemed a vast desert of sage and sand "irredeemable now and forever." Water was not only wanting, it was fruitlessly swallowed up by gulches and deltas. California supplied three river "fountains," the Walker, Carson, and Truckee. They were "like angels of mercy to bless Nevada." The remainder of the state seemed to be lost in "savage isolation." There was "no singing water, no green sod, no moist nook to rest in—mountain and valley alike naked and shadowless." But "Nevada is beautiful in her wildness," and "nature may have other uses" for the desert "besides the feeding of human beings."

Muir was most pointed in noting "Nevada's Dead Towns." He saw with great clarity what Henry De Groot, Sir Charles Dilke, and others had already observed.

> Nevada is one of the very youngest and wildest of the States; nevertheless, it is already strewn with ruins that seem as gray and silent and time-worn as if the civilization to which they belonged had perished centuries ago. . . . Wander where you may throughout the length and breadth of this mountain-barred wilderness, you everywhere come upon these dead mining towns, with their tall chimney-stacks, standing forlorn amid broken walls and furnaces, and machinery half buried in sand, the very names of many of them already forgotten amid the excitements of later discoveries, and now known only through tradition—tradition ten years old. . . .
>
> But in the case of the Nevada miner, he too often spent himself in years of weary search without gaining a dollar, traveling hundreds of miles from mountain to mountain, burdened with wasting hopes of discovering some hidden vein worth millions, enduring hardships of the most destructive kind, driving innumerable tunnels into the hillsides, while his assayed specimens again and again proved worthless. . . .
>
> The dim old ruins of Europe, so eagerly sought after by travelers, have something pleasing about them, whatever their historical associations; for they at least lend some beauty to the landscape. Their picturesque towers and arches seem to be kindly adopted by nature. . . . They have served their time, and like the

weather-beaten mountains are wasting harmoniously. The same is in some degree true of the dead mining towns of California.

But those lying to the eastward of the Sierra throughout the ranges of the Great Basin waste in the dry wilderness like the bones of cattle that have died of thirst. Many of them do not represent any good accomplishment, and have no right to be. They are monuments of fraud and ignorance—sins against science. . . . Like prayers of any kind not in harmony with nature, they are unanswered.[8]

Most observers believed tha the mineral discoveries redeemed the desert and Nevada. John Muir believed they presented "a most vivid picture of wasted effort." Most observers found the Comstock and Nevada mining camps the center "of a thousand excitements"; for John Muir they were "retrogression and decay." For Muir, the old mining camps seemed a sort of obscure outrage. Like the mind, they were a time capsule. But where were the stories, the jokes, the music, the practical arts? The past animation had been too brief, the places had become ghost towns and gone into memory too quickly. Man's hopes, like his efforts, had reverted to desert.

With the completion of the transcontinental railway in 1869, Nevada provided an easy passage to the Pacific, but the state also became something of a magnet and a destination in its own right. Engineers and writers, presidents and generals, reformers and revolutionaries made their way to and across the Great Basin. Robert Louis Stevenson entitled his 1879 jaunt to America *From Scotland to Silverado*. His images of the state, however, were neither sensitive nor perceptive. After observing the unfavorable treatment afforded Indians, Chinese, and tramps, he "was ashamed for the thing we call civilization." His response to Nevada geography was largely routine. "We traveled all day through deserts of Alkali and sand, horrible to man." And after leaving Elko: "of all the next day I will tell you nothing . . . I remember no more than we continued through desolate and desert scenes, fiery hot and deadly weary."[9]

Three years later, the twenty-six-year-old Oscar Wilde observed even less during his quick passage across Nevada. Although the *San Francisco Chronicle* declared him "touched with the Promethean fire," Wilde found Renoites "rather intense and lacking in reposeful languor." Later Wilde explained that there were two ways to seduce the reader or the listener, "to shock" or "to amuse." Despite the efforts of the local press to pyramid the brief March 1882 stop in Reno into an occasion, Oscar Wilde neither shocked nor amused in Nevada.[10]

Some English travelers responded erratically to their whirlwind Nevada visit. There were sneers, censure, and obloquy. The state was found to be "shameless" and a horror. Paul Fountain identified "obscene women" and "moral ugliness," while others encountered "yankee desperadoes" and a free-and-easy "hell on earth." A letter from a Nevada miner published in the *Cornish Telegraph* of Penzance on November 15, 1871, was equally direct. "Pioche is the county seat of Lincoln County, a mining camp a year old. . . . There are about 1200 people here, half of whom have been in the state prison and the rest ought to be. Our graveyard has forty-one graves, of which two were filled by death from natural causes. . . . I sleep with a bulldog, a Henry rifle, and a six shooter." Throughout the seventies the story was repeated, and Pioche maintained its reputation until the *New York Herald* could declare that over 200 murdered persons "were in the cemetery," and "retired robbers had become the town leaders."

Even friendly critics observed that Nevada had transparency rather than anonymity, politics devoid of ideology, a reputation rather than a character, and a parade of observers and narrators rather than a few blooming writers. Nevertheless, the state seemed to beckon to important visitors and it generated colorful movements. In 1864 Emperor Louis Napoleon sent C. Guillemin Tarayre to Virginia City to evaluate the mines, and the next year Ferdinand Baron Richthofen published the pamphlet *The Comstock Lode*. Several German states employed Philip Deidesheimer as a private reporter on the mineral prospects of the state. Emperor Dom Pedro of Brazil visited the region in 1876 and General U. S. Grant and his party were received as conquering heroes when they arrived in Virginia City in October 1879. The amiable Grant endeared himself to the locals by "wanting for so long" to see the source of the wealth that had paid for his Civil War victory. Once in Virginia City he reckoned that he had never been so close to hell, not because of Comstock morals but because of the heat in the mines. Only one year later President Rutherford B. Hayes arrived along with General William T. Sherman and Secretary of War Alexander Ramsey. Always the thoughtful inventor-technician, Thomas A. Edison became more interested in the sagebrush than in the mines. "The Lord never put so much of any one thing in a place without a definite purpose."

The clashes throughout Nevada between the French and Germans during the Franco-Prussian War era, the visits by Irish revolutionary leaders, the formation of the Fenian Guards, and the tours by scores of actors, musicians, scientists, and sideshow performers projected an image of a cosmopolitan and lucrative center. Nevada had become a synonym for quick gain and free expression. Newspapers and journals were the key to the far-flung publicity. A single story from the *Territorial Enterprise* was often borrowed, elaborated upon, and repeated from San Francisco to New York City, thus creating an image that was sometimes far removed from reality.

Perhaps no out-of-state newspaper was as consistently responsive to Nevada issues during the Comstock era as the *Sacramento Union*. Founded in March 1851 it quickly grew into one of the most ambitious and balanced regional publications to cover the settlements east of the Sierra. Over the decades reporters stressed the need for Nevada to become a territory and then a state. They followed the Comstock discoveries, encouraged railway construction, and in 1869–70 noted every detail during the construction of the new capitol, from hot air heating pipes to acoustics. The *Union* could proudly declare that "the new structure will compare very favorably with any seat on the coast." Elections, governor's messages, the actions of the legislature, and economic turns were followed in detail. The rise of mining centers from Austin to Eureka, Hamilton to Pioche, and the various plans for connecting the new camps to the Central Pacific by railway were closely monitored. Elko was to "emerge out of a moody mood" to become a "jubilant" center. During the seventies attention was given to central and eastern Nevada and to the need for a system of roads running south to better connect the Meadow Valley Wash and the Las Vegas area with other parts of the state.

A report from Hot Creek, published in the *Union* on March 1, 1873, explained "who and what" Nevada really was. The inhabitants were seen as literate professionals who had turned prospector and whose "dress and address do not go together." They are "patient, yet excitable," their "hope of great gain is as boundless, and often as barren, as the region." The prospector is "the Moses who leads them [Nevadans] about in the wilderness."

During March 1865 the *San Francisco Evening Bulletin* along with the *Weekly Bulletin* presented a lengthy four-part series on central and southern Nevada. The south possessed a "slim chance of ever finding any thing useful." Because "of its sterility and drought [it] can barely be traversed in the saddle." And yet, if water could be found and transportation arranged, the lands of the Colorado and Virgin rivers might provide a setting for tropical agriculture. On the other hand, the *Bulletin* was less kind to the first state legislative session, which ended on March 11, 1865. The *Bulletin* reporter explained that the Nevada assembly "had its full quota of brainless ignoramuses." There were scenes of "half-a-dozen gambling-tables in full blast at one time in the Committee-room of the Assembly." Both attachés and members played "draw poker through the long watches of the night." Much discredit had been brought to the "law-makers . . . and the State at large." Conversely the *Cincinnati Daily Gazette* and the *St. Louis Republican* had followed the elections in Nevada and were greatly heartened by the results of the political process and the strength of the Republican party.

For several years during the late sixties and early seventies, A. D. Richardson was resident correspondent in Nevada for Horace Greeley's *Tribune*. Richardson, sometimes independently and sometimes through the *Tribune*, contributed to a broad array of papers including the *Round Table* and the *Daily Graphic* of New York City and the *Utica Morning Herald*. Other New York papers like the *World* worked closely with the *Territorial Enterprise*. The *Round Table* was a cultural tabloid of magazine size which carried information on theater, music, poetry, new books, chess, and related sophisticated items. And yet in a single issue, of March 6, 1869, there were balanced articles on the labor demands being made on the Comstock, the new mining excitement at Hamilton and Treasure Hill, the output of the sawmills at Fort Ruby, and the future of Elko with its new railroad. The *Daily Graphic* carried a somewhat bohemian if not bizarre mixture of European art, local politics, and American industry. On November 15, 1878, the illustrated tabloid juxtaposed a large map of the Eureka mining district with a picture of a sculpture depicting Samson being betrayed by Delilah. Since the sculpture had won a grand prize at a Paris exhibition in 1878 and Eureka was to be a famous mining district, the editors believed them to be equally illustrative and revealing of the modern age.

During the Comstock decades, the *Utica Morning Herald* used the

Enterprise, the *Union*, the *Tribune*, Richardson, and a correspondent known as B. R. S. to follow Nevada affairs with singular consistency. While there were stories of stock being sold in "a grand swindle" and much attention was given to wanton shootings, the phrase "good order prevails" was commonly used. Along with the *Tribune* and the *Springfield Republican*, the *Herald* was aware that eastern money was being spent unwisely, and of a "rough, wild, cruel . . . bleak, savage, unfriendly" environment. Nevertheless, Nevada was a land of promise and of great opportunity; the miners were "laying the foundation for future cities." During Nevada's first mining epoch the out-of-state press was perhaps less critical and pointed when dealing with Nevada weaknesses than the internal press. The West had become America's vision of the future. Veins of silver and gold were to easterners merely frosting on the cake of manifest destiny. In sum, newspapers did much to publicize, to dramatize, even to glorify Nevada.

In reflecting the Nevada story, American periodical literature burrowed beneath the headlines and yet projected a mixed account similar to that of the newspapers. The May 1869 issue of *Atlantic Monthly*, entitled "The Pacific Railroad Open: How to Go: What to See," set the tone generally exhibited by railway tourists for three decades. It was recommended that travelers cross Nevada "as speedily as possible" since that portion of the route was "cheerless and dreary," with only the "sluggish and muddy" Humboldt River providing a "sickly oasis." Obviously "sensation-loving" types might wish to visit the mines, which were "disappointingly" successful. Disappointing because they "even threaten to perpetuate her [Nevada's] existence as a State in spite of the lack of everything else that makes and maintains states." In short, less than five years after admission to the Union, important voices were questioning Nevada statehood. Nevada was not merely barren, she "revenges herself . . . for her lack of all the ordinary natural graces" by creating "great hopes, large prospecting, and small returns." The only "pleasure before the traveler [is] the end of the road." Even the Humboldt "sneaks off among the hills, to die in the sands."

If the *Atlantic Monthly* of Boston was consistently snide and eloquently critical of the "monotonous landscape" and inhabitants "devoid of human graces," *The Overland Monthly* of San Francisco was far more paternalistic. The new journal, founded in July 1868, generously covered Nevada. Indeed there were six pointed articles on the state during the periodical's first year of publication. Many were short pieces like the one emphasizing the glories of Reno, where 14 stores, 4 hotels, 12 saloons, and a French restaurant were conceived, built, and opened within a period of six weeks. With a graceful, oblique, and muted Victorianism the article showed Reno as "a rough but honest place." San Francisco welcomed it into the family of towns. In traveling along the Humboldt in "Whirlwind Valley" (present-day Argenta), "the scene before us was romantic and stirring in the extreme." As the railroad crossed Nevada, "The cinders, ashes and smoldering embers of the burned up world of the dead past, were behind us, before us the life, action, energy of the living present—the abundant promise of a glorious future."

But there were also stories by sensitive if somewhat vindictive critics. In May 1869 *The Overland* presented an article by Louise M. Palmer on "How we Live in Nevada." Palmer rather jarringly suggested that in the past the areas may have been uncivilized, but *"nous avons changé tout cela."* As the wife of a mining superintendent, Palmer was unhappy on the one hand with the unfinished nature of the region, and on the other hand she found the mines and mills ugly and unsettling. She even flirted with the idea of leaving nature alone. She was perhaps the first to argue that the works of man "invaded this peaceful spot," and destroyed the birds of the hills and the fish of the river. "Let them [the mines] perish." But like John C. Van Dyke three decades later, she suggested that man's efforts are "but of a day" and the "barbarians" can seek treasure elsewhere while Nevada will revert to nature and "will yet be but a howling wilderness." Palmer wrote in part out of tongue-in-cheek criticism, in part out of a personal exasperation, and in part out of prophetic understanding.

Later the same year Hilda Rosenblatt of New York City moved the discussion from provocative cynicism to artistic mysticism in her "For Three Weeks" published in *The Overland* of December 1869. She, like so many other sensitive types, saw Nevada covered with "ruined castles" as though it had at one time in the past been occupied by druids. The alkali plains became "vast, illimitable, undefined— no Alpha, no Omega." Past experiences seemed a dream, "and this was Eternity." Rosenblatt admitted that she was unprepared "for the absolutely new appearance of the country."

Mixed in with the impressionistic articles of *The Overland Monthly* were the scientific and economic treatises prepared by Henry

De Groot, Taliesin Evans, and others. De Groot, in an article of August 1871, recognized the tremendous expense and waste in trying to develop Nevada mines—a land of "Dead-Sea apples, that turned into ashes on the lips of those who sought to taste them." In using the divining-rod to find silver and gold, "more is spent than is recovered." The whole laissez faire approach to mining discoveries "was a delusion and a mistake." Nevada was "a sinister joke" being perpetrated on New York capitalists through the "misapplication of means." Eventually Nevada mines would produce "a land of silence—an industrial Sahara—a valley of dry bones." [11]

Although an authority on metallurgy, Taliesin Evans also emphasized that every region required a balanced economy and particularly a healthy agriculture. Indeed, years before the establishment of a university, Evans, in October 1871, stressed the need for an institution with chairs in agriculture and horticulture, an active cultural program, and studies in economics. Although a miner, he argued that permanent prosperity could not flow from a "boom and bust" mining economy. The *Mining and Scientific News* had long noted the De Groot and Evans concerns. As early as January 1864 the San Francisco weekly cautioned the mining world about unreliable reporting and disastrous and futile developments being attempted in Nevada. A phenomenal wealth in machinery and supplies had been assembled at camps which failed to produce a single dollar of silver or gold. Nevada was becoming famous as a "dead-weight of intellectual inactivity."

Throughout the seventies there was a flurry of attention given to Nevada in *The New York Illustrated Times*, *The Illustrated Police News*, and most notably in *Harper's Weekly*. Colorful, well illustrated, and generally informative, the articles were mainly of a specific and factual nature. Charcoal burning, the manufacture and transportation of smelting furnaces, labor conditions, log flumes of the Sierra, the future of mining in southern Nevada, and even the possibilities for outdoor sports in the Great Basin were given extravagant coverage, sometimes not faithful to the facts.

In the decades immediately following the "Washoe Excitement," Nevada became a much-publicized region in the British press. English and Scottish investments helped to finance Nevada mines, and the Wild West travel accounts by British writers and aristocrats were eagerly sought by their local public. Large numbers of

Irish and Welsh eventually found their way to the state; however, it was the Cornish more than any other ethnic group who established a direct link with many of Nevada's most remote mining centers.

Cornwall's two largest newspapers, *The West Briton and Cornwall Advertiser* of Truro and *The Cornish Telegraph, Mining, Agriculture, and Commercial Gazette* of Penzance, literally became the Nevada miners' mouthpiece—accidents, wages, working hours at Pioche, Eureka, Austin, Cherry Creek, Lewis, Galena, Treasure Hill, Mineral Hill, and elsewhere became as well known in Cornwall as they were in the American West. And when *The West Briton* carried weekly news columns for many of the local communities like St. Ives, St. Agnes, Liskeard, Redruth, Camborne, and Camelford, they often included Nevada as one of the Cornish parishes. Collections were regularly made for holidays, charities, and the miners' fund, and the contributions "in cash" from Nevada provided one of the more impressive accounts.[12]

Since the Cornish papers had a wide circulation within the state and required less than a month in transit, the Cornish of Nevada remained closely tied to home and friends. In addition, Nevada newspapers were carefully studied and reported on by the Cornish press. However, the majority of space was devoted to letters to the editor or personal letters which local families presented for publication. There were travel accounts like "The Cornish Miners Journey to the Summit of the Sierra Nevada Mountains" and "A Journey from Quebec to San Francisco." There were cautionary letters like "A Hint for Intending Emigrants" and "Trouble Brewing for the Mormons." But most often the reports told of personal disaster like "Accidental Death in Nevada of a Native from Redruth" and "Fatal Accident of a St. Just Miner in Nevada" and "A Cornishman Lynched in America." Accidents and natural calamities like fires, snowstorms, water shortages, and the failure of a mine were often covered with surprising detail.

Sometimes there were local stories like "The Exodus" and "One Who Remains At Home" in which all were cautioned that the Cornish were far too anxious to rush to the American West. The *Redruth Times* quoted a Nevada miner as declaring, the "people of America do not walk in carpet slippers. You will find that in order to succeed you will have to elbow your way through thorns and thistles. All the vinegar of labor isn't left in England." The editor of *The West Briton* assured the readers on July 17, 1872, that a letter from Pioche had been written by an intelligent, thrifty Breage man: "I think I told you in my last letter that Pioche is about 350 miles from *everywhere*. There is a big desert to cross from Utah territory to this place, and many fast boys who have run through the last dollar, and are not able to get work, attempt to foot it out. Some go right, others miss their way and are not heard of again—either killed by Indians, or die of starvation. . . . The whole of America is in a constant commotion; there are but a few men in this great country who find any rest for the soles of their feet. They are always hearing of greener fields ahead and a host of pretty butterflies."

It should never be assumed that the Cornish were always chasing "pretty butterflies." In early Nevada thousands of men were almost completely self-governed and dozens of isolated communities were self-directed. Some immigrants were sure to engage in irresponsible confrontation rather than fruitful cooperation, in destructive rivalry rather than creative enterprise. At least a dozen Nevada authors have noticed the traditional animosity between the Cornish and the Irish. The often amusing and exaggerated areas of enmity grew up during the California gold rush and were quickly reflected and even intensified in early Nevada. On the Comstock, Cornish and Irish boxers pounded each other into pulp, and on at least one occasion, the respective trainers engaged in an even more deadly rivalry with pistols.

In July and August of 1870, the Irish and Cornish embarked on a week-long conflict which resulted in Gold Hill becoming known as Bloody Gulch. In one saloon every door was torn off, every bottle of liquor broken, and fists became numb; therefore pistols were introduced. But while a score of men were injured, not a single Celt was killed. Many companies issued orders to employ Cornish and use Irish only when absolutely necessary. Partly as a result of the policy, in April 1867 Belmont experienced destruction of property and many injuries. Eventually a protective league was formed and the Ku Klux Klan organized to keep Nevada safe for "Americans" (the Cornish were "American"). Once, in April 1877 at the Brunswick Mill on the Carson River, the Irish wrecked much of the machinery while demanding the removal of a Cornish factory superintendent. In short, the Cornish migrants to Nevada provided adequate stories and controversy to maintain the Nevada column in the Cornish press as a lively feature.

Unfair treatment of Cornish miners, the requirement to work on

Sunday, and the absence of churches disturbed a few of the migrants. However, most agreed that the mines were in "remote, wild, mountain regions" far from "church and school-house and the family," and therefore that Nevada was much like Australia, or Mexico, or South America. And one Cornishman explained that no one went to Nevada to enjoy the "humanizing influences" of her culture.

The West Briton often published verse and poems as well as letters and editorial comments. A female visitor to the Comstock wrote:

> Paint me Washoe, as you see it,
> Tinting with a truthful touch;
> Line it with a faithful pencil,
> Do not colour overmuch.

George Wharton James, the Methodist minister to a dozen Cornish mining camps in central Nevada, became one of the more famous examples of being "painted" by Washoe and the West. James came to call the desert "God's color Showroom" and a "divine exhibition salon to which He freely invites all men." Although James remained in the state less than six years, he returned often in the early twentieth century and became one of the most aggressive defenders of Nevada institutions and the wonders of the desert. As a vocal twenty-three-year-old Englishman, James arrived in Nevada in early 1881 and, although from Lincolnshire, not Cornwall, quickly proceeded to Battle Mountain to preach to the Cornish "Cousin Jacks." Over the course of many months he moved up the Reese River to Galena, Lewis, Austin, and finally on to Eureka, which had been founded by the Cornish a decade and a half earlier.

Over the years James underwent a transition from Calvinistic Methodism to a worshipper of the natural freedoms of the desert. He was to become a man of all talents interested in astronomy, geology, the humanities, and the arts; he became a Chautauqua lecturer, an editor of journals and newspapers, and the author of over forty volumes on science, philosophy, politics, and, most particularly, the desert southwest. Toward the end of his life James became a pitchman for desert promotion and settlement; his writing skills and enthusiasm were thrown behind Nevada developmental and reclamation schemes.

But James and the Cornish communities created yet other images for the state. Alice Ward Bailey wove her plot for *The Sage Brush Parson* (1906) around James's early evangelistic experiences in central Nevada. She showed a sensitive Englishman drawing strength and courage from the buoyant atmosphere of the young West. In Nevada the gray clouds of Calvinistic prudery were replaced by a beautiful "nakedness of nature." The Cornish also inspired Zua Arthur in *Broken Hills* (1958) to present the life of her Cornish prospector husband as he moved throughout the state. Frank A. Crampton built his Goldfield reminiscence around the Cornish mining phrase *Deep Enough* (1956), and Charles O. Ryan's attractive autobiographical essay *Nine Miles from Dead Horse Wells* (1959) concentrated on an age-old superstition supposedly brought to Nevada by Cornish miners, about Johnny Knockers and Piskeys, who haunted the mines as ghosts, ghouls, and ill omens and kept underground workers always on guard. Jean McElrath's *Aged in Sage* (1964) often used the Cornish in the book's thirty-six short stories set mainly in Elko County; Mark Requa's *Grubstake* (1935) set in the Eureka of 1874 employed the Cornish; and Anne Burns used Cornish characters as she focused on the central Nevada mines in her book *The Wampus Cat* (1951).[13]

The Cornish painted a portrait of Nevada that was harsh and muscular; their letters did not create loose ends, fluid concerns, opaque images. They saw themselves as raw material, ideal for a state with growing wealth and unsophisticated sinews. The almost one hundred letters, brief editorials, and photographs researched tell an unassuming and very personal story. Nevada was neither a miracle nor a backwater, neither an intrepid land nor a quiet bucolic place. One did not argue about the landscape or the climate; almost no one spoke of culture or freedom. Rather Nevada was simply a place to work, and if your mine was demolished by fire or your camp closed, you accepted word-of-mouth rumor and often alone, but with resignation, pushed on to the next mine head. And yet few Americans, indeed few people of any nationality, provided a better record of their wanderings on the frontier. The Cornish of Nevada both reflected and absorbed, but mainly they supplied and they created yet another image of the state.

Numerous diverse and often blatantly promotional books were published during the Comstock era. Typical was Henry T. Williams's *The Pacific Tourist*, first issued in 1876 and specifically designed for the transcontinental railway trade. Over forty artists, engravers, and writers were used to make the 312–page work into the most elaborate guidebook of its time. The tour writers relied on legend and history, myth and fact, fable and detail. They were both derivative and superficial. Sometimes their account was a pretentious parade of the highest mountains, the largest streams, the customs of Indians.[14]

Fifty-two pages of the text were devoted to Nevada. Lands were being opened to irrigation, fish and game were plentiful, expeditions to the mines were arranged, and Indians were a source of wonder and study rather than annoyance and fear. Chief Winnemucca was even christened "Napoleon of the Piutes." Highlights, like bloody Gravely Ford and below it the well-tended Maidens Grave, allowed the railroad to claim a deep "devotion to women." It was, however, at Humboldt House, twelve miles west of Mill City, that Nevada was able to reveal her true identity. "The Oasis in the Desert" had been built by George Washington Meacham in 1868 and was later to become famous as the girlhood home of Nevada's first woman of letters, Idah Meacham Strobridge. In 1876, trees, green grass, "shady bowers and flowing fountains" proved that "the desert can be reclaimed and made to bud and blossom as the rose." Fruit was as beautiful as that of California "but superior in flavor." Apples were prolific and peaches, pears, plums, and cherries supplied an eastern ambiance. Trout, wild geese, mandarin ducks, as well as a shipping yard for cattle served to replicate in Nevada a bit of "God's country" like that in the East or the Midwest. Many editions of The Pacific Tourist were to follow down to World War I, and the agrarian possibilities of Nevada were routinely and repeatedly stressed. The listing of 95 curious and colorful place names along the Central Pacific track may have failed to create the desired image for future homesteads. Dead Mule Canyon, Gouge Eye, Lousy Ravine, and Loafer Hill were not to blossom into major centers, but neither was Humboldt House.

John J. Powell also used the centennial year of 1876 to extol the state in his Nevada: The Land of Silver. According to Powell, the "cloud of ignorance was at length dispelled." The suggestion that the state "was unproductive, dreary, desolate; an arid waste, incapable of supporting a civilized community; a sea of sand—the Sahara of America" was, according to Powell, being reshaped. Powell played on the thread of past injustices, but in 1876 Nevada was "the physical wonder" and "the great treasure-vaults of the world." Past misconceptions could be overlooked. "Instead of monotonous plains of sand, we find mountains of sparkling silver." Triumphant Nevada had "bones of silver and veins of gold."

In the years after the Civil War, the federal government followed up on its earlier explorations to sponsor four great surveys of the West. Both Clarence King and George M. Wheeler supervised geographical explorations over large areas of Nevada. Both published several scientific volumes on their findings. King was to conduct a scientific survey of the 40th parallel from the California-Nevada border to the Great Plains. He arrived at the first base camp, Glendale, Nevada (near the future Reno), in July 1867. He followed the route of the transcontinental railroad and sought water resources that could provide for base settlements along the line and eventually "establish irrigation throughout."

His report on Nevada probably did not entice migrants to the area. A local hermit kept preaching "desolation, thy name is Humboldt," some men claimed the wells gave them gonorrhea, other locals declared the Humboldt Sink "the worst place between Missouri and Hell," and many in the party became ill with malaria. King was struck by lightning while surveying a peak near Stillwater. Finally, back in camp in November 1867 he declared, "this is in every way the most difficult and dangerous country to campaign in I know of on the continent."

During an 1885 congressional investigation of the surveys, Representative Hilary Herbert declared that there had been far too many reports on Nevada. Nevertheless, Eliot Lord, an assistant to King, had written *Comstock Mining and Miners* in 1883. Lord was a brilliant, Harvard-trained scientist, but even he found the Comstock an "Arabian Nights Tale," and "a story of Aladdin." And yet he admitted that in Nevada "fortune sometimes favors fools." The speculators were always over-sanguine and "faith, capital and skill" were necessary for prospecting, but seeking wealth in Nevada was "essentially a gambling venture."

Perhaps an even more graphic result of the geographic surveys was the photographs of John K. Hillers. The German-born Hillers met John Wesley Powell in 1871 and immediately joined the expedition down the Colorado. In 1872 he became Powell's official photographer and embarked upon a thirty-year career depicting American Indians and western landscapes. Moving inland from the Colorado to the site of present-day Las Vegas, Hillers, in September 1873, photographed four Southern Paiutes engaged in a quiet gambling game and three Indian maidens carefully posed with breasts showing. Hillers's gamblers and nudes were of the nineteenth century. He could not have envisioned the future motif of Las Vegas. But as Don Fowler, presenter of *The Photographs of John K. Hillers,* has suggested, "Las Vegas has a longer history of gaming than the present-day Chamber of Commerce realizes."[15]

Nevadans have never accepted the old aphorism about sticks and stones breaking bones, but words never hurting. Words, stories, jingles, and the national press were viewed as powerful forces, and Nevada long remained particularly sensitive to any type of economic or cultural criticism. Perhaps the most notorious and prolonged incident of image making occurred during the late 1870s. In April 1877 Frank Leslie, one of New York's leading publishers, left Madison Avenue for an excursion across wild America and on to the Pacific Coast. Accompanying Leslie on his private train, which had his name emblazoned on all coaches, were his wife, two close friends, and six staff writers and artists. Leslie not only published *Frank Leslie's Illustrated Newspaper*, he was also owner of an impressive chain of magazines, founder of the German-language *Frank Leslie's Illustrated Zeitung*, provider of articles for *The Illustrated London News*, supporter of a Dutch newspaper, and a dominant figure in some six other publications.[16]

Born in England in 1821 and christened Henry Carter, he had been apprenticed to a wood engraver associated with the London press. Changing his name but maintaining his technical skills, he emigrated to New York City in 1848 and rapidly matured into a successful businessman. Growing wealthy during the Civil War, he burst onto the publishing world as a producer of gaudy, fast-paced papers full of mental pabulum. Leslie became involved in politics, was appointed commissioner of the Philadelphia World's Fair, and, after a divorce, married the young wife of an employee. At the peak of his form and after much advertising and a highly touted champagne party, Leslie's train started across America. The party arrived in Nevada during May

1877. The newspapers and tabloids had already published numerous articles about them and provided many drawings of the state; and Mrs. Leslie had achieved a level of notoriety because she had traveled with Lola Montez, even performing with her on stage and claiming to be Miss Montez's sister. Consequently, Virginia City literally rolled out the red carpet. In addition to providing the party with free accommodations and escorts around town, pure silver lumps were given to the members; and as a mark of a special distinction "the chief" was given a solid silver brick, thus "conferring honor" on a "distinguished visitor."

Late in 1877 and throughout 1878, *Frank Leslie's Illustrated Newspaper*, a weekly, along with his other publications, featured stories on the transcontinental excursion. From December 1877 to June 1878 the lengthy and colorful illustrated accounts dealt with the Nevada crossing. Most of the stories about Nevada, whether about corrals being built at Wells, stockyards at Halleck, the palisades near Carlin, or the Humboldt House, were well executed and positive. Upon leaving Virginia City the writers were polite, even eloquent. "It was, however, with regret that we took leave of the enterprising city." The inhabitants had been "kind and attentive. None of the alleged roughness of Western manners was perceptible." The Comstock had become a "rapidly growing and important landmark of human progress."

Mrs. Leslie occasionally contributed to the articles and took extensive notes which were pulled together as a *Pleasure Trip from Gotham to the Golden Gate*. In addition to authoring such articles as "The Gracious Life of the Palace Car Traveler," she employed French phrases and spoke romantically of the moon rising over the desert and the ever-shifting sands. Most of the book was a masterpiece of superciliousness, even arrogance, but for some unknown reason Virginia City became the focal point of scorn. "To call a place dreary, desolate, homeless, uncomfortable, and wicked is a good deal, but to call it God-forsaken is a good deal more. We never found a place better deserving the title than Virginia City."

The climate, the geography, the buildings, all presented a "dreary scene." The city boasted forty-nine gambling saloons and one church; the latter was used frequently for funerals. She said of the town, "Every other house was a drinking or gambling saloon, and we passed a great many brilliantly lighted windows where sat audacious-looking women who freely chatted with passers-by or entertained guests within."

Devout Londoners claimed to have felt a series of earth tremors on the day that Henry Fielding's ribald *Tom Jones* was published; all of Virginia City felt the mountain move the day *Gotham* arrived in town. Leaders on the Comstock, peculiarly sensitive to criticism, were humiliated and claimed to have been deceived and betrayed by the Leslies. Rollin Daggett, editor of the *Territorial Enterprise*, participated in an investigation of Mrs. Leslie's life and career and on July 14, 1878, issued a special edition of the paper accusing her of being an adventuress, a bastard, a fornicatrix, and a snob. With trenchant ridicule and irony Daggett savaged Mrs. Leslie, her friends, her past lovers, and her literary and social accuracy.

The "biography" was bound into a brief pamphlet and widely circulated in Nevada and California and especially in New York City. Information on Mrs. Leslie had been obtained, in part, from her former husband, the famous archaeologist Ephrim G. Squires. According to the pamphlet she had been born Miriam Follin of unmarried Creole parents in New Orleans in 1836. She married and was divorced as a teenager. After traveling about the world with Lola Montez, and having lived with congressmen and others, she married Squires in Central America. When Squires was employed by Leslie, she quickly was given editing and publishing positions on various periodicals. Upon marrying Frank Leslie, her fame as a party giver and as owner of diamonds and other fine jewelry became widespread.

With Daggett's reply to *Trip from Gotham to the Golden Gate*, along with labor troubles, the depression, and excessive expenditures, Frank Leslie's empire was beginning to crumble. After a series of economic misadventures, Leslie died in January 1880. Mrs. Leslie seized control of the several publications, defeated his sons in litigation, married Oscar Wilde's brother, claimed she was a baroness through her French ancestry, and died an avowed feminist in 1914. The Leslies' weekly magazine survived until 1922.

Nevada's rather excessive response to both real and simulated criticism was to continue for a hundred years and invariably ended in a tarnished triumph.

Differing from Utah or California, there was no utopian image for Nevada of a city built upon a hill or of a town carefully founded in a lush, humid valley. There were no statues, no cherubs or angels or saints, no monuments to Indian chiefs, no memorials to military heroes. Few Nevada settlements were augmented with spiritual, ideological, or social zeal. No one possessed the wonderful putty or conviction or the natural bond provided by the land— land which so often held a community together in adversity.

Nevada's towns had not evolved in a thoughtful way. Rather they were accidents of geology. If the streak of silver was found at 7,000 feet on a barren mountainside 200 miles from a major road or railhead, a camp was formed, but it seldom flourished as a regional or trading center. Neither the residents nor the reporters came to think of these camp-towns as a permanent home where families and children would live and work and retire and be buried. None of Nevada's more than a hundred railway camps and sidings was any more permanent. Well over 90 percent were swept away within a decade. None grew rapidly and it was the twentieth century before any became centers of industry or magnets for sustained commercial activity. After the Comstock, Nevada became a wasting land where the few residents either prospected for a new bonanza or clustered along the railroad or the California border to be within striking distance of economic or cultural life. The remainder of the state became part of a moldering edifice, a ghost town, dissolving into some dark and deadly sleep.

Unfortunately, throughout the Comstock period the image makers found neither leaders nor a vision, neither a spokesman nor a statement, neither a mover nor a movement. A populist reformer and reclamation advocate of the eighties could sum up the all too transitory era with a benediction from Isaiah.

> Your silver has turned to dross,
> Your wine is watered.
> Your princes are rebels,
> Accomplices of thieves.

The eulogy, however, was premature. As the nineteenth-century mines collapsed, they trailed in their turbulent wake a hyperactive tale of grandeur and disillusionment. And another equally idiosyncratic mining era was to follow in early twentieth-century Nevada.

CHAPTER III

I am too poor to afford bending.

—Charles de Gaulle

C harles de Gaulle once told Winston Churchill during the dark days of World War II, "I am too poor to afford bending." Nevada was in much the same position during the dark decades ending the nineteenth century. As the mines collapsed and no economic substitute was found, the population decreased by a third. The state became peripheral, static, and solitary; the largest town, Reno, had only 4,500 people in 1900. There was little literature of hope and little unity of purpose; there were few examples of solidarity by the citizens and few experiences built upon or remembered. Occupations, classes, and ethnic groups became little more than individuals lost in a chilling sea of isolation and economic uncertainty. The Comstock slowly evolved from action to memories, and from memories to floating myth and legend. Nevada became a land of arrested gestures and declining certitudes, of phasing out, closing down, and moving on.

And yet, during these long decades the people of the state built for themselves a paradigm, an image, which was to influence their thinking for half a century. They saw their economic stagnation as a result of outside empirical forces that, having drained the state of its riches, were unwilling to replenish, rebuild, or replace what they had taken. They saw themselves as independent, self-sufficient citizens with crude but noble characteristics rather like those of the indomitable frontiersmen. They saw their state as set apart, unjustly scoffed at and scorned, and sorely misunderstood. They felt justified, therefore, in establishing peculiar institutions and in promoting their own unique, if questionable, livelihood. They saw themselves at one and the same time as America's greatest patriots and the most profound critics of governmental injustice and federal indifference. Most Nevadans sincerely believed that the mining industry could be resuscitated if outside interests only had more faith and the imagination to invest. And after being caught up in the reclamation movement, they came to assume that the state would become an agrarian paradise and a western model for the small farmer.

During the depression, however, even railway promoters grew uncertain as to whether it was possible to combat the negative image. A jingle in the Chicago press typified the eastern sarcasm.

> We strike the Great Desert
> With its wilderness howl,
> With its cactus and sage,
> With its serpent and owl,
> And its pools of dead water,
> Its torpid old streams,
> The corpse of an earth
> And the nightmare of dreams.[1]

Before the twentieth century's rediscovery of the glories of a "wild and woolly West," or the later respect for desert ecosystems, the eighties and nineties provided a truly Gilded Age for formalized western travel. There was elegance in ornate palace cars and much dignified reporting as the rich made excursions to the sumptuous hotels of California. The tourist and travel industry became big business in western America. Earl Pomeroy in his *In Search of the Golden West* has noted the problems faced by railroads when encouraging the trip to California. According to him, in 1886 the Santa Fe Railway claimed that the Arizona and Mojave crossing was "no worse than Nevada." Indeed, the Santa Fe deserts were "the narrowest and cleanest of all those howling wildernesses which, by a peculiar dispensation of Providence, every transcontinental line must cross." In *Our Country's Scenic Marvels*, published in Boston in 1893, J. W. Buel could write of Nevada, "Nature has denied to this wretched region any compensation of flower, stream, bird, or even curiosity. . . . It is the very nakedness of bleak desolation, and stretches its cursed length through a distance of 600 miles."

The travelers found the plush, upholstered, palace cars with their varnished wood and silver-mounted interiors a slice of Eastern civilization cutting through the uncouth, tasteless shantytowns of the desert West. The English and the nouveau riche Americans could find adventure and excitement; indeed, as Walt Whitman admitted in 1879, it was "a fierce wild pleasure" to be inside your Pullman and observe the outside world. But the Nevada image seemed to repel most observers. Rather than the train exemplifying the magic of commerce, wealth, and culture for the state, only the burning desert heat and the alkali dust filtering through the cracks in the windows and onto the rich velvet upholstery and heavy clothing were to be remembered. In an era when three-fourths of the country lived close to the soil, the object of most rich Americans was to escape the boredom of the outdoors, especially the tedium of the forlorn desert.

Nevertheless, throughout Nevada's great depression decades there remained a romanticism of place and nature, heightened by both geological and literary writing. Israel Cook Russell in a lengthy 1885 study entitled *Geological History of Lake Lahontan* repeated the earlier evaluations of the Great Basin. On the one hand its valleys were "absolute deserts" like Arabia and the shores of the Dead Sea, yet the mountains were "sometimes marvelous, especially when . . . composed of the purple trachytes, the deep-colored rhyolites, and the many-hued volcanic tuffs so common in western Nevada." There was a "grandeur of this rugged land . . . a world of sublimity."[2]

The impressive railroad guide, *The Pacific Tourist*, was republished several times, each edition using much of the original material. The 1882–83 edition noted the University of Nevada at Elko, but in general Nevada was described only in terms of scenery and the pleasures of life in a palace car. It was not until after the turn of the century, during a new mining boom and the prosperity that came with America's first federal reclamation project, that railroad literature again became eloquent in describing the wondrous opportunities of Nevada.

Henry R. Mighels, the editor-philosopher-politician, to some degree countered the boisterous tourism-and-geology image of Nevada with a series of sensitive and underplayed characterizations. Mighels was born in Maine, studied medicine in Cincinnati, and traveled to California in 1850 where be became a painter, printer, and publisher.

First an editor of small papers in Butte and Oroville, he eventually became an editor on the *Sacramento Bee*. After failing in California politics he returned to the East and later joined the Union army. Injured in 1864, he immediately returned to California; in 1865 he assumed editorship of the *Carson Daily Appeal*. He served in the Nevada State Assembly as a liberal Republican but was defeated for lieutenant-governor in 1878. Most of Mighels's contradictory writing was published in 1879 in *Sage Brush Leaves*. He was one of a handful of intelligent, sensitive, even mystic men, rather like Henry De Groot, J. Ross Browne, and John Muir, who drifted across the Nevada scene.[3]

Mighels admitted that in his craving for learning he tried to pattern himself after the English historians Thomas Macaulay and James Froude, and yet quoting from "An Apology for Idlers" he declared, "Books . . . are a mighty bloodless substitute for life," and he found few books worth a pound of good tobacco. Mighels believed Nevada to be like all new settlements, peopled "with a hardier, more industrious and more seriously occupied race." And yet he saw nothing wrong with "the art of living without work." The "Fellow of the College of Indolence" was better for society than the "dull, plodding blockhead." He conceded that Nevada had remained on "the outskirts of the region of Vagabondage" and thought Nevadans had perhaps correctly been "bullied and scowled at and pointed out as dreadful examples." Although a Republican, he regretted that the state did not enjoy a "sweet, rebellious tone." Indeed, even the term "Nevada" should be eliminated and replaced by "Washoe," a "propagating, virile noun and not a mere sexless adjective." The "aboriginal substantivity" should replace the "lisp of ill-understood, second-hand Spanish." But perhaps most telling and unique for anyone with political ambitions was his view of mining. He bemoaned the discovery of new mines because nature was the greatest of all forces and should not be disturbed. "We know how hard the times are, and how much there is need of some developments." But "we hope [Nevadans] will find never a speck of gold in any stream whose laughing waters leap into that lake [Tahoe] nor on any hillside or glen thereabout; for we are not willing to contemplate the fair face of that loveliest of sheets of mountain water stained and muddied with the turgid rinsings of flumes and rockers and sluices and long-toms."[4]

Henry Mighels lived in Nevada for a little over a decade, and was not markedly successful as a politician, a businessman, a humanist, or a newspaper editor. He was inconsistent, and according to closest friends "his faults were glaring." But he was a practicing thinker and stubborn critic when there were few of either in the state. Everything from art to temperance, from poverty to urbanization, attracted his attention. His vision of Nevada was cultural as well as corporeal, aesthetic as well as materialistic.

With the collapse of the mining booms, the Eastern press often used Nevada for sensationalism, sports opportunities, and colorful illustrations. The *New York Illustrated Times* ran articles on "Sports in Nevada," *Harper's Weekly* noted the old mines and the new lumber industry, *Frank Leslie's Illustrated Newspaper* maintained interest in the state and occasionally published gaudy and bizarre illustrations of the area's natural wonders, and Cyrus Currier and Sons provided illustrations on Nevada smelting equipment for the *Daily Graphic* of New York. On March 1, 1890, the *Illustrated London News* overshadowed its American competitors with a front-page article entitled, "A Day's Antelope-Hunting in Nevada, North America." Four drawings depicted a horse frightened by a snake and the dazed rider picking himself out of the cactus and preparing to walk out of the desert. In print and from a distance, Nevada had become a sportsman's paradise.

On the West Coast, *Sunset* carried the very occasional poem, picture, or brief impressionistic short story like "Battle Mountain Bill" or "A Glimpse of Lake Tahoe." In a September 1899 *Sunset* article entitled "Across Nevada," Dougherty Coulter pointedly attacked the long decades of negative image making about the state. Dismissing the repeated tourist quips that in crossing America "Nevada is the minor chord," Coulter recklessly declared that before the railroad our grandfathers would "tell you that the pleasantest part of the journey was following the Humboldt." Although Nevada lost its wealth to out-of-state raiders, the natives desired neither sympathy nor pity. "We have no cyclones, tornadoes, blizzards, earthquakes, nothing to disturb the harmony of a peaceful life. . . . We have been deserted by our millionaires and can boast no palaces, no cathedrals, no museums of art," but there are "no homeless, no destitute, and few ignorant and lawless." Coulter also made gallant attempts to explain the success of Nevada's sheep and cattle ranches. *The Irrigation Age* not only noted the short stories of Mary Hallock Foote and Idah Meacham Strobridge, but argued as passionately and illogically as Coulter that the West was the last best hope for America. Without agriculture in the desert "the last safety valve is closed."

Western Americans were also coming to read *The Californian*, founded in San Francisco in January 1880. Of the first six issues of the literary, political, historical, and personal-interest journal, eight of the articles in whole or in part addressed Nevada. In prose and in poetry they noted Indians, sheepherding, lynchings, small town life, lakes, rivers, and mountains. Later in the eighties, the Basques, the Paiutes, and historical notes on Mark Twain, Adolph Sutro, and labor unions were emphasized. *The Californian* and *The Overland Monthly*'s coverage of Nevada were designed for thoughtful and questioning readers, whereas *Sunset*, *The Irrigation Age*, *The Progressive West*, and *The Land of Sunshine* (later to become *Out West*) were promotional, upbeat, and designed to influence and direct the reader's actions.

During the late nineties *The Land of Sunshine* published a series of stories by Idah Meacham Strobridge and occasional Nevada vignettes by other local writers. However, the journal also gave much attention to railroad development in southern Nevada and to irrigation. In a December 1896 article entitled "The Irrigation Congress," by Fred Allers, the argument was pointed and passionate. Irrigation was the only major issue facing western America. Far more important than silver or the tariff, it had become the "rainbow of promise." Only water could change "a voiceless desert, into a place fit for homes for millions of now homeless people." There would be a new class of citizens, the "Lords of the desert" who would no longer be reduced to poverty or the "lottery" of nature. This new desert West could accommodate "sixteen million families"—a population larger than the entire United States in 1890.

During the late nineteenth and early twentieth centuries a disparate group of progressive promoters came to believe that through a massive infusion of federal funds, the vision of *The Irrigation Age* and *The Land of Sunshine* could become a reality and "the American West [would] yet provide the truest picture of Acadia." Most of the irrigation crusaders were optimists loyal to the ideal of the Eastern and Midwestern family farm and believers in the populist jingle, "Come along, come along, don't be alarmed, Uncle Sam is rich enough to buy us all a farm." In Nevada a faith in irrigation eventually tended to pull together those with reclamation, agricultural, progressive, reform, and educational interests. The broadly accented movement remained an attractive image of Nevada public life until after World War I.

Nevadans had long been aware of the capricious nature of the weather. During the first decade of settlement they had undertaken irrigation projects and the physical control of water. As early as 1859 Horace Greeley spoke in terms of millions of farmers settling in western Nevada as quickly as major dams and irrigation canals could be constructed. And during the Comstock era an advanced water system for Virginia City was devised and many utopian plans for damming the Humboldt, Carson, and Truckee rivers were suggested.

In *A History of the Comstock Silver Lode and Mines*, Dan De Quille argued that Lake Tahoe should be used as an immense natural storage reservoir. Borrowing from John Wesley Powell's ideas, De Quille proposed that a four-foot dam at Tahoe could provide water for 500,000 acres. A similar dam at Donner Lake could irrigate an additional 150,000 acres, and flowing wells yet other thousands of acres. Furthermore, only a railroad and a controlled water supply were delaying southern Nevada from becoming a tropical paradise. In the absence of private investors, De Quille believed the Nevada state legislature should organize the first great irrigation thrust for the state. By the end of the nineteenth century, however, it was obvious that the massive undertaking that would be necessary to make a significant impact upon the local economy would require a commitment by the federal government.[5]

While many careful observers noted the need for giant irrigation projects, it was Robert Fulton who, because of his enthusiasm and position, helped to launch the idea. Born in Ohio in 1847, trained as a pharmacy clerk and a telegraph operator, Fulton worked in Wyoming as a railway dispatcher during the late sixties before moving to Reno in 1875. He invested in railroad properties, purchased the *Reno Evening Gazette*, became a land agent for the Central Pacific Railroad, was responsible for establishing Joseph Stubbs as president of the University of Nevada, lead both the Anti-Gambling and the Womens' Civic Leagues, and was cofounder and first president of the Nevada

Historical Society. Fulton had been reared a Calvinist by his Scotch-Irish father, but in Nevada he found religion "the most ineffectual of human activities." A Progressive Republican, he came to support governmental involvement in major public works projects. Upon his death in October 1920, the *San Francisco Examiner* eulogized him as "The Father of the Irrigation Movement" in Nevada. Fulton became the bridge between railroads and reclamation, between business and education, between agriculture and Nevada culture, between the Historical Society and the community.[6]

In early 1877, shortly after arriving in the state, he stood at a vantage point west of Reno near the Truckee River, envisioned a dam, and drew a plan for an irrigation works that would "emblazon history with the conquest of peace . . . and unite the world in one social family." The nearby valleys would bloom with "fertile farmlands and productive cattle ranches, orchards, and grape arbors, bringing a prosperity to the new state that would endure." Fulton, reflecting the ideas of fellow newspaper editor Henry Mighels, quoted the English poet William Collins, "Curst be the gold and silver which persuade weak men to follow far-fatiguing trade." Biographer Barbara Richnak in *A River Flows* found Fulton "a writer obsessed with his craft, and history was his favorite topic." As a contributor to *Sunset* and other magazines, as an opponent of prizefighting and the Silver party, and as a detractor of most "European traditions," Fulton became an early supporter of Nevada's federal reclamation project.

As the eighties progressed and mining continued to decline, Nevada embarked upon several faltering attempts to diversify the economy. The actions at first created only limited outside notice, but slowly they were to build into the reclamation movement and eventually reorder both the internal and the external image of the state. The first formal proposal for the state legislature to undertake state-supported irrigation or reclamation projects was made in 1885. In 1887 a State Bureau of Immigration was created with the governing board composed of the state controller, the state surveyor general, and the state superintendent of public instruction. No funds were allocated for the bureau's promotional activities, however. Therefore, the agency did little more than write copy for newspapers and alert the West to the opportunities to be found in Nevada lands.

The Reno Chamber of Commerce, Robert Fulton of the *Gazette*,

L. H. Taylor, the future engineer for the U.S. Reclamation Service, and Orvis Ring, the state superintendent of public instruction, blended with the Bureau of Immigration and attempted to make contacts, to advertise, and to solicit potential migrants. Sometimes they overshot the objective. The immigration "bureau of 1888 engaged in considerable hyperbole and overstatement. A brochure declared the climate of Nevada to be "the most delightful and salubrious in the known world."

> The warmest days of summer are modified by soft southwest winds, laden with the sweet odor of wild flowers and the invigorating aroma of the indigenous sage, while the nights are seasons of transcendent loveliness, rendered so by the gentle mountain breezes that waft health and vigor to the sleeper.[7]

In 1889, soon-to-be congressman Francis G. Newlands organized the State Board of Trade. As an unofficial body including the governor, Senator William Stewart, and the Central Pacific Railroad, it worked with private citizens and local organizations throughout the country to encourage rural settlement in Nevada. After a series of newspaper articles, letters, and brochures were circulated, an eighty-eight-page booklet called *Nevada and Her Resources* was published by the State Printing Office in 1894. The pamphlet represented a joint effort but was written and compiled by Fulton and Taylor and became the pattern for numerous similar publications that were to appear over the following two decades.

Although presenting the opportunities and inducements for settling in Nevada, the work, nevertheless, was surprisingly candid and informational. "Our own state has so long been the subject of adverse comment and hateful criticism that the Scripture has been paraphrased and men instinctively ask 'Can any good thing come out of Nevada?'" Since there had been no official response to the innuendoes, the state "has but few who understand or sympathize with her." While Nevada was not to be compared with wealthy California, both capitalists and homeseekers, the poor and the workers, should investigate. "Nevada will find work for idle hands."

Turning to history, the authors readily admitted that "no one ever considered the feasibility of building a state here." But the mines and the railroad created a society. And with sheep, cattle, and farming, the area would be planted "so firm and solid that the true era of the State's prosperity . . . and . . . integrity . . . will be dated by it." The "rotten borough" was but a memory, the millionaires were gone. They only left "inverted shafts and holes in the ground for monuments."

During the early nineties, parties of prospective migrants contacted the Board of Trade or the governor, and occasionally farmers visited the state and inspected the lands. The results seem to have been uniformly unsuccessful. On one occasion representatives for over a hundred Tennessee families were induced by Newlands to travel to Reno, but the first morning after their arrival, an unseasonal September snowstorm ended the negotiations.

One group of wanderers, who actually tried to fashion a Nevada Elysium, provide a more tragic story. In June 1897 the 5,000-acre Wymore ranch in Smith Valley was offered for sale. On August 12, Ephraim Deinard, secretary of the Hebrew Agricultural Society of the United States, wrote to Nevada's German-born governor, Reinhold Sadler, requesting "encouragement and moral assistance" in their plan to settle hundreds of migrants in Nevada. The Philadelphia-based philanthropic group was helping Russian and Polish Jews to colonize.[8]

With the governor's encouragement, two Carson City merchants claimed to have purchased the ranch and by October had signed an agreement to settle an initial cadre of seventeen families. But by November, twenty-five families had arrived in Reno and were anxious to move on to their new home. Dishonesty, mismanagement, and misunderstanding led to the immediate collapse of the settlement and by December 1898, the Hebrew Benevolent Society of San Francisco was assisting the colonists to move to California. The thousands of Russian, Polish, German, and Austrian Jews, some of whom had already traveled to Canada and South America, were not to make Smith Valley into the new Israel, and Nevada failed to "triple in population in the next five years" or become the Jewish State of America. Nor was the state symbol changed from an engraving of mining and industry to one embossed with grain and vegetables, as had been prophesied by flamboyant newspaper articles.

At the national level, Nevada's Senator William Stewart, after being returned to the Senate in 1887, reviewed for that body the serious problems facing the arid West and had himself named chairman of a Senate Committee on Irrigation and Reclamation. Stewart and John Wesley Powell, head of the U.S. Geological Survey, toured

Nevada in the summer of 1889. The federal action was fortuitous since earlier in 1889 the Nevada legislature had established a Board of Reclamation and Internal Improvement and authorized $100,000 for the construction of reservoirs and canals. The senate committee met with the newly created state board in Carson City. The board not only requested federal aid to develop Nevada as an agricultural economy but declared local conditions to be more desperate "than at any time since its organization as a state." The board recognized and readily admitted that Nevada was impotent to save itself. "Can the General Government refuse to render assistance or will it allow one of its sovereign states to languish?"

Despite its moving appeal for federal assistance, the Board of Reclamation and Internal Improvement was terminated by the Nevada legislature in 1891. However, the National Irrigation Congress founded in September 1891 helped to keep the irrigation issue in the forefront of western politics. The National Irrigation Congress also contributed to the dramatic rise in prominence of Francis G. Newlands and William E. Smythe.

Born in Mississippi, educated at Yale and Columbia, and admitted to the bar in California, Newlands moved permanently to Nevada in 1888. He recognized that irrigation could become a key to political success and immediately spoke out on the issue of water and reservoirs; becoming a friend of Robert Fulton, William Smythe, and others devoted to the issue, Newlands toured with Senator Stewart's committee on irrigation in 1889 and became head of Nevada's delegation to the first National Irrigation Congress, which was held in Salt Lake City in September 1891. During 1892 Newlands ran for Congress as the nominee of the newly formed Silver party and won over three times as many votes as his nearest competitor. After the failure of the Carey Act of 1894 to meet the needs of the arid states, and with the reclamation-minded Theodore Roosevelt becoming president in September 1901, the Newlands Reclamation Act became law on June 17, 1902, and the Truckee-Carson Irrigation Project was born. Congressman Newlands moved to the U.S. Senate in 1903. Newlands, Stewart, Fulton, Taylor, Ring, and other reclamation advocates were political and pragmatic, ambitious and successful. They were not preservationists, nor did they worry about the shrinking wilderness. They found the desert useless unless touched and used. It was to be redesigned and improved for the public good, an example of man's achievement and not a sanctuary or God's preserve.

As a precocious youth and son of a wealthy Worcester, Massachusetts, shoe manufacturer, William E. Smythe was editor of his own newspaper at nineteen. In 1888, at age 27, he moved to Nebraska but in 1891 hurried on west to found *The Irrigation Age* and to organize the first National Irrigation Congress in Salt Lake City. Since Newlands led the Nevada delegation to the congress, he and Smythe became colleagues in the great reclamation crusade. But Smythe, quickly tiring of a single crusade, founded a colony in Idaho in 1895 and then pushed on to Lassen County, California, where, on an isolated ranch near the Nevada border, he wrote the first edition of *The Conquest of Arid America*. In 1900 he located in San Diego where he ran for Congress; later he attempted to establish more agrarian colonies, and finally he accepted employment in the Interior Department and settled in Washington, D.C.[9]

During the nineties Smythe became a leading advocate for reclamation in Nevada and an impassioned critic of the state's many detractors. Although he often noted Nevada in articles, speeches, and letters, his two great defenses of the state were a response to a *Chicago Tribune* article and the 1905 re-editing of *The Conquest of Arid America*. The suggestion that Nevada be deprived of statehood was made many times between the 1860s and the 1950s; however, the humiliation appeared most likely to be achieved during the depressed 1890s. The population of the state had been reduced to about 40,000, the largest town could claim fewer than 4,000 persons, and only the railroad seemed to hold the widely scattered communities together. In an editorial, "How To Deal With Nevada," the *Tribune* like many other publications noted the state's lack of minerals, agricultural resources, and industry and concluded, "she is flickering out." The two senators could be excluded as was done with the Southern States during the Civil War and Nevada could be easily merged with Utah.

Smythe, in a piece headlined "Shall Nevada be Deprived of Statehood," answered the *Tribune* in April 1897, in *The Forum* of New York City. In his nine-page rebuttal he argued that such "radical" and "perilous" steps could lead to the "dissolution of the Union." He suggested that the argument was selfishly and politically motivated. But he devoted most attention to Nevada's potential to become "one of the great States of the Union." Nevada was wealthy in mineral ores and would again become a mining state, but most important, the Irrigation Congress of 1893 had studied the lakes, the rivers, and the wells of the state and scientifically determined that they could irrigate 5,000,000 acres. All of the fruits and grasses of the temperate zone as well as the figs, olives, almonds, and English walnuts of the semitropical zone could be grown. For Smythe it was the greed of mine operators and banks and railroads that bled Nevada of its capital. "Nevada's decadence is due to economic evils common to the arid region." Since the federal government held over 90 percent of the land, the federal government must act to redeem it.[10]

Smythe first wrote *The Conquest of Arid America* in 1899, but revised and expanded the work in 1905. He devoted a chapter to most of the western states but argued that "No division of the Union has been so persistently and grossly misunderstood" as Nevada. He repeated the story about the Pullman car travelers who found the place "only fit to hold the earth together" and quoted "a recent novel."

> Nevada! But the name is all. Abomination of desolation presides over nine-tenths of the place. The sun beats down on a roof of zinc, fierce and dull. Not a drop of water to a mile of sand. The mean ash-dump landscape stretches on from nowhere to nowhere, a spot of mange. No portion of the earth is more lacquered with paltry, unimportant ugliness.

To counter the novelist, Smythe turned to John C. Van Dyke, who as an aesthetician, not a pragmatist, had no wish to reshape the desert or to see it turned into Midwestern farms. Van Dyke had published *The Desert* in 1901 and Smythe applied it to Nevada.

> Not in vain these wastes of sand . . . they are beautiful in themselves . . . what land can equal the desert with its wide plains, its grim mountains, and its expanding canopy of sky! You shall never see elsewhere as here the dome, the pinnacle, the minaret fretted with golden fire at sunrise and sunset; you shall never see elsewhere as here the sunset valleys swimming in a pink and lilac haze, the great mesas and plateaus fading into blue distances, the gorges and canyons banked full of purple shadow.[11]

Smythe's image of Nevada was important not only because he was positive but because he reflected deep and popular American values. He firmly believed that agriculture was the basis for civilization. He firmly believed that irrigation would redeem, renew, and re-invigorate the West. He firmly believed that scientific methods would bring about abundant harvests. He firmly believed in Uncle Sam, who as a noble innovator was equalled only by God. In brief, Smythe was a classic product of his day and he helped to bring the popular faiths and accepted beliefs to bear on Nevada.

The difference between the miner's Comstock and the progressive's reclamation was the difference between the hedgehog and the fox. The Greek poet Archilochus recorded the enigmatic lines which Isaiah Berlin used in a famous essay: "The fox knows many things, the hedgehog knows one big thing." Nevada mining was one big thing, for the state was tied to a single industry; but reclamation had many facets and spawned cultural, social, and economic movements that were to create a broad and diverse mosaic. Without knowing it, a large segment of state activity meshed with and drew upon progressive reformers. For a brief period they became the dominant Nevada image, an image that placed Nevada for the first time, and, some might argue, for the last time, in the mainstream of Western American enterprise.

Before the nineteenth century came to an end, however, Nevada became associated in the public mind with one of the most notorious and controversial "sin enterprises"—an enterprise that was to make Nevada famous and economically viable during the twentieth century.

The intense excitement surrounding prizefighting in Nevada started during the summer of 1896, with an evaluation of a confusing 1893 law which had been designed to legalize such events. The discussion was prompted by the San Francisco Examiner's suggestion that the Athletic Club of that city stage a fight in Nevada and that perhaps the state would become a sports center, with the Olympic Games soon to follow. Later in 1896, Arkansas, Montana, Wyoming, Mexico, and various off-shore California islands were suggested as possible sites for boxing matches, but on January 13, 1897, Carson City was selected. The Glove Bill, to legalize the contest, was rushed through the legislature and signed by the governor, a stadium was constructed, and on Saint Patrick's Day 1897 Jim Corbett and Bob Fitzsimmons started a tradition and created an image for Nevada that was to stimulate controversy for the following three and a half decades.[12]

By the late nineties Nevada had been so reduced in population and so limited in natural resources that even a modest promotional activity could result in substantial economic gain. The estimated $20,000 to $100,000 contributed by the Southern Pacific Railroad and Western Union Telegraph to stage the event in Nevada, the scores of reporters who publicized the 17,500-seat stadium, and the sports fans who filled hotels provided a much-needed economic stimulus. But countering the raw economic pressures was a vocal and growing moral element composed of cultural, religious, and reclamation leaders and many of the newspapers of the state.

The peculiar resurgence of puritanism and middle-class rectitude reflected in rural America from the turn of the century to the Great Depression had taken deep root in Nevada. There was an element of Victorian prudishness and Kiplingesque cant, but there were also the educated, the clergy, and many businessmen who provided the movement with a solid grounding. The robust "win or lose" character of the Comstock generation had been to a large degree replaced by a new morality which stressed family, home, abstinence, church, and school. Even more pointed was the refrain by part of the local press that claimed that the weak had left the state and that the strong and courageous, "by God's grace," had endured and were to be congratulated for their "Christian steadfastness."

Obviously the pro-fight forces controlled the legislature, but it is worthy of note that as Nevada started on the path toward prizefights, easy divorce, and legalized gambling, a large and for a while vocal segment of the citizenry bitterly opposed such "inhuman sports" and "immoral social practices."

Throughout the late winter and early spring of 1897, Nevada newspapers filled their columns with nationwide press reports. Although a consistent supporter of the fight, the *Daily Appeal* of Carson City was scrupulously careful to print the national opposition. As the state's most vocal opponent to the fight, the *Silver State* of Winnemucca apprised Nevadans of their misguided actions. In late January the *Silver State* spoke of "Nevada's Dishonor" and argued that by "legalizing what is a crime in all other states," Nevada had made herself "a target of ridicule of every newspaper in the United States." We have "bartered away the state's honor for a mess of potage." Throughout February and March the tempo continued to mount. The *Los Angeles Herald* cried, "For the sake of womanhood it is to be hoped that females who may be found in the pavilion" will henceforth be restricted from the virtuous and respectable social world. Nevada had made women ashamed of their sex.

By February a Hartford, Connecticut, resident was complaining that Nevada had captured the attention of American journalism; there were twenty comments about Nevada in the local paper to one comment about nearby New England states. The *New York Journal* worried about "declining civilization" and how Nevada made "even Kansas respectable." The paper found it necessary to dismiss the state as a "Holy Horror." Closer to home even the *Truckee Republican* became a regular critic of its boisterous downstream neighbor.

The *Philadelphia Public Ledger* took two approaches. First, it found "a disgraceful spectacle in a country which claims to have reached a high tide of civilization," and of course, to have invested Nevada with statehood was "a grave mistake." Unfortunately, weaknesses in the federal Constitution forbade remanding Nevada back to territorial status. After the fight the *Ledger* saw the crowd at Carson City as "a study in degeneracy not often witnessed outside the barbarous, churchless, and schoolless communities." But second, the *Ledger* attacked its own city. In a series of articles it declared boxing a common pursuit in private clubs across America and discussed two young Philadelphia men who had recently died from the sport. "How the spirit of William Penn must writhe." The editor suggested that Pennsylvania send missionaries to civilize Nevada so that Nevada could send missionaries to civilize Pennsylvania.

The churches of the West mounted the most sweeping and vituperative campaign. Milbourne Parker Boynton of the First Baptist Church of San Francisco thanked God that the population of Nevada was small. And yet, the "disgrace of one is the shame of all. . . . The filth cast by Nevada's Legislature upon the skirts of Columbia scents with its polluting odor the whole raiment of the Goddess of Liberty." Joseph Hemphill, pastor of Calvary Presbyterian Church of San Francisco, explained that Nevada was "a dying state" with only alkali, sagebrush, and jackrabbits. "Let her blot out from her seal of State the rising sun and put in its place a falling star, or the faces of the brutes who are soon to fight for a prize." The Reverend T. Magill of Reno's Congregational Church founded a series of "Indignation Meetings" which were joined by churches throughout the West. And apparently as a result of his principles, Magill resigned his pastorship, preaching his last sermon in Nevada on March 28. Various clergymen took as their text "America on the Down Grade" and the meaning of "Manliness." Several Methodist churches kept their bells tolling throughout the March 17 affair, and the Law and Order League of Nevada requested that the attorney general stop the fight. Francis Nash, writing for the *Christian Endeavor* in February 1897, explained that Nevada had never been a Christian state and had never recognized the Sabbath. "Saloons and gambling halls make more money on Sundays than all the other days of the week. . . . Wives and mothers dread the day." Sundays in Nevada represented drinking, carousing, horse racing, and murder.

The *San Francisco Monitor*, widely quoted in the *Reno Evening Gazette*, was particularly outraged that two Irishmen were to fight on Saint Patrick's Day. "To put the seal on their infamy, they have chosen to desecrate a festival sacred to the highest interests of the Irish race. . . . It is to be made a holiday for men whose names stink in the nostrils of civilization." Partly as a result of the *Monitor* article, the Irish of San Francisco launched an official protest on March 7 and urged that no Irishman travel to Nevada. Opposing the almost uniform trend by religious groups, Father Gartland of Saint Teresa's Catholic Church in Carson City thought the fight no worse than a football game and believed it would "put money in circulation."

A scattering of newspapers seem to have been, at least in part, supportive of the fight. The *Chicago Chronicle* argued that man was foremost an animal; therefore, fights for "primal manliness" were inevitable. Since most of America was neither intellectual nor thoughtful, why not let Nevada have the bloody sport? The *San Francisco Bulletin* thought Nevada the ideal place, "keep the affair going." Nevada's location could provide the perfect weekend for Californians. The *Sacramento Bee* also rushed to defend the state. Nevada had "refused to be a hypocrite" and was a "sparkling jewel of consistency." Following the same reasoning, the *San Francisco Post* disapproved of the event but said, "if it is to be tolerated . . . Nevada is best adapted to it." Following a different logic, the *Salt Lake Tribune* consistently opposed the fight but defended its good neighbor and bitterly attacked papers in New York, Chicago, and St. Louis for their "unanimously sneering" superiority when viewing the West.

Perhaps the most vituperative and pointed defender of Nevada was Alabama's *Tuskaloosa Realist*. "From the amount of tommy-rot that is being souped and spat about . . . an uninformed person might be led to suppose that the citizens of Nevada had entered into a covenant with the Devil to crucify their mothers, to choke their offspring and wind up with the commission of the unpardonable sin."

By early February Governor Sadler had received telegrams from many governors requesting that he stop the fight; eleven states officially denounced the affair, and Texas called a special session of the legislature to outlaw what Nevada approved. The issue was introduced on the floor of Congress and demands were made locally for a state constitutional convention to prohibit prizefighting. But in the meantime Wyatt Earp, Tom Sharkey, John L. Sullivan, and even the future governor of New York, Al Smith, had arrived for the festivities. Bat Masterson was placed in charge of police and given full authority to maintain order. Pinkerton agents had arrived, one group of counterfeiters had been apprehended, and Reno jails were filled with tramps.

The Southern Pacific offered special low fares to Reno, and Carson City bars were lengthened by 12 to 18 feet to accommodate the crowds, but no new hotel was built. By February 24, almost a month before the fight, thirty of the leading sports writers in America were in Nevada. On February 13 an order for a block of seats had been received from London, while fans from New York, Chicago, and other cities purchased sections of the stadium. Hearst newspapermen arrived with a traincar of wine, and five moving picture machines reached Reno on February 22. Over six and one-half miles of film was exposed at a cost of $60,000, and by late March the fight was being shown throughout the country except in states like Maine where the "Nevada experiment" had been specifically banned. For over a month there were cockfights, rumors that Mexicans would introduce bullfighting, and extensive plans for dog racing.

For a half century Nevada's rivers had been called "fraudulent pretenses," her forests "sagebrush preserves," and her entrance to the Union "a corrupt political scheme," but with the introduction of prizefighting Nevada became "the Black Sheep of the States." The 1897 extravaganza was Nevada's first major "sin enterprise," and it established an image that was not to completely disappear during the twentieth century. For many, Nevada had become a place of "immorality and debauchery."

After 1880 most of Nevada's highly publicized but short-lived mining booms proved to be chaste prostitutes. They entertained many, but disappointed all and granted favors to none. The clients drifted away, seemingly anxious to be again deceived. On the other hand, the vision of massive reclamation projects was somewhat less illusionary. A score of observers imagined that water and therefore vegetation could transform the wide Nevada valleys into farmlands of abundance. The populists, the progressives, and the agrarian mentality of America could not but dream of the barren wastes becoming populated with sturdy farmers. Slowly the progressives took the pragmatic view; they would with government help and modern engineering remake a desert into an oasis. There would be a renaissance, a proof of man's ability to bring life; technology and Uncle Sam held the answers.

But throughout the era many itinerant writers and travelers were frightened or repelled by the absence of vegetation and saw no hope for domesticity. For them Nevada could only be emptiness and ugliness, a place where one coped constantly with a landscape that reduced, degraded, and exposed. And finally moralists and publicists from across the country saw Nevada's legalization of prizefights as an earthy action that placed the state outside the bounds of civilized norms. Starting with the caustic comments and indignation of 1897, many Nevada image makers began to redirect their criticism. During the twentieth century they found increasingly less fault with the natural landscape and relatively more fault with Nevada's human character and institutions.

CHAPTER IV

Nevada: beautiful desert of buried hopes.

—Anne Martin

From the turn of the century to World War I, Nevada not only commanded outside attention, it evoked widespread excitement. Throughout most of western America its water project elicited genuine surprise and admiration. No longer did the geography intimidate, rather the myth of opportunity and western exceptionalism seemed to dominate the state. The great Buddha's admonition that "life can change as quickly as the swish of a horse's tail" seemed to apply in a most positive way. Twenty years of depression was replaced with a boom psychology. In addition to Nevada's second major mining rush, agriculture was seen as the new opportunity. Indeed, the state enjoyed a peculiar agrarian marriage between such diverse interests as advocates of reclamation, political progressives, Reno's intellectual community, the Southern Pacific land office, several machinery and wholesale houses in San Francisco, cooperative and utopian colonies, and some Salt Lake City business and church interests. All envisioned a new, prosperous rural society; all saw democracy, federal technology, and taming the arid lands as a moral and material resource.

After the passage of the Newlands Act in 1902 and the attendant western publicity, a local newspaper could amusingly note that "Nevada agriculture is becoming more respectable every day." And as work on the giant project proceeded on schedule, it attracted increasing notice, perhaps reaching an initial zenith between 1904 and 1907. *Sunset*, published by the Southern Pacific Railroad, regularly returned to the subject in articles like "Redeeming the West," "The New Nevada," "The Reclamation of Nevada," and "Irrigation as a Social Factor." Both fact and hyperbole were crowded into the stories. A February 1905 report claimed that letters from prospective homemakers were flooding the office of the state engineer. "Thus the lonely Sagebrush State will awaken from her slumber to listen to the gladsome shouts of youth in fields and orchard." Equally as important, irrigation farming was to produce a spirit of serving which was to exert an unusually healthy influence upon both local and national life. The *Land of Sunshine*, the *Californian*, and the *Overland Monthly* followed the lead of *Sunset* and for some years emphasized Nevada's agrarian opportunities.

On the national scene, *Harper's Weekly*, *Leslie's Weekly*, and *Collier's* covered Nevada's mines but also spoke lengthily and positively of Nevada irrigation. Senator Newlands wrote for *Collier's*, while *Harper's* in a florid and melodramatic story of February 2, 1907, spoke of "titanic labors," "unbounded imagination," "performance of miracles," and "marvellous jugglings of rivers and mountains." After quoting scripture extensively the writer stressed that the members of the Reclamation Service were practical men who proposed "to convert two-fifths of the area of the United States from arid land into fertile farms."

As the irrigation publicity seemed to crest, on May 23, 1905, the *San Francisco Call* published a special Nevada edition consisting of sixteen pages with seven columns per page. The *Call*, "the washerwoman's paper," was by the 1860s known as California's most popular and cheapest newspaper. Mark Twain reluctantly took a job with the *Call* in June 1864 and was most unhappy there as a police-court reporter. The paper insisted that Nevada was "witnessing the dawn of a new era." Along with pictures and articles on oats, alfalfa, creameries, and beet sugar refineries, Robert L. Fulton explained that the state "runs south into the fig, orange and cotton country. Nowhere is there such celery, such mealy potatoes, such juicy berries." Nevada was "trembling on the rise and not in a thousand years will she offer the inducements to settlers that she does to-day."

Perhaps the most sophisticated image provided by the new agrarian movement was the founding in Reno, in June 1905, of the state's first professionally designed and edited magazine, the *Progres-*

sive West. The journal was an indirect outgrowth of various publications fostered by the Reno Chamber of Commerce over the previous decade and a direct outgrowth of *Nevada's Natural and Industrial Resources.* First printed in Reno in January 1904, *Nevada's Natural and Industrial Resources* was the state's entry at the 1904 St. Louis World's Fair. With a lengthy introduction by Robert L. Fulton, it emphasized the university and livestock farming and told quaint stories about the "jewel of great prize," which was, of course, Nevada. *Greater Nevada: Its Resources and Possibilities,* published in early 1905, expanded upon the 1904 issue. About that time it was decided that a monthly publication would create a more widely circulated and sustained image of the state.

The *Progressive West* combined the several new forces which had been drawn together to build a more traditional "mid-western-like" agrarian culture. Editors for the magazine were J. E. Stubbs, dynamic president of the University of Nevada; J. A. Yerington, son of railroad executive Henry Yerington; and John Sparks, governor of Nevada. The managing editor and motive force was the creative M. M. Garwood. Mrs. Garwood, also executive secretary of Reno's Chamber of Commerce, enjoyed the local assistance of newspapermen like Sam Davis and John L. Considine of the Carson *Appeal* and the ever-active Robert L. Fulton of the Reno *Gazette.* The journal well expressed the progressive optimism of the day; it was "intended primarily and ultimately as means towards the reclamation of the desert." The editors believed that the publication was "the logical outgrowth of a demand from every part of the world." Therefore, the first number was circulated throughout the United States and in England, France, and Australia.

Reversing the long and persistent justification for failure and claims of colonial exploitation, the magazine found that "no State has yet received such a vast impetus, nor such actual material assistance as has Nevada." The contribution was such that "not even the next generation will witness the climax of its achievement." June 17, the day President Roosevelt signed the reclamation bill, must become a Nevada holiday; Dat-so-la-lee, the seventy-year-old Indian basket maker, was a state treasure; and Reno's Mardi Gras, from June 29 through July 4, 1905, was seen as a clean, healthy, spirited celebration. Not surprisingly no comment was made about Nevada's second major prizefight, held in Reno on July 3. The progressive forces were successful in their demands that the affair not be scheduled for July 4.

Garwood was convinced that the newly established Las Vegas was going to succeed as a center for southern Nevada; she christened it, perhaps borrowing the title, "The Gateway to Goldfield." Commercial conflicts and jealousies between Reno and Tonopah-Goldfield, between agricultural interests and the mining boomtowns, between temporarily prosperous camps and those of past glory were to be reduced to good fellowship and understanding. Industrial advertisements were a major financial underpinning for the publication. The eighteen in the first issue represented Chicago, New York City, Los Angeles, Sacramento, and San Francisco. Salt Lake City businesses soon became supporters of the journal. However, the advertising grew only slightly and San Francisco remained the chief advertiser of machinery, transportation equipment, tools, and other hardware.

By late 1905 a few newspapers like the *Deseret News* of Salt Lake City and smaller sheets from Inyo, Mono, and other rural California counties praised the objectives and positive attitude of the *Progressive West*. Unfortunately, by 1906 Mrs. Garwood had withdrawn as editor and the journal was rapidly becoming self-conscious, garish, and apologetic for not maintaining deadlines. Although Garwood briefly returned to the editorship later in 1906, the high hopes and tasteful quality rapidly slipped away. A noble attempt to assure the country that Nevada's physical reclamation had also introduced an era of broad cultural reformation had been short-lived.

Fortunately, the Nevada State Historical Society, also a product of the expansion and reform of the decade, was more successful as a cultural association. Its founders and supporters were from the same small knot of progressive-minded Renoites who wished to eliminate what one of the group characterized as "the negative quality in Nevada's history." In the creation of the society, the "negative quality" was to be assaulted by the "man of all seasons," Robert L. Fulton, and a "woman with a missionary zeal," Jeanne Elizabeth Wier. In addition to their social concerns, the two were brought together by their fierce respect for Frederick Jackson Turner. Writing for *The Irrigation Age* in January 1902, Fulton encapsulated the doctrines of the western historian in a simplistic, although theoretical, way. Fulton explained that in the past "the public lands were open and the tinker and the tailor, bookkeeper and the barber, the laborer and his sons knew that if worst came to worst, they could go west and find a quarter-section and make a home on it." Misery, riots, anarchy, class hatred had all been averted in America through western land. But now "the safety valve is closed."[1]

Jeanne Wier, a new history instructor at the University of Nevada, may have worked with Fulton on the article. Coming from Iowa by way of Oregon and California, she had become an ardent Turnerian while a student at Stanford University. As an activist, she along with other academics like President Stubbs and sociology professor Romanzo Adams found Fulton and his community of friends invaluable supporters of the proposed agency. (Fulton was also responsible for Stubbs moving to the university; they were relatives and both from Ohio.)

In May 1904, the Nevada State Historical Society was founded with Fulton as the first president and Wier the secretary-curator. The society under the persistent Wier, the university under the progressive Stubbs, and an active group of business and political leaders formed an unusually concerned, vigorous, and enlightened force within the state. They were a small beacon, an attractive image, which introduced leading scholars and publicists to western Nevada and brought the society some little outside recognition. Wier's dogged determination to make the association into a reputable, professional organization led her to embark not only upon invaluable collecting ventures but to take her story to meetings of historians, to publish professionally, and to catalogue an impressive body of her findings. For the first time Nevada began to enjoy outside academic attention. It was a new image. Jeanne Wier believed that Nevada must cease being a frontier and a wilderness because "The American frontier zone has moved into the midst of the Pacific." Nevada must cease being a desert and with reclamation "Nature shall reap . . . even where she has not sown." After observing the retrogression and decay of a hundred Nevada communities, she declared, "We are not willing that Nature should come to her own again here." Jeanne Elizabeth Wier enjoyed a William E. Smythe type of enthusiasm; however, she held fast to one objective.

Certainly the National Irrigation Congress, and its crowning achievement, the Newlands Reclamation Act, widely publicized the opportunities for western settlement. But almost as significant was the new wave of experiments being undertaken by advocates of co-operative settlements. By 1916 at least 250 such communities had been established in the United States with the majority having collapsed in infancy. By the turn of the century the West had become the Mecca for scores of bizarre and generally unrealistic social experiments. Many saw one of Nevada's remote valleys as a Shangri-la which could easily be converted into a productive and self-sufficient paradise. Although substantial sums of money were spent on several of the projects, most never proceeded past the planning stage.

As early as 1892 there had been a plan to settle a thousand Danes along the Walker River. In 1907 Father T. W. Horgan proposed to locate a thousand Irish near the Carson Sink, and in the same year four hundred Polish families were to found a settlement near Fort Halleck in Elko County. In 1911 much publicity was given to a planned Italian vineyard near Unionville, and Russian Americans considered farming opportunities in northeastern Nevada during 1915. The Dunkards, under the leadership of George L. Studebaker of the famous wagon-automobile family, almost left Muncie, Indiana, in 1904 to take over Spanish Springs and Lemmon Valley in Washoe County, and the House of David considered leaving Benton Harbor, Michigan, in 1907 for Rhyolite. According to the group's religious prophecy, 144,000 persons would be drawn together in southern Nevada before the millennium. A half-dozen plans to locate Russians, Finns, or Estonians on the lands of the Nevada-California-Oregon Railway were typical of the short-lived or stillborn ventures of the era before World War I. A proposed South African Boer colony in northern Nevada, a Hindu colony in Churchill County, Japanese colonies in the Ruby Valley, at Fallon, and at Las Vegas, a Siberian Baptist colony in Washoe County, a Norwegian colony on the lower Carson River, and a Greek colony near Reno further suggest the attractive rural image and colonization mania that had overtaken Nevada.[2]

During the last half of the nineteenth and first years of the twentieth century, the Mormon Church contributed in a quiet and selective way to Nevada's agrarian image. Church affiliates had fostered settlements in southern and eastern Nevada, and around the turn of the century it again became involved when the Nevada Land and Livestock Company secured property at Georgetown, near Ely. Although this experiment was short-lived, the church fostered the purchase and settlement of numerous other ranches along the White River in White Pine and Nye counties.

The most widely publicized and best financed semi-Mormon colony was that of Metropolis, ten miles northeast of Wells in Elko County. Building the community was a joint effort by the Southern Pacific Railroad and Salt Lake City businessmen. In 1911 the Pacific Reclamation Company of Salt Lake City, Reno, and Ogden secured large tracts of land, mainly from the railroad, and constructed a major reservoir on Bishop Creek. It was declared the third largest earthen dam in the United States and designed to irrigate over thirty thousand acres. The town was built on an impressive scale with a large hotel, a railway station (Southern Pacific constructed a branch line eight miles long), fire hydrants, sidewalks, parks, schools, and a cooperative marketing system. Prospective settlers from all over the West and Canada came to visit the "farmers' paradise." By 1913 the community had grown to approximately a thousand persons, the majority of whom were from Utah, Idaho, and Canada.

Along with the usual problems of dry years, rodents, and crop failures, the Lovelock Valley Irrigation District quickly brought suit against the Pacific Reclamation Company for taking water from the Humboldt River. After a lengthy legal battle, Lovelock won the case; most of the colonists were Mormon, however, and since they were encouraged to remain by church leaders, Metropolis was slow to die. In 1924 some thirty-five families still remained in Metropolis. The town officially disbanded during the 1930s, but twenty-seven residents still occupied the land in 1960. The promotional brochures, the land salesmen, and the advertised fourteen inches of rain per year had given way to drifting sand, sagebrush, and jackrabbits. Another widely publicized image of a "genteel life on the fertile plains" had been abandoned.[3]

The largest and most widely publicized cooperative colony to be founded in Nevada was located in the heart of the new reclamation district some four miles east of Fallon. The leaders, who enjoyed extensive contacts throughout the country, had most recently participated in the Llano del Rio Colony in Antelope Valley, forty-five miles northeast of Los Angeles. Numerous Nevadans, including several farmers and ranchers who turned over their lands for co-

operative settlement, joined the visionary promoters. Indeed, it was
a strange mixture of utopians, populists, Marxists, and dirt farmers
who founded the town of Nevada City, Nevada, in 1916. World War
I heightened the drama. Within a few action-packed months, persons from thirty-three states, Alaska, Hawaii, Cuba, Canada, England,
Germany, Sweden, France, Hungary, and Switzerland had arrived at
the new Eden. Most colonists were opponents of the war, and many
assumed that Nevada's isolation would shield them from the conflict. From the first, the Marxist-oriented, German-speaking, semi-
intellectuals had difficulty relating to the half-starved farmers from
the Great Plains and the rebellious fruit pickers and lumbermen from
the Pacific Coast. Between 1916 and 1919 some five hundred persons
actually settled in Nevada City, and over two thousand other heads
of families joined the cooperative in absentia and made preparations
to migrate to Nevada.[4]

Colony leaders gained access to a dozen lengthy mailing lists.
Some, like the world-famous socialist newspaper the *Appeal to Reason*, enjoyed a circulation exceeding 525,000. Nevada City published
two widely circulated monthlies, *Nevada Colony News* and the *Co-
operative Colonist*; the editor of the *Colonist* placed advertisements
"in all of the Socialist papers of the country." From the *Daily Call*
of Seattle to the *Leader* of Fitchburg and Boston, from the *Star* of
Frackville, Pennsylvania, to the *Co-operative News* of Everett, Washington, and from the *Sword of Truth* of Sentinel, Oklahoma, to the
Weekly Bulletin of Butte, Montana, the story of Nevada's new order
was told. In local papers like the *Argosy* of Belper, Kansas, in regional
journals like the *Home and Farmer* of San Francisco, in specialized
publications like the *Angora Journal* in Portland, Oregon, in the *Socialist Year Book of Cuyahoga County* of Cleveland, and even in a women's
weekly printed only in Finnish, *Toveritor*, readers were informed that
there was a community in Nevada that soon would have "greater
power and influence than the Standard Oil Company."

The *Appeal to Reason* of Girard, Kansas, the *Cooperative Herald*
of St. Paul, the *York Labor News* (Pennsylvania) and the *Miami Valley
Socialist* (Ohio) seem to have provided an extensive correspondence
list of potential colony members and genuine interest in "America's
new Socialist home." Not all papers, however, welcomed the colony's
business and promotion. For example, the *Co-operative Consumer* of
New York City canceled the Nevada advertisement in May 1918. They

had previously given it a prominent display on the back of their journal, but the advisory council composed of John Dewey, Edward P. Cheyney (the historian), Walter Lippmann, and others checked the colony's references and financial statements and concluded that the project was unsound.

For three brief years the image of Nevada, at least for thousands of the disaffected, was not of an arid landscape or a booming gold town, or controversial prizefights, or easy divorce, but rather Nevada was "the new socialist center of America" and a haven for those frustrated by drought, capitalism, and war. The dispossessed longed for association and felt a need for material and sentimental comradeship. They were in revolt against loss of status and the disappearance of frontier relationships. Ownership in common, use of a commissary, and participation in the commonweal were as American as Jamestown and Plymouth Rock and now were to be rediscovered in the fertile Lahonton Valley of Nevada. An optimistic Frenchman once declared, "No map of the world is worth looking at unless it contains an island of utopia." The nationwide image of Nevada as the poor man's utopia was tragically short-lived.

William Bradford stepped off the *Mayflower* at Plymouth Rock in 1620 and recorded in his journal that he had arrived at a "hideous and desolate wilderness." Nearly three hundred years later scores of observers stepped off the train at Tonopah-Goldfield and recorded the same impressions. Rex Beach, the novelist, had been a pioneer of the Klondike and at Nome, and yet he wrote in *Everybody's Magazine*, "It was two hours after midnight when we piled out of the Pullman into the whirling snow that the desert wind whipped into our faces . . . this frozen gale flapped my fur coat about my legs, numbed my nose, and destroyed illusion utterly." The Yale man Frederick Palmer, writing for *Collier's*, found that at Goldfield "you step out of the world of the whole of America into the world of a mining camp." Only "two branch lines of steel disappearing into the mystery and silence" tied one to civilization. And when Barton W. Currie of *Harper's* decided to rent a car at Goldfield to travel the seventy-eight miles to Bullfrog, he said, "It was a burning day. The indoor thermometers scaled well above 100. Outside, dust that stung like lime-powder wove about in eddies and spiral clouds."

Occasionally, writers and image makers jokingly declared that the new mining districts had embraced the proposition that it was "unwise to become overcivilized," and that the camps were synonyms for "frontier barbarity." And yet most writers preferred to produce highly illustrated articles suggesting that a spirit of the Old West was being blended with modern technology, and although the camps presented a desolate outlook, tons of supplies were gorging all wagons and freight cars headed for the rising mining towns.

Although at first there was a shortage of food, water, timber, and related necessities, an extensive and efficient freighting system was quickly inaugurated. Railroads became a high priority, with the first train reaching Tonopah in July 1904, less than three years after the initial discovery became generally known. Almost all of the two score active camps founded early in the twentieth century followed the traditional pattern of birth, boom, and decay; however, the speed of development and rapidity of decline were unique. The total human history of a majority of the camps was less than two years. The most vocal individual publicists were often the speculators, stock salesmen, and business promoters. Many were not only excessive in their praise, but fraudulent with their schemes.

Of the many journals rushing to record and reflect the new Cinderella of the West, *Sunset* probably provided the widest and most popular coverage of the Nevada scene. The magazine had been founded in May 1898, and in addition to advertising Nevada's agrarian opportunities it printed blandly written stories, poems, and bits of history about the state. Its editors were surprisingly slow to notice the Tonopah-Goldfield strike. The first mining article, however, "Tonopah and Its Gold," of May 1903, opened an era of over four years in which everything Nevadan became a journalistic imperative. Authors quickly changed the thrust of their articles from Tonopah to "The Goldfield Way" and "Money Makers of Goldfield," and then to "The Gold of Fairview" and to "Finance in Fairview." In late 1906 and early 1907 the magazine published a series of articles on Manhattan, Round Mountain, Wonder, Ramsey, Olinghouse, Bullion, Silver Peak, Bullfrog, and similar widely celebrated and short-lived strikes. Most journalists noticed the "forlorn prospectors," the "dusty burros," and the dugouts, tents, and "huts of beer bottles." Nevertheless, Nevada had again become "a land of prodigals," of "fair play," of "adventurous spirits," where "the last of the gun-fighters" from Texas and Alaska,

Australia and South Africa had come to die. The new mining boom had stimulated a strange, bizarre, rough-hewn romanticism.

The lack of journalistic restraint and judicious limit reflected in *Sunset* was surpassed by the newspapers' exaggeration of the day. The *Call* of San Francisco was perhaps the first widely circulated paper to actively promote, indeed to ballyhoo, Nevada mining. On May 23, 1905, it supplied several fairly balanced statements by President Stubbs and five other professors of the University of Nevada, and then it blared headlines like, "Opulent Nevada Amazes Mankind," "New Era Dawns on Land of Gold," "Capitalists Invest Their Millions in Belief That Returns Will Be Good," "Story of Wealth and Progress Wins Admiration of the Entire World," and "Prosperity Attends Forward March of Fabulously Rich Commonwealth." The *Recorder* of San Francisco was soon to equal the *Call* in prodigious exaggeration. On June 20, 1907, it ran an anniversary edition on "California and Nevada Mines." The 28-page supplement became an encyclopedia of Nevada's mineral wealth. The articles were wildly exaggerated. There was "Searchlight is Without a Failure," "Manhattan, the Goldseekers Mecca," "Wonder Camp, of Wonder," "Goldfield, the Great Golconda, Richest Camp on Earth," "The Thriving Camp of Rhyolite," "Copper Wealth of Ely District," and "Candelaria Mines Carry Rich Silver."

Even surpassing the *Record* and the *Call* in an attempt to build Nevada's mining image was the formation of two papers totally devoted to propagandizing the West. On June 10, 1906, a newspaper-size publication entitled *Manhattan* was issued in San Francisco. As a Sunday mining edition, it was to be complete with pictures, advertisements, and directions on how to invest in various Nevada stock options. *Manhattan* was a mere continuation of the many attempts to stimulate investment. *Tonopah* had been launched in San Francisco as early as May 1903. The first paragraph of the first article set the tone for the 32-page journal. "Never have Nature, and Fortuna, her handmaid, spread their treasures with more munificent hands and never has their largesse been more equally and fairly distributed between man and man, than in that new and wondrous mining district, Tonopah." Articles on the health, the soil, the university, the officials, and, of course, on the mines of Nevada followed. Over a dozen poems were tucked into the first issue. Few were as short as

> The Goddess of Gold flew o'er the earth
> And pitied the desert bare;
> A kiss she pressed on the desert's breast
> And the wealth of a world was there!

Although *Tonopah* was to be "circulated throughout the American Continent," it was discontinued after the first issue.

By the turn of the century, the *New York Times* had become the premier mirror of the nation's industry, finance, labor, and politics. The paper's response to Nevada tended to project the eastern image of a western state awash in mining booms. Clearly the *Times* focused on issues which concerned the nation as a whole, so in the case of radical labor as well as mining investment, Nevada was merely mirroring western America. But conversely, reporters occasionally saw unique personal and social issues worthy of special emphasis. Between 1901 and 1912, the *Times* carried more than a hundred articles on the state, excluding sports. More than eighty of these dated from between 1907 and 1910. Roughly 28 percent were centered on White Pine County and the corporate investments in the copper camps. Twenty-six percent of the articles were devoted to radical labor: the Goldfield shooting of John Silva by Morrie Preston on March 10, 1907, the subsequent strikes and introduction of federal troops, and the bizarre nomination of Preston for president of the United States by the Socialist Labor party in July 1908 while he was in the Nevada State Prison.[5]

The 1907 strike and the shooting of Silva elicited over twenty articles in the *Times* and a similar broad-based response in most of the national press. With President Roosevelt ordering federal troops into the state in December 1907, coverage of the Goldfield labor problems continued to mount. In early December the mine operators asked Governor John Sparks to introduce federal troops to preclude the violence anticipated by the mining unions. Sparks informed the president in a telegram that troops were necessary since "domestic violence and unlawful combinations and conspiracies" existed. Popular opinion across the country accepted the claim and tended to support the official action. Indeed a kind of national hysteria swept the country on December 7 as the first troops arrived in Goldfield. Within a week, however, it became clear that the miners were not threatening, or were unable to take violent action, and newspaper coverage of the incident rapidly declined. By December 20 both the president and many responsible papers openly questioned the facts that Nevada officials had presented and doubted the necessity for the introduction of troops. Later in the month, the president became convinced that something was gravely amiss in the state and pressured the governor to call a special session of the legislature. A state militia was quickly organized and in March 1908 the federal troops were withdrawn.

Over the period of a month the *Times*, like the president and most of the eastern press, had moved from support of the Nevada officials and mine operators to serious doubt and questioning of their motives. There was a general feeling that the mine owners had manipulated the nation. The Goldfield affair became a cause célèbre for the radical press. The Industrial Workers of the World's official publication, the *Industrial Union Bulletin* of Chicago, and *Miners' Magazine* of Denver, carefully covered the dispute and castigated the president for being duped by the rag-tag state of Nevada. Even Emma Goldman's *Mother Earth Bulletin* of New York City denounced "the capitalists of Nevada" and the "White House Tsar." Senator Newlands, who owed much to the president for Nevada's reclamation, found himself embarrassed by the now emerging Nevada image. And within a year Nevada officialdom again became involved in a national, indeed an international, conflict with President Roosevelt and the central government.

Early in 1909 Nevada's demands for Japanese exclusion became a thorny issue for the local legislature and a major irritant for President Roosevelt. In a lengthy series of articles, dating from February 2 to February 10, 1909, the *New York Times* closely followed Nevada's attempt to exclude the Japanese from holding land within the state. The Roosevelt administration, which at the time was negotiating with Japan, found both the Drew Bill of California and the Nevada resolution unwise interference in national policy. But the Nevada resolution "criticising President Roosevelt, and designating the Japanese as 'parasites of the world' and a menace to civilization and progress" particularly infuriated the White House. A "very high Administration official" declared that Nevada would be amusing in her outburst if it didn't create so much serious trouble for the federal negotiators. He noted that the "good manners" of the Japanese contrasted favorably with "the boorishness of the Nevada Legislature," and he was pleased that the Japanese people and government well understood the relative unimportance of the Nevada debate.[6]

During the controversy the Roosevelt administration reminded the state of the labor troubles of 1907–08 and suggested that its citizens misunderstood their position and the role of the central government in the labor dispute and that they had again misunderstood their position in relation to the Japanese. In the face of the federal pressure, the state senate on February 9 referred the bill to the Judiciary Committee where it was to die quietly. Again, Nevada officialdom had created a lasting image of a thoughtless, provocative, inept government.

The *Times* often found it impossible to limit a discussion of Nevada prizefights to the sports page and praised F. M. Lee, vice president of the Nixon National Bank of Reno, and Senator Nixon for being opponents of prizefighting, divorce, and gambling. Lee was interviewed while staying at the Waldorf-Astoria and easily dismissed the peculiar Nevada sports as "tiresome."[7] Both the physical location of gambling establishments and the future of divorce were issues that often competed for space with mining stories. But occasionally the paper, like most of the press, failed to retain its quiet, underplayed reporting. For example, on June 21, 1908, it devoted an entire page along with photographs and cartoons to "Romance and Reality in the Rush to Rawhide." Smaller headlines were equally flamboyant— "The Boom, Outranking the Klondike Stampede," "The Cowboy who Named Rawhide," and "The Man who Might Have Been a Tenderfoot." With seven columns to the page, the *Times* supplied facts and history, personal experiences of early inhabitants, and finally wild stories about escape from snakes in Rooky Gulch.

Like moths to a flame, journalists seemed to be drawn to exotic hellholes from Leadville to the Klondike, from Butte to Bisby. And yet they produced a most uneven collection of essays. Although they sought the bizarre and the mundane, the incomprehensible and the offensive, few of the articles showed a practical wit built on intimate details or were literarily provocative. In short, the major articles in the established eastern magazines were lengthy and well illustrated, but neither humane nor historic. They were of temporary camps on yet another last frontier and only casually influenced America's image of Nevada.

The White Pine County copper-mining boom differed dramatically from mining developments in other parts of the state. Copper, discovered in 1870, was first processed in 1873, but it was not until electrical appliances demanded large quantities of the metal that the Guggenheims established the first permanent furnaces in 1900–01. The industry enjoyed a steady growth over several decades while Greeks, Serbs, Croatians, Italians, Basques, Japanese, and other immigrants provided labor for the new industry. Racial and nationalistic clashes occurred, but outside newspapers and journals seldom created an image of local discord; with full employment and the adult population of White Pine County being over 50 percent foreign-born, ethnic clashes were quickly forgotten. Labor bosses supplied large blocks of the foreign manpower for the mines and railroads; an image of Nevada as a land of hope where all could work was easily sold to the prospective migrants. Although not always understood by the local press, the foreign-born supplied Nevada with a majority of its labor force for sixty years prior to World War I.

Between 1963 and 1965, seventy-eight older immigrants from White Pine County were interviewed by the author and asked for their image of the state. Clearly not all immigrants were reflective, nor were their ideas newsworthy or unique; but the publicity given to the state by mine owners and stock jobbers should be balanced against the opinions of the often illiterate workers. All of the interviewees had migrated to Nevada as adults at least twenty-five years earlier, i.e., before World War II. The average migrant questioned was retired and sixty-seven years old. Thirty-five percent were women, none had graduated from high school, and several could not write in any language.

After a lengthy residency within the state and retirement, most presumably felt comfortable or they would have left. Sixty-five percent of all men interviewed did project a positive perception of Nevada. They emphasized the rough and masculine nature of the country, the opportunities to hunt and fish, and the lack of controls. A typical comment was that of an Italian who had worked as a school janitor for over forty years. "The day I arrived in Nevada I felt like an eagle. I have felt that way ever since." Over half of the men admitted, however, that their arrival was an accident of employment. The response of an eighty-five-year-old Cornishman was typical. In his first letter home he emphasized that "under no circumstances will I remain in this state for more than five years." He had not been out of the state for more than two days at any one time since 1906.[8]

In 1923 a London-born woman who had been converted to Mormonism arrived in McGill. She wrote to England, "If we had gone one mile further into the wilderness we would have dropped off the earth." She became despondent, tried to starve herself to death, and feigned tuberculosis so that she would be sent to a city for treatment. After forty years in Nevada she still "hated and despised" most aspects of western life. A Swedish girl was drawn to the desolate camp of Blue Eagle, southwest of Ely, to become a schoolteacher. Sixty years later she contended that "sagebrush, drunken Indians, and overwork" was her perception of Nevada.

For some three years, 1906–1908, *Harper's*, *Collier's*, *Leslie's* and other similar publications seemed to compete for coverage of Nevada mines with photographs, drawings, tabloid art, and titles like "The Millions at Tonopah," "Gateway to Goldfield," "Nevada, the Western Eldorado," and "All that Glitters in Nevada." In addition there were many articles devoted to railroad construction, automobiles in the desert, labor conflicts, electrical and water systems, and prizefights.

After the turn of the century, several national journals devoted all, or a major part, of an issue to publicizing a particular state. *Harper's Weekly* allotted its June 20, 1903, number to Nevada. It was ideal timing since both reclamation and mining strikes were newsworthy developments. In addition to the traditional photos of new camp sites or of twenty-mule teams hauling lumber into and ore out of Tonopah, the lengthy article glorified pioneers, exaggerated the state's progress, and supplied a detailed encyclopedia of mining discoveries. Two years later Winifred Black had greater access and new material when compiling "Gold of the Burning Desert" for the September 1905 issue of *Cosmopolitan Magazine*. Although a good story teller, Black was led to exaggerate when explaining that the camp of Bullfrog "sells more stamps in a week than the city of Sacramento does in two weeks." Black declared that Bullfrog, when only three months old, had nearly 10,000 inhabitants, a $50,000 water system, electricity, an ice plant, and a forty-room hotel. *Collier's* did its giant spread on Nevada on January 26, 1907. Frederick Palmer was arrogantly clever, but amusing and probably accurate. He noted the boosterism and attempted to analyze some of the "horny crocodile" types who were trading stock, dissolving million-dollar companies, selling office furniture, and pandering to eastern speculators. As more new strikes were publicized, Nevada had "turned mania into dementia."

National interests in and journalistic coverage of Nevada mining declined almost as rapidly as it had burgeoned; however, national magazines continued in their various series to highlight the state. By October 1916, *American Magazine*, in a series called "The Glory of the States," provided a sidewalk coverage of historical and commercial issues. The author was particularly impressed that as early as 1875 the Encyclopedia Britannica could give a paragraph, although rather critical, to the state and that in 1885 Nevada apples were shipped to Windsor Castle for Queen Victoria. Almost totally ignoring the state's mining past, the article concluded that "What Nevada needs more than anything else is about two million hogs, cows, beef cattle and sheep, [and] another half million acres of cultivated land."

Two years earlier, in April 1914, George Wharton James applied William Allen White's famous article "What's the Matter with Kansas?" to Nevada. In *Out West*, formerly *Land of Sunshine*, James provided a lengthy, pointed, and surprisingly accurate image of the state in "What's the Matter with Nevada?" James was the Calvinistic Methodist leader of the Nevada Cornish; he had arrived in America in 1881 and over the years had become equally devoted to ecology and growth, to industry and beauty, to nature and Christianity. After dismissing the geography, climate, and migratory problems of Nevada, James suggested that there was an outside perception that "every city, town and mining camp [was] a rendezvous for the gambling and demi-monde elements." It had become "a State born of fraud and lies, cradled in pollution and corruption, nurtured by graft and swindling, . . . shunned [by] good men and women, [but] the paradise of the corruptionist, the gambler, the pimp, the abandoned and the degraded." Nevada was viewed as "a menace to the progress of civilization, the despair of the church, the anguish of the angels, and the anathema of God,—what good could possibly come out of Nevada?" Outside the state the very word "Nevada" called "forth a laugh, a sneer, a blush, or an oath." In the minds of Americans, Reno had become "the awful cesspool" overwhelming even Dante's *Inferno*.

In an attempt at emphasis, James repeated the already famous doggerel associated with Reno divorce. The first of several verses suggests the tone of the jingle.

> Nevada, 'tis of thee,
> Sweet state of liberty,
> Of thee I sing.
> State where our fathers flee:
> State that sets mothers free—
> Marriage, because of thee,
> Hath lost its sting.

James noted the problems, but he failed at solutions. His unsatisfactory conclusions argued that the "illmated *from other states*" should no longer "flaunt their domestic infelicities before the unwilling eyes of the pure men, women, . . . and children of Nevada. They must stay at home [and] cease from making Reno the wash-house of the nation." Perhaps the aroused and decent people of Nevada were in the process of a bold and defiant challenge to eradicate immorality and evil. Although no longer in the pulpit, George Wharton James was always facing personal contradictions; for him religion was to be tailored to size and use. He had converted desert aridity into beauty and novelty; therefore, Nevada behavior was not beyond an indulgent and friendly God and morality need not create conflict but rather could elicit something of a free-floating approval. In a strange and unreal way, James revealed many of Nevada's contradictions.

Finally, the *Nation* ran its "These United States" series in 1922, and the widely traveled tennis champion, former history instructor, and candidate for the United States Senate, Anne Martin, wrote "Nevada: Beautiful Desert of Buried Hopes" for the July 26 issue. Martin was both thoughtful and devastating; she demonstrated that Nevada had not progressed in three decades. The brief agricultural and mining booms did little to change the image of the state. "'Youth' cannot explain away her backwardness and vagaries, her bizarre history, her position as the ugly duckling, the disappointment, the neglected step-child, the weakling in the family of States."

Martin even reverted to the casual traveler who saw the "wonder or weariness" of the "'desert' plain," the "straggling towns" and "drying bed of a river." Nevada possessed "a peripatetic male electorate," half of whom drifted out of the state every two years. Nevada,

with venereal disease and prostitution, had placed a greater percent-
age of her citizens in jails, prisons, almshouses, and insane asylums
than any neighboring state. Martin also attacked the "Mackay millions," the "Comstock lode," and the "Guggenheim" interests. They
were all gone except for a few exploiters who were "still picking the
bones." Indifference by the national, state, and local governments to
the plight of starving farmers and the greed of the large livestock
interests infuriated Martin. And finally she offered a prediction that
boosters' clubs and chambers of commerce could not change Nevada.
The people must rise up, otherwise "She will continue to lie, inert
and helpless, like an exhausted Titan in the sun—a beautiful desert
of homeseekers' buried hopes."

H. L. Mencken, William Allen White, and Edmund Wilson,
among others, contributed to the *Nation*'s series, but none equalled
Martin's passion. Over the previous ten years, she had created an
image of a privileged, educated, rebellious suffragette who had been
led to jail in both England and America. But after her leadership of
the National Women's party and defeat for the United States Senate
in 1918 and 1920, she moved to Carmel-by-the-Sea in 1921 and with
some bitterness remembered Nevada and herself as a "tangle of weeds
and pond lilies" moving "without pattern."

Eloquent and depressing, angry and sad, Nevada's most famous
female was devastating when evaluating her state, but "Beautiful
Desert" was not to quietly fade away. After the essay appeared in book
form in 1923, Governor James Scrugham was naively approached by
the publishers and asked for an endorsement. Scrugham found the
article to be a "gross libel" on the "devoted and self-sacrificing" citizens
of the state. The editor of the *Nevada State Journal*, former governor
Emmet D. Boyle, was even more sarcastic and uncompromising in his
attacks. Eventually both Martin and Scrugham agreed to a written
debate rather than "a fistfight." The issue died after a flare of notoriety
and publicity, leaving the American image of Nevada in even greater
confusion and doubt.

After the bitter moralistic controversy surrounding the Corbett-
Fitzsimmons fight in 1897, it was surprising to find that the Marvin
Hart–Jack Root heavyweight championship of July 3, 1905, created
scarcely a ripple of dissent. Indeed, Reno almost concealed the fight
with a six-day Mardi Gras celebration that included bicycle races,

trapeze performers, a carnival with a beauty queen, a trout-fishing contest, horse races, and local Indian participants wearing colorful marching apparel. The elderly Mark Twain was invited by Robert Fulton to preside over the entire week's performance and was assured there were "no objectionable shows." As the city rather successfully controlled the entire celebration, Reno was able to declare itself "a center of legitimate sport." It was difficult to criticize Nevada when major fights had been held in San Francisco in 1902 and 1903 and with both Los Angeles and Coloma, California, scheduled to stage fight events over the next few years.[9]

National reaction was more critical when Joe Gans and Battling Nelson fought for forty-two rounds in a lightweight championship match at Goldfield on September 3, 1906, and again when Gans and Kid Herman fought at Tonopah on January 1, 1907. Both fights were designed to revive a flagging gold rush. Mixed in with Goldfield's fight promotion was the successful attempt to move the county seat from Hawthorne, and enthusiastic locals even speculated that the state capital would soon be moved from the north. The *Los Angeles Record*, *Chicago Chronicle*, *San Francisco Bulletin*, and other papers found the mining camps to be "wildcat country" where legitimate "sports have held their nose at the mention of sagebrush." The *Salt Lake City Telegram* declared that nations which have bullfighting could now "look down upon the Anglo-Saxons with . . . commiseration . . . and contempt for our civilization." The *Butte Evening News* thought the entire affair a stock swindle: Nevada "must be losing its red blood." Before the Goldfield fight, the *Tonopah Weekly Bonanza* claimed that "hundreds of letters from preachers" across America were sent to Tex Rickard and the Goldfield Athletic Association opposing the contest and its related events. The Young Men's Christian Association, the Ladies' Benevolent Association, and many other groups across the West published bitter denunciations of prizefighting. Supposedly because of the outcry, Goldfield canceled the planned bullfights and substituted auto races across the desert.

Despite criticism of Nevada and of prizefighting, the sports corps representing major papers from New York, Boston, St. Louis, Philadelphia, and the West Coast cities converged on Goldfield in August 1906. Many reporters received shares of worthless mining stock in return for a favorable account of the town. A further complicating image was that Gans and his unusually attractive wife were black and Nelson was a declared racist. On August 25 Nelson proclaimed: "While I can ever crawl, I will not let it be said that a nigger put me out." He refused to shake hands with Gans before the fight and assured his supporters, "I am going to go after him while I've got a breath left in my body." Poems about "coons" circulated along with suggestions that Gans would star in *Uncle Tom's Cabin.*

Tex Rickard and other promoters spent somewhere between $5,000 and $18,000 to build the stadium and to send out 37,000 illustrated postcards, 30,000 circular letters, and 8,000 souvenir cards; but only some 8,000 spectators arrived in Goldfield. Although he was in Nevada, President Theodore Roosevelt did not visit the event; Nevada retained its image as the "carpetbagging kingdom" and set the stage for the greater racial disturbance that followed in 1910.

On July 4, 1910, Reno staged the most widely publicized and eventually the most racially controversial fight of the century. During the early summer, the publicity steadily increased while Reno became infamous and Nevada again "broke with nationwide moral and religious opinion." Again, the state was viewed as an unfortunate black sheep, off limits but "less to be scolded than to be pitied."

Many issues overlapped to create the harsh characterization. Nevada's persistent permissiveness clashed with the national distaste for prizefighting. Jack Johnson, the easy victor over Jim Jeffries, was black, his wife and his many girlfriends were white. Differing from Joe Gans, Johnson seemed vain, even arrogant, and showed a baffling confidence. And finally Reno could not absorb the many different social problems and basic need for facilities created by an influx of somewhere between 14,000 and 25,000 people. By July 4, special trains were lined up trying to find switch-yard accommodations. Reno faced its first traffic jam with automobiles descending upon the town from California and perhaps from Utah. Jack Johnson drove his personal "solid steel" motorcar. There were occasional fights and very heavy gambling, but according to journalists, "little blood was spilled."

Scores of telegraph operators were imported so that the fight could be reported round by round in other states, and thousands of people jammed armories, movie theaters, and parks across the country. The *Detroit Free Press* of July 5 typified the national reaction to Johnson's Reno victory. On the front page were headlines such as "Race Riots Follow Big Fight in Many Cities," "Several Killed and Many Hurt; Blacks Chased in Streets," and "Negro Tenement Burned

by a Great Mob in New York." With the Johnson victory in the fif-
teenth round, rioting broke out across America. Two blacks were
killed at Lake Providence, Louisiana; a black constable was killed
in Mounds, Illinois; two blacks were shot in New Orleans, and one
in Roanoke. A third lynching in twenty-four hours was threatened
at Charleston, Missouri, but even after the first two Negroes were
hanged, the governor still found no further need for police protection.
In almost all eastern cities, as well as in Little Rock, Houston, Pueblo,
and others further west, rioting occurred. Whites were infuriated by
the Johnson victory and by the blacks' attempt to celebrate. In New
York City there were seventeen major clashes before midnight; trol-
leys were stopped and blacks pulled off to be beaten. Groups like the
"Hounds of Hell" and "Pearl Button" gangs accosted Negroes while
others chanted "Let's lynch the first nigger we see." Blacks fought back
in many towns and urban regions and several whites were injured or
killed.

Jack London described the fight round by round for the *Daily
Picayune* of New Orleans, the *New York Herald*, the *St. Louis Republic*,
the *San Francisco Chronicle*, and several Canadian papers. He found
tragedy in the defeat of the white champion. He also tried to explain
"the yellow streak" in Johnson which he had noted before the fight.
Of course, London had assistance in his racism. The *Chicago Daily
Tribune* for July 5 ran a large cartoon entitled, "Sambo Remo Rastus
Brown—On His Way From Reno Town." Blacks were depicted in the
railway dining car after the victory, demanding "poke chops—an' . . .
some watermelon."

Most of America's leading sports figures were pleased with Reno
hospitality. The ten reporters from the *San Francisco Chronicle*, two
of whom were women, continued their defense of the state of Nevada.
Helen Dare, one of the woman reporters, stated, "Never have I seen a
crowd more kindly . . . It was a good-looking crowd, the well dressed,
well groomed, well set up men, many of notably distinguished bearing were in preponderance." Most of the press corps agreed with
the referee when before the fight he had called for "three cheers for
Nevada, the only free state in the Union." An English observer even
found Reno similar to London and to Epsom Downs on Derby Day.

 During the Johnson-Jeffries fight observers spoke glowingly
of the automobile traffic arriving in Reno from California

and Utah. Their reports, however, seem somewhat exaggerated since only about fifty transcontinental motorists traversed the state four years later, in 1914. One of the last cars to make the trip in that year was driven by Paula and Ned Davis; they were traveling from their home in Oakland to Albany, New York. Fortunately Paula Davis kept a diary and carefully recorded their experiences while crossing Nevada.[10]

They entered the state at Verdi on September 5, 1914, and seven days later reached the Utah border. Although from the West, they were shocked by the total absence of trees and grass, by the burning heat, and by the isolation and primitive character of the communities east of Reno. It was a land of "bare dry valleys and mountains . . . with old decrepit mining towns . . . to break the monotony." The Davises focused most of their attention on their 1913 Chalmers automobile and the rocks, chuck-holes, and ruts which laced the roadway from Reno to Utah. East of Fallon they found "desert with a vengeance." They drove across "a big bare crust, which would crackle every foot of the way" and was "absolutely impassable" when it rained. In short, the Nevada segment of the soon-to-be-famous Lincoln Highway was intolerably bad, with not more than "fifty-miles of even graded roads through the whole state."

The Davises and other tourists repeatedly joked about the poor 80,000 citizens of the state who constantly complained about their financial inability to properly build a highway. The motorists declared the unmarked alkali wastes of Nevada and Utah, where the cars sank in lonely bogs and sand pits, the worst stretch on the entire transcontinental road. Indeed, in response to a promotional scheme by the Lincoln Highway Association imploring tourists to "See America First," the motorists, after crossing Nevada, often critically advised people to "See Africa First" or "See the Moon First." Henry Joy, president of the Lincoln Highway Association, was forced to admit that a twenty-five-mile stretch of sand and marsh east of Fallon was the worst road on the entire American crossing. Nevertheless, by 1915 World War I had diverted eastern tourists from Europe to California, and some five thousand autos crossed central Nevada in that year.

While profiting from the travelers, Nevada was marked as being the most backward place in America in road construction. Fortunately, the Federal Road Act of 1916 was to inaugurate an extensive highway-building program, and by the early twenties the state had,

rather by accident of location and the largess of the federal government, captured an image as a major auto-tourist attraction.

The sparse rural society of the early 1900s drew as much
from a national identity and outside involvement as from
the local setting. The land that had been so uniformly disparaged
was beginning to claim attention, even a reverence. The Mormons
could see a chance to expand their social ideals of family, church, and
brotherhood; the utopian socialists had visions of cooperative action
propelling them into a position of economic and political power. Both
land promoters and intellectuals borrowed the agrarian dreams of
Cato the Elder, of Jefferson and of Smythe, and they saw the land
and its occupants blooming while the children were being taught and
the righteous were praising God. It would be a mistake, however, to
apply Robert Frost's poem to Nevada. "The land was ours before we
were the land's." Only at major reclamation sites like the new town
of Fallon, in a few irrigated areas, and across the cowboy country of
the northern counties did the land come to shape a regionalism and
permanently create a distinct way of life and thinking.

In short, Nevada generally failed to kindle the magic power of
place so often prophesied in the barrage of early twentieth-century
literature. Although likening themselves to a Columbus locating a
new world and conversely assuming the mantle of a Montezuma
with a room full of gold, the visionary promoters and investors were
soon gone. And Nevada with an estimated population of 100,000 in
1907 had declined to only 77,000 persons in 1920. Despite the boom
psychology of World War I, drift and disillusionment were again to
prevail. From the mines to Main Street a cruel feeling of helplessness
confronted both businessmen and the jobless. Neither did observers
find a rich and stable social order. There seemed little interest in
belonging and a lot of lengthy discourse on rugged individualism.
There was much freedom and much space, but little sense of place or
shared memory. For a decade Nevada had fit Gertrude Stein's view
of America: "Conceive of a space that is filled with moving." But mo-
bility had always seemed the primary reality for Nevada, and with the
collapse of the mines and the many agrarian experiments there was
another exodus. It was again time for the forlorn, lost, scruffy towns
and camps to be reclaimed by the desert.

CHAPTER V

Vice is merely catering to the

underground desires of virtue.

—Walter Lippmann

Of the dozen towns thrown against the Sierra in western Nevada, Reno was the largest. According to Walter Van Tilburg Clark's *City of Trembling Leaves* and the University of Nevada's advertising brochure, it was a pleasant little city of green trees, quiet residential streets, and many churches. But tourists did not travel to Nevada to read Balzac at the bar or to smell the June roses. They came because of Nevada's gambling and divorce and because of its glamorous heritage. As Americans between the world wars, they were trying to define themselves and break from their many poverties.

The twenties and thirties were decades when the boys paid a nickel at the local gas station to play the punchboard and maybe win a baseball glove; when young couples danced for days in a marathon so that they might have use of a Ford V-8 with a rumble seat for a few hours; when city fathers ignored the local abortionist and the gambling in the back of the drugstore. Perhaps the often crass and crude reports on Nevada were in keeping with the broad, depression-ridden American life.

In a Marshall McLuhanesque manner, the medium had always helped to shape the product in Nevada. And after World War I the media, more than the citizens, created the new state dimension. In particular, they elevated Reno almost to the status of Hollywood; they made Nevada into a stopover for the country's gangsters; they provided ammunition and purpose for moralists and preachers; they glamorized a floating desert for early motorists; and they kept a barrage of sensational stories coming for the nation's curious. Observers disagreed as to whether the state had abandoned American values and traditional institutions. But the friendly media insisted that Nevada was a mere variation within the federal framework and that the state's open-mindedness was the continuation and even the recapturing of the integrity of the Old West. And finally, there were journalists who insisted that Nevada was expert in discerning nonsense and charlatanism and that it would not employ the smoke-and-mirror hypocrisy of most of America.

Clearly the scores of ambitious articles reveal much zigging and zagging on the state's institutions but almost never suspense or surprise. Apparently, nothing in Nevada provided protective secrecy or needed to be contrived. The geographical spectacle and urban plan beckoned all to see and participate. The little towns stood baked against the bare mountains, ridge on ridge against the sky. Even the generous plain had a harsh and dusty look; the silhouettes of the forlorn towns were flecked with the green of trees, the rusty ocher of old bricks, or the grey of decaying wood. Although located in the center of the Far West and becoming famous for divorce, gambling, and tourism, Nevada had come to feel like a small country, it was so separate and so far. It was expansive if not fulfilling, indifferent and humanly incomplete, and when most visitors entered the state they stole into another self.

During the nineteenth century, Nevada was not known for its liberal attitude toward divorce. While the state's six-month residency requirement was lenient by contemporary standards, it conformed to the citizenship requirement and brought the state little notoriety. During the first decade of the twentieth century, however, Nevada became the divorce center of the country. The change in image was, in part, the result of three divorce scandals. The first decade revolved around the second Earl Russell who, after being awarded a Nevada divorce in 1900, promptly remarried. He was later accused of bigamy by his first wife and the English courts set aside the Nevada decree and imprisoned the earl for three months. In 1906 Laura Corey, the wife of the president of United States Steel, sued her husband for a divorce in Reno. America was outraged by stories of an unfaithful husband pursuing a younger woman, and Nevada again became notorious for its lenient attitude and institutions.

By 1910 Reno had become "an infamous divorce Mecca," and the national press was debating the moral and philosophical issues involved in the practice. Attorney W. H. Schnitzer published a series of articles in the *Reno Evening Gazette* starting on September 24, 1910, in which he laid a rather thoughtful foundation and presented arguments that were to be repeated for the following forty years. Schnitzer believed that "a narrow puritanical people which represents an infinitesimal fraction of the great freedom loving" American community made most of the public "commotion." No legislative body should totally control the personal and intimate aspects of human beings, and marriage was particularly personal since it was for "enjoying companionship, making a home and reproducing" the species. Experience, not religious doctrine, should be used to evaluate vital relationships. Besides, the "sophists" were hiding behind controls that denied women freedom from men who were often "brutal and repellent." A careful study of personal and social experiences was a better guide to understanding marriage and divorce than the edict of clergy or legislative fiat.

Despite arguments like those of Schnitzer, in 1913 reform elements in Nevada demanded a more stringent divorce law, and a statute was passed granting divorces after a six-month residency only when both parties lived in the state. If only one of the parties resided in Nevada, a one-year residency was required. In a strong reversal of thrust, the new restrictive legislation brought a nationwide reaction. The *New York Times* devoted an entire page on January 11, 1914, to an article entitled "Farewell to Reno's Supremacy as a Divorce Centre." Much was said about Nevada having been in the spotlight and "attracting the attention of the world" after 1910, but with the new legislation, the Reno divorce colony "shall have become a memory."

The divorce "farewell," however, was to last only until Nevada's next legislative session. In 1915 the legislature reinstated the original six-month proviso and the state's reputation as America's divorce capital seemed assured. In 1920 Mary Pickford, taking advantage of a loophole in the Nevada law, was granted a divorce after a stay of only a few weeks in the state. The nation was incensed, Nevada was ridiculed, and reform elements renewed their struggle for a more stringent law. In 1922 an initiative to change the statute was placed on the state's ballot, but it went down in ignominious defeat. Liberal divorce had become a way of life in Nevada.

In 1927 the divorce industry was threatened by competition from France and Mexico; the legislature therefore almost without debate lowered the residency requirement to three months. But a local and a national outcry followed in which almost all of the Nevada press became involved. The *Elko Independent* declared "The better class of the people of this State will experience disgust over this coup of the Reno business men who prey upon the nation's wedded failures." A few lawmakers had "hoodwinked the people of this State and sold their good name." The *Humboldt Star and Silver State* of Winnemucca was certain that Nevada would lose trade. The *Reno Evening Gazette* was confident that the legislation would "only operate to lessen the respect in which our courts will be held by its own people and the esteem in which we are regarded by our sister States." The *Elko Free Press*, the *Carson City News*, the *Ely Daily Times*, the *Tonopah Bonanza*, the *Carson City Daily Appeal* all bitterly opposed the legislation. Even the president of the Nevada Bar Association called the law a "cold-blooded bid for the dollars of unhappily married men and women from other States."[1]

If Nevada comment on the new divorce law was caustic, outside editorials were scathing. The *Philadelphia Inquirer* found it a "sinister history of trickery." The *Chicago Daily News* thought Nevada wanted more patrons, more clients, more divorce-seeking strangers to fuel a derelict economy. The *Providence Journal* believed the legislation to be dangerous. The *New Haven Register* predicted that "the Soviet Government of Russia will inaugurate divorce mills that will grind out decrees at greatly reduced rates without any residential requirements at all." The *Minneapolis Tribune* sensed that the law would be attractive since it would reduce the "pain of living in Nevada" by three months. The *Arkansas Gazette* of Little Rock predicted that Nevada had "written the record for all the world to see, and the State will be largely judged by that record." From New Hampshire to California, from local weeklies to the *Literary Digest* of New York City the "midnight legislation" was found to be "parliamentary footpadism."

Only four years later, in March 1931, when economic problems led several states to lower their residency requirements in an attempt to win a piece of the divorce action, Nevada again acted. By adopting a six-week residency requirement, the state won the "trade war" and her preeminent status as the nation's divorce capital was not again to be called into question. America, however, was overwhelmed by yet another Nevada transgression and this time the negative reaction was to extend for decades.

As Ralph J. Roske noted, gambling has a long history in Nevada. The Anasazi and the Paiutes wagered long before the first white settlers came to the region. As early as 1850, an enterprising resident of the Carson Valley set up a gambling table to prey on California-bound emigrants. When gold was discovered on the Comstock and California miners rushed to Washoe, the gambling habits they had acquired on the Mother Lode expanded into Nevada. Games of chance flourished in the early mining camps even though they were technically banned first by territorial and later by state law. In 1868, the Nevada legislature bowed to the inevitable and passed an act that permitted licensed gaming in the state. Legal gambling thrived in Nevada until 1909, when the state legislature, momentarily infected by the reformist fevers of the Progressive Era, once again banned it. However, in 1911 legislation was enacted that eased restrictions on "social games." Again in 1913 the state's reform elements rallied and passed legislation designed to restore the stringency of the 1909 law. In 1915 the pro-gambling forces reasserted themselves, and another statute that loosened restrictions on social gambling was enacted.

The national press valiantly tried to follow the Nevada legislature with headlines like those in the *New York Times*—"Nevada Open to Gamblers" and "Nevada Closed to Gamblers"—and long and unclear discussions as to where and how and what gambling games could be pursued. The 1927 divorce bill also included the legalization of gambling until hours before its passage by the legislature. The effect of the legislative vacillation was not to eliminate gambling but to force it underground, where it flourished until 1931. Indeed, illicit gambling establishments operated by underworld figures proliferated, while state revenues derived from gaming were curtailed.

Motivated by the ills of unenforced laws and the Great Depression, as well as by the belief among some segments of Nevada's business community that the legalization of gaming would be good for the state's tourist industry, the practice was legalized in March of 1931. After a rather slow start during the 1930s, gambling became the unquestioned symbol of Nevada following World War II. The casinos in all urban centers and eventually in a half dozen border towns were to drive shafts of light into the clear night sky. Nevada finally achieved an unquestioned nationwide and worldwide image.

The immediate image, however, was far from favorable. Nevada's changing of the divorce and gambling laws had amused but also irritated many American groups. If the nineteenth-century English traveler Paul Fountain found the state a "shameless horror," a "hell on earth" filled with "Yankee desperadoes," "obscene women," and "moral ugliness," the twentieth-century epithets were equally biting. Nevada was labeled "the paradise of the corruptionist," "a menace to the progress of civilization," the "despair of the church," the "anathema of God," the endorser of "progressive polygamy," and "a roadhouse for matrimonial joy riders." The *Dallas Morning News* envisioned "flushed and shaken men, women, and youths" being sucked in, drained dry, and then the husks of humanity flung carelessly out. In 1931 the headlines across America blared, "Nevada Goes the Limit," "Pandora's Box," "Gambler's Heaven Opens," and "Nevada's Infamy." Chancellor Elmer Ellsworth Brown of New York University told the Newman Club at their commencement breakfast in 1931 that Reno and Moscow were "the two great danger centers that threaten American society."[2]

The intellectual dogma supporting Nevada divorce and gambling did not suggest abandoning universal values or national standards. Nevada did not argue that there were no permanent truths, no moral code; rather, verbal emphasis on family, church, and school, if anything, was heightened during the twenties and thirties. Of course, all must concede that any community or state was the product of specific historical and geographical circumstances, and the outside world must therefore understand Nevada's peculiar traditions and needs. It was argued that the mercenary and present-mindedness of the society was only one side of the coin; implementing and recapturing the integrity of the state's frontier institutions was the other side. Unfortunately, as observers evoked a reflective mentality, they tended to confuse fact with mythology, pragmatism with tradition, and truth with arbitrary fashion.

By World War I it was obvious to most local residents that neither mining booms nor reclamation agriculture was to make the state consistently prosperous. Therefore, migration, settlement, tourism, and industry slowly became the internal objective for the progressives and other responsible business interests. Some four quite different forces became, each in its own way, major positive image makers during the twenties and thirties. A long-term publicizer and advertiser for the state's culture was the *Nevada News Letter and Advertiser*, a Saturday weekly started on February 14, 1914, and continuing through the 1920s. Boyd Moore, the editor-publisher, not only provided political comment but also followed the social and economic health of the state. Once a year the *News Letter* issued an impressive special edition designed for outside consumption. It not only noted *economic* opportunities, but as a representative of the progressive forces still active within the state it stressed *cultural* growth and opportunities. For example, the 1916 special edition featured the Nevada Historical Society and carried an in-depth article by Jeanne Wier on Mark Twain. The issue was even dedicated to women and emphasized Nevada's better known and active women. Kindergartens, women's insurance companies, Dat-so-la-lee baskets, and other female-oriented enterprises were noted. Anne Martin and her Women's party were an embarrassment for the paper, especially because she received much unfavorable attention in the *New York Times* and the national press.

By 1920 the *News Letter* had grown more self-conscious with articles in the special edition like "The Real Reno and the Real Nevada" and an uninspired comment by Governor Emmet D. Boyle entitled "The State of Nevada: First in Virgin Opportunities." Nevertheless, the lengthy (about 100 pages) report on the state was a cut above normal advertising and promotional copy. There was much on the streets, sidewalks, and shade trees of Reno, philosophical discussions as to whether Nevada was a new or an old state, and a great amount of sentimental poetry. George Wharton James supplied a lengthy article, "Reno: City of the Sierra Foothills," for the 1922 edition. The city was not "Wild West woolliness" or "hell-roaring freedom" or even a "pioneer town"; rather, it was a "well-ordered, beautiful, well-paved, well-lighted, well-conducted western city." James declared himself a "cosmopolitan traveler of wide range" and he could say "unhesitatingly and deliberately, Reno is one of the most beautifully located cities in the world." When he first saw the Sierra and Reno forty years earlier he was "entranced and full of longing." In the meantime, Reno had become "a progressive California city . . . cheered by the singing of a thousand Sierran birds." It was rapidly becoming a Berkeley or a Stanford for "the better class." In a second article in the same issue, James wrote with similar lavish excess about Lake Tahoe.

By 1924 the special edition was no longer on the cutting edge.

Rather it was dominated by poems that were dated and artless, but perhaps representative of the era. Typical was Carlton L. Stevens's "Nevada: Beautiful Land of Sunshine." Two verses will suggest the local romanticism.

> A wondrous state is our Nevada,
> Land of sunshine, little rain.
> To the West the high Sierra,
> Towering o'er her vast domain.

> Proudly flows the winding Truckee,
> On her course from lake to lake;
> From the highland to the lowland,
> Bringing progress in her wake.

Sherwood Anderson's "So This is Reno" was almost as vacuous as the poetry. He stressed the skyrocketing popularity of the place and said you could hear "Reno" in the French Market of New Orleans, in New York, Boston, London, and Paris. As he put it, the world remembered the fights, the crowds, and the money, while the artists remembered the coloring, the shapes, and the hills; but they all said "I'm going back there some day." For tourists, Reno was "human adventures," "sudden wealth," and "a sense of fun in life."

The *Nevada News Letter* and the yearly special edition were a cultural remnant, incorporating the progressive era, the agrarian hopes, the intellectuals and artists, along with the promoters and salesmen. All very much wanted Nevada to be respectable, appreciated, and even sanctioned by the American middle class.

A second imaginative and sophisticated effort to promote a Nevada image was undertaken during the mid-thirties. The First National Bank and the *Nevada State Journal* came up with a slogan and title for a booklet generally known as *One Sound State*. The first pamphlet of forty pages and eighteen articles was issued in 1936 and sent to over ten thousand rich prospects who might wish a residence in the state. All were assured that there were neither "reds" nor labor agitators in the region. Even most of the New Deal could be escaped in America's "least taxed" outpost. Richard Kirman, the governor, wrote the first article; Christian Arthur Wellesley, Fourth Lord Cowley, the second; the president of the university, the State Superintendent of

Schools, the highway engineer, and others reinforced the suggestion that Nevada was the "cyclone cellar" and protector against taxation.

The first edition drew some fifteen hundred letters of inquiry and later editions continued to elicit favorable response. During the late thirties *Collier's, Barron's, Business Week, Time*, the *Wall Street Journal*, the *New York Times*, and other national organs all noted the Nevada tax oasis favorably. Reno was compared with Westchester County, outside New York City, or San Marino, California. All sections of the state were noticed, and by the 1943 edition Las Vegas with its new El Rancho Vegas casino was emphasized and articles like "Southern Nevada, America's Investment Frontier" and "100,000 Square Miles of Playground" became commonplace. But conversely, several California newspapers followed the lead of the *San Francisco Chronicle* when it rhetorically inquired whether Nevada was "getting ready to secede from the Union."

Between 1936 and 1944 the brochure was reissued under different titles and stressed slightly different issues. It changed shape and size and content but remained an elaborate invitation to the rich to establish a second residence, a *situs* or place of abode, and thus avoid the taxes of other states and communities. Richard G. Lillard in *Desert Challenge* listed over two score of the wealthy, the socialites, the old families, the industrialists, the successful literati, and the titled Europeans who flowed into Nevada during the late thirties. Although the population was only 91,000 in 1930, the state grew by about 21 percent between 1930 and 1940.

A third and most successful image maker for the state was Harolds Club. Despite the national comment, gambling, after legalization in 1931, remained for a decade supported by the participation of local residents and a few venturesome tourists who experimented with the games. In 1941 Harolds Club started the first significant advertising campaign in which Nevada was taken to every corner of the continent. Harolds first constructed twenty-five signs within 500 miles of Reno but over the early and mid-forties expanded the operation to more than 2,000 signs scattered everywhere in the civilized world. The covered wagon symbol with its "Harolds Club or Bust" slogan awakened casinos to the idea of aggressively promoting business and not waiting for the skeptical tourists. Club officials even asked NASA to have a Harolds Club sign placed on the moon during the first lunar landing. The club also embarked on a series of news-paper advertisements based on Nevada's pioneer history, and from 1946 through 1951 every weekly and daily newspaper in the state carried the anecdotes. The state quickly became a hub with its many spokes feeding tourist business into its expanding hotels and casinos. Nevada had created a truly unique industry and was to change its image from that of "boom and bust" or chronic depression to that of Howard Hughes and spectacular urban wealth.

A fourth positive image maker for Nevada was to become in-finitely more dramatic and economically rewarding than the other three. The Boulder Canyon Project focused favorable attention on the state during construction of the dam, and after World War II it attracted an increasingly large flow of tourist-visitors. By the late eighties some three-quarters of a million people were yearly escorted through Hoover Dam. While always associated with Las Vegas, the dam, along with Lake Mead and Boulder City, has for sixty years maintained a unique status as a commanding western attraction.

Historically, explorers and emigrants had found southern Nevada even more desolate and forbidding than the Humboldt crossing. Dur-ing the nineteenth century the Colorado River country had been in-spected, surveyed, and studied, but because of climate and geography it was dismissed as hopelessly inhospitable for human settlement. In-deed, Lieutenant J. C. Ives's comments typified the American image of the region. In 1857 Ives took a government steamboat up the Colo-rado for four hundred miles. Upon returning he reported to the War Department: "The Region is altogether valueless. . . . It seems in-tended by nature that the Colorado River along the greater portion of its lone and majestic way shall be forever unvisited and unmolested."[3]

Soon after the turn of the century, Theodore Roosevelt declared that "one of our greatest national duties is to change the waste of the Colorado River into controlled use." The president's Reclamation Service took the first steps towards river control in 1902 when hy-drographers and geologists began to identify potential sites for a dam. For two decades the feasibility of such construction was debated and a dozen proposals discussed. At one point the project was to be as-sociated with the Panama Canal; at another the French were to be invited to cooperate in planning and construction. By 1906 a Repub-lican convention in Nevada voted to ask Congress for assistance in the undertaking, and in 1914 the secretary of the interior granted a permit to build a dam in the canyon to private interests to be financed by the Rothschilds. By 1921 the Nevada legislature was considering working with other western states to finance the construction of a dam. After the creation, in 1922, of a federal commission with Secretary of Commerce Herbert Hoover as chairman, there was general agreement that a dam would eventually be built by the federal government.[4]

Finally, after years of negotiations, Congress approved the project and the first bids were let in December 1930. The government wished to employ as many jobless Americans as possible, and by April 1931, 800 men were working in the canyon. On July 20, 1934, the number reached a peak with 5,251 men engaged in some form of construction. President Franklin Roosevelt spoke at the dedication ceremony on September 30, 1935. All of Nevada's congressional delegation, six governors, and many federal officials were present. Despite the depression, America had produced another miracle; again the pioneering West, imagination, and engineering technology were to make the desert bloom.

The national press found the entire episode worthy of prolonged and repeated attention. Starting on June 18, 1922, the *Los Angeles Sunday Times* devoted entire pages to the meaning of the project. There were maps, drawings, pictures of Uncle Sam, and colorful headlines. Publications like *Sunset* were more explicit and pragmatic. In "When Boulder Dam is Built," dated February 1926, Edward A. Vandeventer argued that the greatest engineering enterprise since the Panama Canal would supply "water to make fertile many millions of acres of land now parched by the desert sun." The dam's cheap electrical energy would bring back Nevada's mines and make that industry again profitable. It would light cities yet to be built, move trains, hoist elevators, propel streetcars, and lift water. Indeed, an empire greater than that of Alexander the Great would spring from southern Nevada.

Eastern papers were equally expansive in their coverage of the project. Between January 1, 1927, and December 31, 1938, the *New York Times* presented 391 articles on the dam, its construction, and its relationship to southern Nevada. Some 25 dealt with water and irrigation, 36 with electrical power, 30 with recreation and tourism, 29 with labor problems, and 37 were editorials. Nevada's institutions and lifestyles were noted, often praised, and seldom ridiculed.[5]

For example, in "New Pioneers in Old West's Deserts," October 26, 1930, the *Times* found Nevada "the one State in the Union which refuses to admit that the old West ever died. Men are men." Las Vegas "above all other places in the Republic [is] the city where the new type of pioneering has its best chance to rub shoulders with the old." The job hunters already in Las Vegas were "the genuine article . . . old-fashioned cowboys and prospectors." And since both trades "are at a low ebb . . . the real Westerners have ridden down, often hundreds of miles, from forgotten ranches and from near-ghost towns in the hills." They are "the old stock" and hope that their government will offer them "regular work at regular pay." Of course, "the forty-five saloons, in their way," would provide "only an apéritif" for the new pioneers. "Strange he-men in a strange town must also gamble." But both old and new pioneers in their mind's eye see "a lake, blue and charming" and "fields of the Southwestern desert blooming white and green with a vast cotton and orchard acreage."

After the project was completed, the *Christian Science Monitor* explained in "Rediscovering America," on August 19, 1939, that the dam "just about Rivals Yellowstone," but in addition, it provided water for the desert and oranges for the world. It represented America at its finest. "Co-ordination, co-operation, cohesion, and unity have been a basic American principle since 1776." The *Los Angeles Times* in a full-page spread on January 12, 1941, found that the highways, railroad, and airlines to Las Vegas provided a "never-ending parade" to a land of "incomparable attractions" and access to a dam and lake which were "breath-taking." The publicity was effective: during August 1941, 61,623 persons were conducted through the dam. After the war, tourists returned to visit the canyon in ever greater numbers. In August 1946, 64,051 persons officially registered at the dam site and papers like the *Record-Searchlight* of Redding, California, proposed studying the Nevada style of promotion so that tourists could be attracted to Shasta Dam and Redding.

Throughout the thirties there were a few articles like "Fifty Dry Agents Clean Up Hoover Dam Gateway Town" and "Wild West Town Near Boulder Dam." In Washington, Herbert Hoover, always the engineer, and Franklin Roosevelt, always the centralized planner, enthusiastically supported the Colorado project. However, Hoover's secretary of the interior, Ray Lyman Wilbur, and his commissioner of the Bureau of Reclamation, Elwood Mead, as well as Roosevelt's secretary of interior, Harold L. Ickes, could not conceal their hostility to Las Vegas liberalism. The city, of course, prospered, doubling in population between 1930 and 1934. Advocates of federal reclamation, the brainchild of the agrarian progressives of an earlier era, would have been shocked to learn that their rural principles were to help create an entertainment Mecca in southern Nevada rather than produce corn and hogs on Midwestern-type farms.

Counteracting the homey progressive values of the *Nevada News Letter*, of the Hoover Dam builders, and of the all-American advertisements by Harolds Club were the tenacious reporters and their widely circulated exposés. The *Sacramento Bee*'s special investigator found pointed and fundamental failures in the Nevada institutional system. Arthur B. Waugh ran his first revelations on page one of the *Bee* on October 18, 1928. He found that "Bootleggers and Bone Drys Form Unholy Alliance for Hoover in Sagebrush State." The Women's Christian Temperance Union and "crown princes" of Nevada's underworld were working "hand in hand" to "shove Herbert Hoover and the Republican ticket down the gullets of the voters." The "gargantuan conspiracy" was led by the gamblers and "red light" owners James McKay and William Graham, at the same time that the WCTU and Nevada Federation of Women were traveling the state for Hoover. Church leaders and the Ku Klux Klan were part of the same political alliance. Waugh's strange argument stressed the fact that Hoover was "dry" and therefore attracted Christian groups, whereas federal Republican agents had been bought by the underworld and had not attacked a single one of Reno's 121 bootlegging resorts. On October 19 Waugh returned to the charge by arguing that George Wingfield had become "the Silver State Octopus" and the "Sagebrush Caesar," controlling banks, elections, and the underworld.

Waugh often exposed Nevada and in January 1934 bitterly denounced the circuit court and other judicial appointments because the men were from the "discredited" Wingfield Machine. The Wingfield banks had closed and according to Waugh they had "fleeced Nevadans." Both Waugh and Nevada received high profiles when the Pulitzer Prize Committee awarded the *Bee* a gold medal for "the most disinterested and meritorious public service rendered by an American newspaper during 1934." Throughout the period the *Bee* effectively played its dual role as carrier of Nevada news and sponsor of Waugh. Indeed, its editorial page assured readers that Nevada businessmen and officials were honest and that the closed Wingfield banks would work to save Nevada depositors from loss.

The *Bee* offered two pictures of Reno and two Nevada headlines on the front page on November 2, 1932. The pictures suggested high-rise construction and major growth within the city and the captions "Nevada, Fundamentally Sound, Takes Bank Holiday 'Rap-On-Chin' With Smile" and "Nevada's Essential Soundness Assured" were solidly positive. Much was made of Nevada's pioneer western spirit. "The state has a history of staunchly and courageously meeting and overcoming even more serious disasters. . . . The shifts and turns in the winds of fortune have stayed the steady onward purpose of Nevada. . . . Something of the spirit of the old Argonaut still lives in the heart of her people . . . and they will fight their way out of the present crisis with honor to themselves and credit to their state."

The positive image reflected by the *Bee*'s editorial staff was in keeping with the paper's detailed overall coverage of the state during the twenties and thirties. A systematic random sample of the paper between July 1 and December 31, 1931, revealed an average of 6.88 significant articles devoted to Nevada per issue for a total of 1,074 articles during the six-month period. Since the new gambling and divorce legislation had been passed in March 1931, it was surprising to find that only 10 percent of the *Bee* stories dealt with divorce and only 6 percent with gambling. Some 13.4 percent were centered on Nevada mining, 5.6 percent on ranching, and 5 percent on the environment, weather, and natural and man made disasters. Even with the economic and legislative upheavals, the *Bee* scoffed at the suggestion that Nevada had become a "symbol of brutality, vice and antisocial behavior."

After World War I and particularly during the early 1930s, Nevada provoked more expansive and sensational coverage than during the earlier Comstock or Tonopah-Goldfield periods. Typical of the protracted and sensational stories were the twenty illustrated articles which Laura Vitray first printed in the *New York Graphic* between July 1 and July 24, 1931. The entire series was later published in the *Philadelphia Daily News,* and other regional newspapers borrowed bits and pieces from the two more famous scandal sheets. As founder of the second *Daily Graphic*, Bernarr Macfadden in 1924 had inaugurated new ideas regarding decency in poster, magazine, and newspaper illustration. (The first *Graphic* had also published many sensational articles on Nevada but had collapsed in 1889.) Not only was Macfadden an exponent of the strenuous life, vegetarianism, and physical culture, he also published pictures of men and women in the near-nude. He sent Vitray to Reno in part to stimulate the *Graphic's* faltering circulation, but despite the sensual appeal to the masses the paper succumbed after the Nevada exposé.

To introduce the Vitray series, a five-column headline blared "Vice Czar Rules Lust-Mad Reno's Whirlpool of Graft and Corruption." A second headline was equally pointed: "Peon Citizens of Nevada, Outlaw State, Are Serfs in Toils of Rich Politician." For twenty days Vitray maintained her melodramatic exposé style and in general painted Reno and Nevada into a moral and economic quagmire. Vitray found Nevada possessing a "wild, majestic stormy beauty" and called Reno "a full-blown desert flower, brilliant as a poppy." The citizens were the "finest people in the world." However, Nevada was an "outlaw state" where democracy was unknown. One man, George Wingfield, controlled all industry, finances, and the underworld. He had plans to strip "the suckers en masse," but also schemed to bring 4,000 millionaires to the state. "We will show a panorama of divorce and gambling, dope selling and prostitution, merrymaking, murder perhaps, and hijacking, and it will all fit into one harmonious picture."

As the daily fare of graphic language, photographs, and cartoons continued, the sweeping indictments were repeated; but neither proof nor in-depth analysis was attempted. The charges expanded. "Men and women mingle lewdly in hotels," "morality, like democracy, is rapidly disappearing from the state," students were leaving the university, there were swarms of "gangsters and gunmen" on the streets, public officials were bought, there were slot machines in candy stores, and there would soon be "a carnival of blood." Chapter three was directed toward Jack Dempsey and his prizefight promotion of 1931 and toward the colorful mayor, E. E. Roberts, whose famous statement, "I should like to see Reno with a whiskey barrel and a tin cup on every street corner," was repeated a hundred times throughout the thirties. By chapter four, Vitray had found "144 Girl Slaves" in

Reno, but she was equally concerned by the male students who were wrecking their lives.

Occasionally the *Daily News* complemented a Vitray story by running additional articles on Nevada. Statements by religious groups, the International Christian Endeavour, and the *Sacramento Bee* as well as historical sketches of Nevada's violent past were thought to validate Vitray's charges. Perhaps the punch line of the entire series was the last sentence of chapter nineteen. "What Reno—and Nevada—are tomorrow will depend on the help they get from the outside world in their fight against gang control." In short, in addition to selling newspapers, Vitray, like so many other concerned citizens, wanted religious faiths, the federal government, and moral America to eradicate "the Nevada cancer."

Waugh and Vitray typified the position of those who found Nevada so outrageous and excessive that only strong and stark language could transmit the human tragedy. As moralists, they were baffled and frustrated but refused to grant even grudging approbation. They refused to accept the claim that there was no truth, only versions of the truth, and they reacted to Nevada's traditional Manichaeanism which had always accepted some evil as a given. Both Waugh and Vitray were like a play that had its catastrophe in the first act. Their arguments, their positions, became less forceful and convincing the more they talked.

Other journalistic visitors experienced a serendipitous adventure in Reno. They wished to be neither heroic nor judgmental; they laced their stories with a mild and quiet humor. The author of a *Richmond Times-Dispatch* article possessed a kind of fundamental decency. He described Reno in a prose that at times became luminously gentle, always with a touch of understatement and lighthearted banter. He was neither smug, superior, nor self-congratulatory, neither hypocritical nor flamboyant.

On Sunday, April 6, 1930, the *Times-Dispatch* introduced the reader to the Patsy letters. They were to record the "trials and tribulations" of a woman who had "gone through the divorce mill at the Mecca for all those who are . . . bored." Patsy decided to leave her husband because she had become only "a dandelion" and not his "orchid." She listened to platitudes from friends, studied the statistics about Reno, and read about Cornelius Vanderbilt and others who had been

"Reno-vated." Upon arrival at the Golden Hotel she was lonesome and forlorn, but her skillful and adroit lawyer became something of a companion and to her surprise there were flappers from age 17 to 70; there were also women of dignity, with grey hair. She noted the large number of European immigrants, from Spain to Russia, who had sought out Nevada for personal freedom and economic opportunity.

Patsy was also pleased with Nevada's ability to bridge the gap between the old mining camps and the "sophisticated metropolitanism of the Reno of today." She found the personal honor common to the Old West but also a misguided quixotic sense of manliness. It was still a society where you could lose a million dollars and laugh and yet be shot over a minor insult. At the same time, Patsy found something charming about the code of Mayor Roberts, who lost heavily in the stock market with "no hint of shock," but who was visibly shaken when he learned that a wildcat had made off with four traps from his trapline along the Truckee. Patsy slowly came to appreciate that despite talk about the values of the Old West, the current Reno society was culturally insecure, occasionally strident and oversensitive, brash and overreactive to criticism.

Yet another approach to Reno was supplied by Inez Robb in ten tabloid-style articles for the widely distributed Sunday supplement, the *American Weekly*. Starting on May 7, 1944, "Out of This World in Reno" was designed to be gaudy and fast-reading, attractive and appealing to women. Robb arrived in Reno thinking it was "heartbreak house . . . awash with tragedy and grief." The "years of legend and fiction, festooned on Reno, led me to expect innumerable dowdy, middle-aged women, pitiful and alone." She found the place "worldwise," a "gay metropolis" which in 1943 granted a tidal wave of 5,884 divorces, the largest number since the 4,745 of 1931. She agreed that Nevada was truly the "Refuge for the Tax Weary" and she effectively tied wealth to divorce. For example, in 1943 Tucky French Astor divorced John Jacob Astor II; Abbey Rockefeller Milton, daughter of John D. Rockefeller, Jr., divorced David Milton; Doris Duke Cromwell divorced James H. R. Cromwell; Sunny Ainsworth Manville divorced Tommy Manville; and Eleanor Roosevelt temporarily retired to a dude ranch in Washoe Valley. "Uninhibited and unregenerate, lusty and robust, Reno herself seems unaware of how picturesque she is, how colorful her streets to the outsider."

As a prolific writer of human interest stories, Robb loved the well-tailored phrase. Reno provided a "fantastic story of life, liberty, and the pursuit of alimony." Its streets were "jammed with a mixed grill" from Indians with papooses to synthetic cowboys, from old desert rats to professional men and soldiers. Robb told of one woman divorcing two men in two days and marrying a third on the following day. By episode five she admitted that Reno was also filled with "nobodies from Keokuk, Tulsa, North Platte, Birmingham and Grass Roots, USA."

The ten-week series was fast paced, sleazy, overstated, simplistic, and read by millions of Americans. The articles confirmed Reno's image in the minds of the petty bourgeoisie. To many readers it was disconcerting to find that during a most brutal war, when thousands were dying "to preserve a cherished way of life," others continued to glorify the atomistic and hedonistic aspects of society and to discredit traditional American values.

An equally critical but totally different response to Reno was reflected by some of the women at the other end of the social spectrum. Mariette Köevse von Neumann, whose father was one of the wealthier men of Hungary, traveled to Nevada to obtain a quick divorce in 1937. Her husband, John von Neumann, had been born in Budapest, was quickly recognized as a child prodigy in creative mathematics, was educated in many central European universities, and had joined the Institute for Advanced Study at Princeton in 1929. His father had received a title from King Francis Joseph. Mariette was not only wealthy but also highly educated. In 1937, however, Mariette decided to seek a divorce in Reno and upon arrival in the state wrote a brief note, on September 22, from the Riverside Hotel, to her husband in Princeton.[6] It said in part:

> Johnny Sweetheart, I believe that Hell is certainly very similar to this place. It is undescribable, everybody is constantly drunken and they lose their money like mad, 5–6 hundred dollars a day. The roulette table stands in the hall just as a spittoon some other places. The ranch where I allegedly go out to today, a 35 mile journey through the desert, is a wonderful sight for a day but not for six weeks. The place itself is terribly primitive . . . This place is hellish expensive, everything costs about twice as much as in New York . . . I have the howling blues.

A second letter, not dated, was written from the Pyramid Lake ranch apparently in early October:

> Johnny Sweetheart, it is entirely crazy here and I would not feel so miserable if I were not meant to stay here for 6 weeks, I believe I won't survive. I live in the midst of an Indian reservation, there is a beautiful lake and the country is so divine that it is difficult to imagine. But these horrible females, it is impossible that there are so many kinds of women in the world. . . . Riding is very beautiful but the evenings are deadly; imagine dinner at six and night goes until 10 o'clock.

Mariette's stay in Reno did not remain a secret in Budapest, where the daily *A Reggel* (*The Morning*) reported on October 18, 1937, that von Neumann, who had "married the daughter-with-a-million" and worked with Einstein, was to be divorced in Reno, Nevada. In 1938 von Neumann returned to Budapest for a second marriage, but Hungarian authorities forced him to renounce his Hungarian citizenship, and only after much confusion and legal difficulty were he and his second wife able to leave Hungary just before World War II. Reno was not only viewed as famous but also as infamous by upper-class Europeans. The governments, from the British House of Lords to the Hungarian courts, refused to accept Nevada divorce decrees.

During the 1930s there was a barrage of cheap, gaudy, human-interest publications. Most seemed to have no purpose other than to sell a story, but others became organs for religion, politics, and exposés on various social disorders. For example, *The Reno Divorce Racket* appeared somewhat at random during the early thirties; it opposed both divorce and prohibition and was uncertain about gambling. Various brief articles attacked Reno and the famous visitors who frequented the city. The clever headlines like "Reno's Patent Separator," "Reno's River of Doubt," and "Taking the Cure in Reno," along with discussions of free love, polygamy, and paganism, were supposed to discredit the city but probably made it more glamorous and its wickedness more enticing for many readers. Many such disorganized and factually confused attacks on Nevada leave the reader unclear as to the purpose, if any, of the publication.[7]

Established publications like *Real Detective* made their point more directly. In November 1936 Con Ryan, a special investigator, wrote "The City That Sex Built." With pictures of narrow and dirty back alleys and comments on a dozen famous gangsters, prizefighters, gamblers, and "niggers," Ryan still had room to note, "As you like it, is the only law in reeling, rollicking Reno, divorce capital of the world, a desert Gomorrah of shame, shams and flim-flams." Since the "ugly side of Reno's rackets is suppressed," Ryan found it necessary to expose "this city of legalized vice where you can't do wrong." He found divorcees wearing dirty, smelly Levi's covered with "romantic cow-waddy." And yet, "in Vegas . . . the girls sure give the rattlesnakes somethin' to buzz about."

Nevada's seamy reputation had attracted would-be interpreters who could only exaggerate, insinuate, and degrade in an attempt to gain attention. Their emphasis was drawn to the moral wreckage of a place set apart from the world. American education had created a literate or semiliterate audience, and hucksters were available to supply the readers' limited needs. Nevada had made itself into the nation's most available magnet for high excitement and second-rate writers.

Fortunately, the pulp magazines, enormously popular in the thirties and forties, utilized Nevada in a slightly less garish way. Cheap, untrimmed, and about 128 pages in length, they evolved from the dime novels of the nineteenth century and borrowed much from western thrillers and virile super heroes. During the thirties they were filled with cowboys, air aces, detectives, pretty women, and ugly villains. Nevada became a particularly exciting spot for gun battles and speeding cars. There, with "fading sunlight, streaking across the peaks of the Sierras," "cutthroats [plotted] revolution" in remote Nevada valleys and crowds behind the old corral enjoyed horse races and occasionally the blazing guns drawn "from pliant leather holsters." Editors recommended the Nevada landscape for pulp-story settings. The lusty antics of hardfisted men still caught the imagination of millions of Americans. It has been noted that such diverse figures as Harry S Truman and Al Capone were, at the same time, subscribers to the pulp magazine *Popular*.[8]

Of the unusually large number of novels set in and focused on the state, the old mining camps, particularly Virginia City, drew a steady stream of nostalgic researchers and writers. Generally, only a thread of fiction was used to lace together bits of myth and history from the past. While less prolific, cowboy westerns, like the half dozen works by Harry Sinclair Drago that were centered in and around Humboldt County, tended to keep Nevada's cow-country image alive. But the most spectacular collection of novels was inspired by Reno and its designation as "Divorce Capital of the Nation." On average, at least one highly publicized book a year detailing the city's idiosyncracies was published over the two decades from the mid-twenties to the mid-forties.

According to Professor Ann Ronald, "for reasons simple and complex, writers have sold the public a Reno that . . . fascinates most twentieth-century Americans." The fiction, Ronald explained, depicted the author's notion of the city but also was structured around stock characters, stock situations, and stock actions. The repetitive stories were generally centered on divorcees who slowly became aware of the natural surroundings, the Sierra, Lake Tahoe, and the Truckee River. They eventually found a "real Nevada," and after adversity and despair, roadhouses and decadence, they found themselves.[9]

Some of the Reno fiction was produced by persons often in the news like Clare Boothe, Faith Baldwin, Oscar Lewis, James M. Cain, Vardis Fisher, Ellery Queen, and Cornelius Vanderbilt, Jr. Sometimes the local Chamber of Commerce or service clubs became offended and forced a lengthy controversy with the author. But as time passed, the city seemed to accept Walter Clark's description of an "ersatz jungle, where the human animals, uneasy in the light, dart from cave to cave." All agreed that Reno was "set apart from the world" and had become "a universal symbol" of blight and blessing, of nightmare and dream, of futile endings and new beginnings. The stock characters debated and demonstrated the positive and negative, but the novels generally concluded in a wash of ambiguities. Clearly Reno fiction enhanced a questionable image of the city. A majority of the novels were unimaginative; few were reprinted or are still read. They seemed to emphasize a tiresome repetitiveness and the blurred commonplaces of the era. Reno novels between the wars were mainly formula, drawn from an undiscriminating and melodramatic image of an unregenerate and decadent society.

Occasionally, history and fiction were so effectively blended that myth and long-standing image were created. An amusing example was Swift Paine's 1929 publication of *Eilley Orrum, Queen of the Comstock*. Gustavus Swift Paine joined the faculty of the English department at the University of Nevada in 1909. He became a Christian Science practitioner and eventually a member of the board of the *Christian Science Monitor*. He left Reno in 1921 but soon returned and embarked on the Eilley Orrum story. The book was an immediate success, particularly in the West. Dialogue was cleverly interspersed with historical narrative and the work came to be accepted as historical fact. In October 1937, members of the Nevada Native Daughters, while discussing the Admission Day celebration, decided to contact Paine for further historical insights. He replied that his work was not historical. "It amuses me now to see how firmly imbedded in the growing legend of Eilley Orrum are some of my fictions." Unfortunately, few of the books of the era were to duplicate Paine in the creation of legends.[10]

During the twenties and thirties much was written about Nevada and yet seldom did the words become corporeal objects as dense as the rocky hills, or sharp like the drifting sands. One need only reflect on what brilliant writers have done for the American South or for isolated western states, like Montana, to question the many long decades in which talented residents quietly grew old and painted no pictures, wrote no poetry, compiled no memoirs, and told no unique stories. Clearly hundreds of talented and observant people passed through or remained only for a while in Nevada before they withdrew to California or elsewhere to reminisce and at a comfortable distance reflect on the "tarnished pearl" of their experiences.

After World War I magazine coverage of the state became consistent and extensive. Divorce dominated the thinking during the twenties, gambling and divorce during the thirties, and the rise of Las Vegas along with more personalized accounts provided subject matter for the forties and early fifties. As something of a broad sample, forty leading articles were selected between the years 1920 and 1955 as representative of the images portrayed by the journalists. At least eighteen of the pieces were authored by well-known national figures.[11] Only four of the articles were written by persons living in the state at the time of writing, and only two authors, Grace Hegger Lewis (wife of Sinclair Lewis) and A. J. Liebling of the *New Yorker*, had come to Nevada for a divorce. Twenty-five of the forty works were illustrated, while five were primarily centered around pictures, cartoons, drawings, and charts and offered a limited text.

Some eleven articles attempted to view Nevada as a whole or in

a broad historical sense, eleven were centered on Reno, five on the
greater Las Vegas area, and others were primarily devoted to Elko,
Weepah mining camp, Pyramid Lake, Bunkerville, the atom bomb,
or specific gambling clubs or dude ranches. Perhaps most surprising,
only six of the forty articles were clearly negative in their evaluation
of the state; some twenty-eight were positive, and six represented a
confused analysis of Nevada institutions and society. Six of the stories
were written by women and at least six generated a strong response
in the local or national press. The primary subject or major focus
of many of the articles is difficult to isolate since they were highly
discursive and rambling and often mixed history, statistics, personalities, and personal assessment in a confusing potpourri. Nevertheless,
some nine articles focused primarily on Nevada divorce, five on gambling, five on historical detail or vignettes, two on mining, two on
agriculture, one on labor conditions, and one on the law. At least a
dozen writers were merely on assignment to "get a story," and some
eight were critically focusing on human experiences as reflected in
religious activities, social life, education, crime, or cultural outlook.

Bernard Malamud once likened the writing of biography to the
eating of an oak by an ant; in short, it was impossible to truly master
another human being's words and thoughts. The essential complexity
of the thought and purpose that went into the forty articles places
the stories beyond simple statistics. But even if shaded, this outside
slice of personal comment did, piece by piece, build and rebuild an
image of the state. Granted the forty articles often became a hall of
mirrors—often narratives reflecting each other, some written at odd
angles, some in full perspective, some interested in a single event,
some fleeting, some memorable.

For two or three authors, to salvage anything from the mean
and dubious decay and spiritual devastation which they believed was
Nevada became an accomplishment. On the other hand, the overwhelming majority of the authors did not believe that Nevada had
succumbed to temporary pressures, or had spent its capital recklessly,
or had built its house on sand. Indeed, the weakness of most articles of
the twenties and thirties was their lack of originality and thoughtful
criticism. There was repetitious coverage of the reckless quotations
by Mayor Roberts, a tiresome emphasis on the social status of famous
divorces, a floating ambience above the Golden or Riverside hotels,
an alluring night life, a striking ride into the desert countryside, an

inside story of gambling houses, and the cosmopolitan experiences unusual for a small city.

In retrospect, the Nevada image projected to the world during the two decades following World War I seems dulled by shallow overstatement. Although many of the authors had achieved national reputations they often fell into the "Nevada trap" of attempting to be current, clever, and sophisticated. Many, after a week in Reno, reproduced "boiler plate" for their magazines and discreetly glorified their local hosts who had allowed them personal access to family, business, and life-style.

Most of the articles were gaudily illustrated with standard street scenes of Reno, serious gamblers, and receptive women. The stories were formula driven. After World War II there was a new blandness to the articles and an appeal to the safe, middle-class, American values reflected in broad national trends. Nevada had become a colorful, easy, and interesting place to visit, alluringly active and disarmingly open, but at heart it was safely all American and clung to many of the familiar Midwestern guideposts.

A few of the stories stood out as exceptional examples of vision, understanding, and even affection. Others reflected profound distaste. In 1925 Katherine Fullerton Gerould visited Reno to fulfill her "curiosity" and to write a thirteen-page analysis for *Harper's Magazine*. Gerould typified the tiring, sophisticated snob who frequented Reno during the period. She found Nevada dullness "partly the fault of Paris," which was more exciting for divorcées. After a few days the town became "sinister" and "fastened in decay." The men frightened her with their "habit of gambling" and the women were "not fashionable." With its limited jockey club, Reno could not compete with Saratoga or Belmont Park or even Vancouver or Tijuana. In short, Nevada was a "wild country, most of it, pretty well unredeemed to civilization."

Three years later Grace Hegger Lewis arrived in Reno for a divorce and while in the state wrote a ten-page article for *Scribner's Magazine*. Although she found that the local newspapers could not compete with the *New York Times* and that finding an inexpensive place to live was difficult, she slowly came to appreciate a city where a "lordly Rolls-Royce" is parked by a "muddy Ford," where "there is no social class or order," where "divorce is simple" and routine, and where you can order celery soup or abalone at the same café. The two women created an image of Reno, but more particularly of themselves. For one, the town was cold, callous, and indifferent; for the other, it was warm, human, and forgiving. Newspapers across the country responded to the Lewis image and in March 1929 *Scribner's* published some of the comments. The *Reno Evening Gazette* found "the article refreshingly true" and "a human story." The *Fresno Republican* was equally impressed; the article was "full of human observation rather than mere wise cracks." Even the *Indianapolis News* observed that Reno could be a positive experience and that divorce "ought to be obtained in America" rather than in Paris or Mexico.

A measured, yet widely heralded and spirited article on Nevada appeared in H. L. Mencken's *American Mercury* in June 1929. The cantankerous, critical, and gifted Bernard De Voto provided something of a historical and literary image of the state's nineteenth century. He spoke of the first Nevada miners as being "human slag washed backward in failure from the gold fields. The hills had sealed their madness." But men and women followed money and opportunity and in time learned good graces, good cooking, and good behavior in Washoe. But despite the fact that Boston "transcendentalists," "Lyceum nightingales," and famous writers and thinkers visited Nevada, De Voto found "literature has done vilely by them"; therefore Nevada was "without comment in the statuary of the West," and "unacknowledged in the genealogy." Indeed, Nevada had possessed a nineteenth-century potential which could "touch the investigator's heart," but which had been sadly ignored by the sensitive people of the state.

Paul Hutchinson rapidly moved through several religious-oriented schools to become a Congregational, and later a Methodist, preacher in rural Iowa. Within a year or two, however, he became involved in editorial and missionary work and in 1916 moved to Shanghai, China. After a lengthy illness he returned to the United States and in 1924 became managing editor of the *Christian Century*. Hutchinson visited Reno during the unusually hot July of 1931 and prepared four lengthy articles for his publication. Titles like "Nevada—A Prostitute State" and "Reno's Divorce Mill" attracted wide attention among the Protestant readership of America.

Hutchinson admitted that "the nation is full of people who, in the secret of their own hearts" were eager "to escape social regulation"; therefore it was easy to "deflect this tourist tide into the barren,

sparsely settled state." Since there was always "recompense for . . .
immorality," both economic and political interest found advantage in
the Nevada system. In a balanced, if critical, way, Hutchinson covered
almost every aspect of Reno life and admitted that neither the very
limited internal nor the more significant nationwide religious protest
could be effective. The only real cure "must come from without."
Only federal action through more uniform national laws could curtail
Nevada's economic advantage and social immorality.

Over the weeks following publication of the four articles, the
Christian Century carried responses. They were mainly legalistic, however, and clearly demonstrated that despite the fulminations of Bible-
Belt preachers, there was almost no organized or thoughtful opposition to Nevada's peculiar institutions.

In April 1934 *Fortune* published "Passion in the Desert," one
of the most extensive; colorful, and bizarre pieces ever to appear on
Nevada. There were fourteen large cartoons, drawings, and photographs as well as maps and a complicated chart showing "Divorce:
Where, How and to What Avail" for every American state. History
was woven into current affairs; hock shops, Jack Dempsey, and the
Truckee River were blended with mining, tourist traffic, and divorces.
Life on the dude ranches, Nevada statistics, George Wingfield, General
Grant, and Mayor Roberts were all wedged into the story. The authors
found Reno "still fundamentally Puritan and conservative." And yet it
was "all but an independent state." A map was labeled "Reno: A Free
Principality on U.S. Soil." However, it was no longer a cult city for
"fashionable divorcées"; rather it had "to cater to the poor to keep its
business." The very flamboyance of the article attracted national attention and it almost single-handedly created a dozen different images
of Nevada.

By World War II Las Vegas was beginning to capture some of
the headlines formerly reserved for Reno. The city, however, was bitterly resentful of "Wild, Woolly and Wide-Open," which appeared in
Look in August 1940. The article, interspersed with fourteen pictures,
argued that "sin is a civic virtue" in the city. The first sentence set
the tone for the story: "Las Vegas, Nevada, is the sort of phenomenon that makes Europeans think Americans are brain-sprung. It is
the most sensationally cockeyed and self-consciously wicked place on
earth." The article noted the twenty-four-hour service, the prostitu-

tion, the gambling, and that a Reverend Sloan had married a couple at the Union Pacific depot while the train's fireman served as an official witness.

The Las Vegas Chamber of Commerce found the piece cheap and offensive and demanded a retraction and restitution for "the smirch on the good name of Las Vegas," which Reverend Sloan declared was "a city of clean living and home loving people." The threats of lawsuits and wide public attention forced journalists to reconsider projected articles of a similar nature, and *Liberty* promptly canceled its "Sin for Sale," an equally salacious story about Nevada. The Las Vegas Chamber of Commerce was also successful in silencing or eliciting apologies from other critics. In 1939 an Idaho legislator had officially declared the city the "cesspool of the world." The chamber invited him to personally inspect their businesses, and the Idaho "statesman," amidst considerable publicity, found Las Vegas a fair city which extended a friendly hospitality to visitors.

By the conclusion of World War II, Nevada assumed both a negative and a positive image. There was a questioning of the divorce business and a resentment toward the state that had prospered as a result of the war. The *Citizen News* of Hollywood on December 27, 1945, noted that "perjury [was] committed in almost every divorce case." On the same day the *Sacramento Bee* claimed that a "divorce racket probe" had snared four Californians in Reno. The *Palo Alto Times* on December 17, 1945, found Nevada divorces "shaky" since a rooming-house operator had testified falsely in the case of fourteen Californians. A shower of articles in California papers in December 1945 carried headlines like "Perjury Conducted Every Day in Nevada," "Perjury is the Rule," and "Concerns of Nevada Strictly Mercenary." And yet the same papers calmly noted: "Holiday Divorce Rush Is in Full Swing in Reno," "Reno Divorce Record Broken Last Month," and "200,000 Reno Marriages are Financial Boon to City."

Nor did Reno's peculiar role during World War II go unnoticed. The *Ogden Standard-Examiner* on October 12, 1949, declared that Reno provided "non-essential occupations" as classified by the federal government. "Work-or-fight" was required by the country and should have applied to Nevada. The paper also suggested that the hiring of women as dealers and croupiers in the clubs was to "stave off effects of the draft." Neither the boom psychology of Nevada nor increasing numbers of divorces processed during the war years was easily forgotten in neighboring communities.

At the same time, a series of positive articles on Nevada received wide notice. In January 1946 the *National Geographic Magazine* published the thirty-eight-page "Nevada Desert Treasure House." Profusely illustrated and in itself a history and current events calendar for the state, almost every page of the account plied Nevada with compliments. There were the "trim Nevada towns," the "spick-and-span town of Minden," the "alert progressive Las Vegas," the "lovely tree—and lake—landscaped hill . . . of the University of Nevada," the "splendid Route 50," and the "popular Pat McCarran," and Elko was "the stockman's capital" of the West.

After the war Elko came to be viewed as an ideal western town of great promise. Temple Manning gave it one of his "Three Minute" editorials in the Oakland *Post-Examiner* on December 16, 1944. He found it "absolutely different" than might be expected. Its streets were lined with beautiful Victorian houses, the physical setting was fascinating, its giant service area was as large as several eastern states, and it possessed a true western culture. The *Salt Lake Tribune* on March 17, 1946, envisioned a rapidly expanding city with a high-rise hotel and prosperity relying on both tourists and cattle. When Bing Crosby was appointed the honorary mayor on February 7, 1948, most of the regional newspapers told and retold the story of his 14,000 acre ranch and his love of Nevada. The *Fresno Bee* even speculated on Frank Sinatra becoming honorary mayor of Winnemucca.

In short, the image of a prosperous rural Nevada had been set when Roger Butterfield published his exhaustive account, "Elko County," for *Life* on April 18, 1949. Butterfield was already famous in Nevada for his positive story on "Harold's Club" in 1945, his almost promotional account of a Truckee Meadows dude ranch in the *Ladies' Home Journal*, and his laudatory coverage of James Edward Church, the snow scientist, in the *Saturday Evening Post*. As a journalist-historian Butterfield was editor for both *Time* and *Life* and a contributor to numerous other national publications. He saw Nevada as a colorful and striking yet prosperous and progressive land. He showed Elko County to be the leading cattle-producing county in the American West, with 10,000 head of white-faced Herefords being shipped each year. Along with the 150,000 sheep and 1,500,000 pounds of wool, it was easy to understand Bing Crosby's purchase of ranches in the area. Butterfield placed much emphasis on the "atmosphere of mutual trust," the selling of $100,000 worth of cattle "with no written record at all," the easy "links with Hollywood and Broadway," and the absence of country clubs and "social snobbery" and "boosterism." All led Butterfield to believe that "God made this nation with a perfect balance," and that Elko County was "at present one of the happiest and most prosperous localities in the whole U.S." Perhaps rural Nevada had finally emerged from the decades of identification with "Passion in the Desert" and "Honky-Tonk Trading Post."

Between March 27, 1954, and January 22, 1955, the *New Yorker* carried seven articles on Nevada. A. J. Liebling first visited the state to obtain a divorce during the summer of 1949. He quickly found a Pyramid Lake guest ranch and centered the remainder of his observations around wild horses, Indians, fellow guests, and the political and social climate of the state. Throughout the early fifties, Liebling carefully followed Clark County politics and particularly the policies of Senator Pat McCarran. At the same time he introduced his second wife to Pyramid Lake goose hunting, fishing, and life in the wild.

Liebling documented Indian claims, water rights conflicts, and mustang hunting along with the many disputes of Hank Greenspun, Senator McCarran, and Senator Joseph McCarthy. Author of a dozen books on everything from French cuisine to New York literary figures, and with almost two decades with the *New Yorker* when he embarked on his many visits to Nevada, Liebling became known as "a peerless chronicler of the demi-monde," a product of Paris and New York City, and yet a person who possessed a peculiar attraction for Nevada. He found the state the ideal terrain for a reporter who did not wish to interpret or pretend to be an expert. But at the same time, he was the epitome of art and exactness in journalism and through his extensive writings he gave Nevada a new dimension and a surprisingly significant and realistic image.

Over thirty-five years, 1920–1955, the declared purpose of a few newspapermen and magazine reporters was to direct aspersions toward Nevada. Others were little more than connoisseurs of the trite and familiar; they seemed profoundly uninterested in ideology, morality, or the complexities of social history. Many stories were simply voyeurism and questionable accounts which the journalist had extracted from a garrulous informant. And yet, most writers found neither a "class nor a caste" system in Nevada; most were impressed with the "successful blending of a diverse economy," most came to appreciate the liberal lifestyle, and most reported favorably on their Nevada adventure.

During the decades following World War I perhaps two grand images of Nevada emerged. First, the critics argued that after the 1931 legalization of gambling and the six-week residency for divorce, Nevada's image became distinctly different from that of other states. The knot of agrarian, intellectual, and promotional progressives that had for almost thirty years envisioned a quiet, middle-class prosperity had withered away. Now culture seemed to have been atomized and desensitized. Only consumer culture, which the state was slowly molding into the sensuous and thrilling, was given a transcendent purpose. Careful history, literature, art, and retold human stories often eluded the state's educated citizenry. The masses were as often crippled as strengthened by insecure claims of personal liberty and inalienable rights. While in some ways harmless, Nevada had embarked upon a rather silly and embarrassing path which reduced and abridged her in the nation's eyes. Although the path led to a kind of economic stability, only major social movements would have united the troubled, fragmented soul of Nevada's middle class, and only a blooming culture could have modified the state's hedonistic consumerism and provided it with a truly favorable image.

A second and more positive view noted that after the decline of the Comstock, the state had failed to forge a new economic alloy. Therefore, with the Tonopah-Goldfield mining collapse and the inability of the agrarian reclamation movement to recreate Midwestern-type farming, the state haltingly and unexpectedly drifted toward the divorce-gambling alchemy that was to turn dross into gold. As is so often the case with social technology, history supplied no guideposts. Rather than truly remembering and learning from its checkered past, Nevada seemed to live and survive very much in a pragmatic present. Rather than developing a traditional mythology and an organized will, the state became iconoclastic and singularly individualistic. Nevertheless, Nevada learned to build on its own successes, it sailed on the spirit of a new liberalized social code, and it came to cater to an almost limitless clientele. Although not acquiring a totally positive image, Nevada found itself "on a roll"; it seemed that it could not fail.

CHAPTER VI

Vanity and luxury are civilizers of the world

and sweeteners of human life.

—William Hazlitt

During the last forty years Nevada continued to capture the nation's imagination. Writers, nature enthusiasts, and muck-raking journalists probed most aspects of its history, culture, and environment. Newspaper exposés, magazine articles, historical tracts, and novels created a kaleidoscope of colorful and contradictory impressions. The images of Nevada emerging from this potpourri were often clichéd, sometimes superficial, and frequently banal. Some, however, communicated a genuine sensitivity and insight into the nature of the state and its people. Together, both the artful and the artless images conveyed the nation's mind in perceiving and judging Nevada.

This diversity of opinion and judgments was matched only by the sheer enormity of literary outpourings. Their scope and scale showed that the fascination of writers with Nevada had been disproportionate to its wealth, its population, its political scandals, and its cultural significance. Nowhere was this more obvious than in the press, where in recent decades Nevada continued to be praised, acclaimed, criticized, and maligned. Despite its relatively modest size, Reno, for example, intrigued both the nation and the world. In 1952 America's three principal wire services maintained bureaus in Reno, several West Coast papers kept stringers in the city, and the *New York Daily News* had a full-time man on the Reno beat.[1]

Representative of newspaper articles favorably depicting Reno was a May 12, 1968, *New York Times* piece by Michael Strauss. Entitled "Reno Divorcing Itself From Divorce," this article claimed that Reno's "image as the divorce capital of America has faded." It pointed out that gambling was only one among many tourist attractions offered and highlighted family-oriented activities such as "snow or water-skiing in the Sierra Nevadas" and "sightseeing at the famous ghost town of Virginia City." Although the Strauss article depicted Reno in a positive light, an older image of sin and perdition was still common-place. Indeed, at one end of the image-making scale simplistic criti-cism of Reno and Las Vegas had changed little over the last seventy years. A scathing review by Linda Grant appeared in the travel section of the May 27, 1990, edition of the *Independent*, a London news-paper with a circulation of 387,000. Reno was blasted for its lack of "cosmopolitan spirit," the "slow" and "rusty" minds of its residents, its "awful" food, and its gambling industry that stripped "America's working poor of their savings."[2]

Although controversy still raged around Reno, during the last forty years its pride of place as Nevada's most controversial town was surrendered to Las Vegas. Like Reno, Las Vegas had both its advo-cates and its adversaries. Its tourist attractions were often trumpeted in travel articles appearing in the *Los Angeles Times* and the *San Fran-cisco Examiner*. A July 1, 1990, article by Dick Alexander entitled "A Legend Opens in Las Vegas," for example, told of the grand opening of the Excalibur, the world's "largest resort hotel." According to Alexan-der "the opening was a media and medieval event," and the Excalibur was a "cactus Camelot that makes Disneyland look like a Mickey Mouse operation." The city was commended, however, for more than its hotels. Articles bearing such titles as "Vegas' Best Tables—For Food" and "Mom and Dad Huxtable Do Vegas" regularly appeared in the *Los Angeles Times* as the paper applauded the city's cuisine and its family-style entertainment.

Although Las Vegas generally received sympathetic treatment in the nation's travel press, it, like Reno, had its detractors. An August 11, 1991, article appearing in the *This World* section of the *San Francisco Chronicle* viewed Las Vegas from the vantage point of a needy child. The author, Christine Feldhorn, grew up in the poor, older northwest part of town with the desert heat "searing my lungs, aluminum-white skies hurting my eyes." She found the town "exists just for adults; it's still phony." And despite "all its image and packaging, it's one of the most unsophisticated places on Earth." Perhaps the most shockingly negative comments came from bartenders, waitresses, and boys in the parking lot, all of whom asked of Feldhorn why she would want to come back even for a visit.

While most of the coverage Nevada received centered on Reno and Las Vegas, many articles featured the state's historic mining camps, ghost towns, and scenic wonders. The *Christian Science Monitor* occasionally ran pieces that highlighted Nevada's deserts and suggested rural communities for potential vacation sites. Included were "Wild-Flower Season in the Desert of Nevada," "Fabulous Virginia City Shines Anew," "Nevada's Short Cut to the Sea," and "National Basque Festival" in Elko. Nevada's historic locales and scenic beauty were regularly touted in the *San Francisco Chronicle*, the *San Francisco Examiner*, and the *Los Angeles Times*. These pieces often carried colorful titles like, "Virginia City Blues," "Desert Hideaway," "The Loneliest Road," "Desert Drama: Nevada's Valley of Fire," and "Where in the Hell is Jarbidge, Nevada?"

The coverage of Nevada by the nation's premier newspaper, the *New York Times*, was typical of the eastern press's treatment. A perusal of its *Index* revealed that while the state's general importance (as measured in number of citations) could not match California's, specific aspects of Nevada's culture, environment, and social life received extensive treatment and slowly built a national image.

Among the most-cited topics was Nevada's growing reputation as the nation's nuclear laboratory and dumping ground. In 1950 the Atomic Energy Commission decided to use Nevada's deserts as a test site for its nuclear experiments. The nation's attention became riveted on the experiments. These tests brought the first postwar wave of reporters to the state's southern deserts. Articles bearing such titles as "7,000 of Military To Be in Atom Test," "New Series of Atom Tests To Be Most Extensive Yet," "New Atom Tests Will Set Record," and "A.E.C. Emphasizes Atom Test Safety" began to appear. During the 1950s and the 1960s hundreds of references were made in the pages of the *Times* to atomic testing in Nevada. It reported on the various experiments conducted at the Nevada Test Site, the important political figures who traveled to Nevada to observe them, the impact of the tests upon Las Vegas's economic development, the concerns citizens expressed over possible contamination, snowstorms and earthquakes caused by the experiments, and the government's subsequent assurances that no danger was involved.

During the late seventies, as nuclear testing declined, there was a move to use Nevada's eastern deserts as launching sites for the nation's newest weapon, the MX missile. Nevadans, exhausted by the blasts of the fifties and the sixties, and becoming increasingly aware of the price that some of them paid for earlier above-ground testing, strenuously protested this move, but the Department of Defense in turn launched a public relations campaign defending the plan. As the political storm unfolded in Nevada, *Times* reporters scampered back to the state's deserts, and articles sporting such titles as "MX Missile System Viewed as Devastating to Nevada," "MX Unwelcome in Nevada-Utah Basin," and "Fears on MX Found in Nevada and Utah" began to surface. Although Utah residents also protested locating the missile system in their state, influenced by the "Sagebrush Rebellion" (an attempt on the part of Nevada's ranchers to reclaim for the state its federally administered lands) a consensus was quickly reached among Pentagon officials and journalists that leadership against the MX was centered in Nevada. The protestors were thus identified as "desert rats, miners and ranchers" and their colorful remonstrances attributed to "Old West" "style and attitudes." Las Vegas—apparently defined as more civilized than the rest of the state, and as sympathetic to the project since its "subcontractors" would benefit economically from the program—was set apart in the *Times* coverage from the "cowboys." Although belittled, lampooned, and maligned, the "cowboys" fought on and with the efforts of Nevada politicians the government ultimately abandoned its decision to use Nevada as a nuclear armory. The "cowboys" had won.

Finally, in the next decade the growing public clamor over the storage of nuclear waste once again brought Nevada into the national limelight. This time the point of contention centered on using Nevada's deserts as a dumping ground for the waste. In 1987 Congress selected Nevada's Yucca Mountain as a storage site for waste from "112 commercial nuclear reactors and weapons plants for 10,000 years." Nevadans protested and bumper stickers bearing the legend "Nevada is not a Wasteland" blossomed on pickups and cars. The federal government had once again been challenged by a restless populace, and turned to the process of reexamining its decision. The *Times* was again on the Nevada beat; articles like "Nevada Sues to Block Nuclear Waste Dump," and "U.S. Will Start Over on Planning For Nevada Nuclear Waste Dump" appeared on its pages, and the nation's attention again turned toward Nevada. The final image in this saga, however, remains to emerge.

Then there was Nevada's pariah industry: gambling. Between 1950 and 1990 over 620 references were made in the pages of the *New York Times* to Nevada gaming. During the entire decade of the 1950s the *Times Index* listed only twenty articles relating to the state's gambling industry. In the sixties, however, *Times* reporters "discovered" Nevada gambling, and the number of citations soared to 159. Also in the early sixties *Times* reporters focused on allegations of "Cosa Nostra" involvement in the state's casinos, and articles exposing the "hidden impact" of Nevada gambling upon the nation's character surfaced. One of the most extensive of these was Wallace Turner's November 1963 series of five first-page articles on casino gambling in Las Vegas. In the series Turner claimed that legalized gambling was a "new force in American life" touching on "the careers of such public personalities as Frank Sinatra . . . the pension fund of the Teamsters Union . . . Wall Street scandals . . . Latin-American diplomats and . . . the criminal conspiracy known as Cosa Nostra." While recognizing that not "everyone connected with gambling in Nevada is a crook," Turner suggested that many of Nevada's professional gamblers learned their trade where casino gambling was illegal, and thus possessed a different "ethical outlook" than "ordinary" businessmen. Many, he believed, were skimming profits before reporting their taxes and were using their "black money" to subvert the nation.

Although exposés of illicit activities in Nevada's casinos continue even today, in the late sixties and the early seventies the most popular gambling topic among reporters was the activities of the elusive "billionaire industrialist," Howard Hughes. The *Times* noted, among other things, Hughes's purchases of casinos, his attempt to halt nuclear testing in the state, his "mysterious $100,000 payment" to Charles G. Rebozo and possible involvement in the Watergate scandal, and power struggles under way in the "Hughes organization." During the Hughes era in Las Vegas, coverage of Nevada gambling began to change. While the colorful, flamboyant, and bizarre Hughes helped to further the state's eccentric image in the national press, his involvement with Nevada casinos tended to balance earlier impressions of the gambling industry as dominated by organized crime. The *Times*'s earlier chilly attitude toward the industry began to thaw, and as it thawed there was a growing tendency to equate casino gaming with other forms of legitimate business.

This changing attitude toward gaming was furthered when the *Times* covered the February 1978 invasion of Las Vegas, "that seeming citadel of sin," by Billy Graham and his crusade for Christ. Although the paper appeared to be amused that the "foremost spokesman for Christian virtue" was preaching the Gospel "in a city often renowned for vice," and it noted that the locals considered Graham's presence in their community " 'headliner' excitement," it did not scoff overly much as it dutifully recorded Graham's observations of the city. Las Vegas, Graham claimed, was "a nice place to visit" and "was not merely a city of casinos." Besides, he added, "Probably the greatest center of gambling in the United States is Wall Street . . . I would not condemn Wall Street, and I did not come here to condemn gambling." Graham's equating of gambling with playing the stock market offended some, yet his defense was significant for it indicated that, in some circles, Nevada's industry was beginning to be viewed as legitimate.

The metamorphosis that transformed gambling into a socially acceptable industry was not absolute, however, and the industry still had its detractors. Nevertheless, due to its evident economic success and the legalization of casino gambling in New Jersey—an event that received much coverage in the pages of the *Times*—gambling and Nevada came increasingly to be viewed as acceptable by a growing number of Americans. Its status had risen so much, in fact, that during the economically difficult years of the late seventies, some writers began to suggest that the licensing of casino gambling and the taxing of its proceeds might solve the fiscal problems of many hard-pressed state governments.

Although the supposedly depression-proof status of the gaming industry was shown to have feet of clay during the economic recession of the early eighties, the generally favorable attitude the *Times* had expressed toward Nevada gambling continued. Indicative of this change in attitude was an article on the industry's economic problems, "Cards Turn Bad for Las Vegas." Appearing on the front page of the business section on December 15, 1982, and written by Thomas C. Hayes, the article offered *Times* readers an in-depth analysis of the problems confronting the "gaming industry." The causes of the economic downturn were enumerated: competition from Atlantic City, "the recession, Mexican credit losses, rising air fares and an oversupply of quality hotel rooms"; and suggestions for improving the situation were made: "a change of image" giving the industry a broader base among middle-class and working-class tourists, and less emphasis upon "high stakes" players. What is of interest in this article is not only its well-reasoned analysis, but the fact that the gambling industry was treated as though it was a major business enterprise. Like any other enterprise, it could fall on hard times, and like any other business it could act intelligently to reverse bad fortune.

Another topic stressed in the pages of the *New York Times* over the last decades was Nevada's tourist attractions. Although the paper had been interested in the state's tourist potential in the past, as the century waned and distances grew shorter it displayed even more interest. Between 1950 and 1990 the *Times* ran over twenty substantial articles featuring Nevada's tourist appeal. Ranging from Lake Tahoe to Lake Mead, and from Virginia City to Elko, the state's mountains, desert lands, and colorful cities were ballyhooed in articles bearing such intriguing titles as "Tonopah—Survivor of Mining Days," "Las Vegas Raises Tacky to a Magnificent Level," and "The Real Thing for Cowboys"—a piece on Elko.

Indicative of its increased importance within the state, the favorite Nevada tourist topic was Las Vegas. An example of the kind of treatment that the city's tourist industry received was an article that appeared in the *New York Times Magazine* on June 26, 1955, covering Noel Coward's opening in Las Vegas. After noting that Coward was "an international figure of terrifying and purposeful chic," this article gently lampooned Las Vegas for its obsession with image, and noted the hopes expressed on the part of some of the city's residents that Coward's presence in the community would add a little "polish" and "class" to the town's image. It also recorded Coward's observations of the city. "Las Vegas," Coward stated, "is like a vast cruise ship . . . there is lettuce for every dish . . . The bands are playing swing, jazz, progressive and retrogressive and the people move from hotel to hotel . . . all having a whale of a time."

Another example of the *Times*'s treatment of Las Vegas was found in a May 31, 1964, article appearing in its Sunday travel section. Entitled "An Ace In the Hole for Las Vegas Tourists," this piece applauded the city's "Varied Diversions." Highlighting its architecture, swimming pools, golf courses, close proximity to the Lake Mead Recreation area, and Valley of Fire State Park, the article suggested that there was something in Las Vegas for the entire family, even the children. This article also indicated a trend in the *Times* to periodically remind its readers that there was more to Las Vegas than gambling. One such article appearing on March 16, 1958, was even entitled "Las Vegas Is More Than the 'Strip,'" and it emphasized such things as the importance of nuclear testing to the city's economy, its proximity to Hoover Dam and Boulder City, and the Lake Mead National Recreation Area.

Although newspaper journalists helped to define topical interest in Nevada, the major work at image building was performed by writers contributing to popular magazines. The *Reader's Guide to Periodical Literature* listed over six hundred articles written on Nevada subjects between 1950 and 1990. Since many professional journals and local and regional magazines were not indexed in the *Reader's Guide*, the actual number of articles written on Nevada during these decades was much larger than this figure would indicate.

From among the more than six hundred accounts, and others encountered in the process of research, some eighty-two were selected for analysis. They explored virtually every aspect and region of the state. Twenty-seven focused on greater Las Vegas, thirteen on the Reno-Tahoe area, twenty-three on rural Nevada, and nineteen on the state as a whole. Their subject matter can roughly be divided into six overlapping areas: Nevada's economic development, twenty; political life, three; history and natural environment, eighteen; gaming and tourism, twelve; and cultural life, eighteen. Eleven delved into Nevada's social problems: crime, compulsive gambling, prostitution, and welfare. The format of the articles and their authors' attitudes toward the state varied greatly. Fifty-six included photographs, five had maps, and nineteen contained graphs, charts, or other illustrations. Ten examined Nevada in objective or scientific terms; fifty-one expressed enthusiasm for its natural wonders, its cities, and its people; and twenty-one could barely restrain their contempt.[3]

Out of this melange of images and attitudes three distinct constellations emerged. The first revolved around the idea that Nevada was one of America's "last frontiers." Images relating to this theme were derived primarily from the state's wilderness environment and its mining heritage. The second collection of images related to modern Nevada. It centered on contemporary analyses of Reno and Las Vegas, and focused upon the gaming industry and its impact upon Nevada's social and economic life. The third constellation centered on the notion that Nevada and its people were somehow among the culturally "avant-garde." This last depiction was found primarily in recent artistic and literary analyses of Las Vegas.

The image of Nevada as a last frontier was largely the work of history buffs and nature enthusiasts. Although professional historians continued to write critical studies of the state's multifaceted past, in the popular press Nevada's history was still identified primarily with the state's mining heritage. Articles that boasted such titles as "Glittering Legends Surround the Swaggering Cosmopolis that was Virginia City," "Go it Washoe!," "A Street That IS Paved with Gold and Silver," and "Railroad Days" are typical of this genre and were usually published in such journals as *American Heritage*, *American Mercury*, and *American West*.

Here Nevada's history was frequently retold in the form of amusing anecdotes about hard-rock miners, silver kings and silver senators, tin-horn gamblers, and gunslinging newspaper editors. The men and women described often assumed epic proportions, as the narratives skirted both legend and myth. "Washoe's redeeming feature," one of the authors told us, "was that it was never dull." And, another added, "the legend of the Comstock Lode . . . is possessed of so many fascinations, so much drama and highlight that [it still commands the attentions of] numerous historians." The image that emerged in these articles was of a youthful frontier state—raucous, rowdy, and turbulent. In short, "West is hell" and, implicitly, Nevada remains so today.[4]

While writers of popular history told heroic and humorous tales about the state's first citizens, nature enthusiasts were busy constructing an intellectual landscape upon which Nevada's mythical history— both past and present—could unfold. Few aspects of Nevada were explored more thoroughly during these years than its natural environs. Articles on Nevada's topography, geological formations, caves, desert and mountain lakes, and vanishing rivers appeared in such periodicals as *Smithsonian*, *Holiday*, *Natural History*, *Travel & Leisure*,

Nature, and *Sunset*, while articles touting Nevada's fish and wildlife populations appeared in *Outdoor Life* and *Field and Stream*.

Two contrasting sets of images emerged from the various perceptions of the Nevada wilderness. One group of authors was obsessed with the barren character of the Nevada waste. Representative of this group was Walter Van Tilburg Clark. In "Nevada's Fateful Desert," a November 1957 article for *Holiday*, Clark evoked the emotions a traveler experienced as he crossed the state's "lonesome" lands. The desert was "forbidding," mysterious, an "Unknown Land." Its "frightening distances" and "pale" expanses of wilderness were indifferent to the needs of the traveler, and when confronting the desert "barrens" he experienced a "loss of self" and a "diminishment." The "sameness" and the "oneness" of the desert destroyed the voyager's "sense of distance" and "sense of time," stripping him of his illusions and confronting him with his own insignificance. For Clark the desert was "the eternally unconcerned."

Although he noted a variety of life forms in the Great Basin, the barren character of the Nevada wilderness was underscored by Donald Dale Jackson in a November 1987 *Smithsonian* piece on the Great Basin National Park. Jackson described the Great Basin as "a kind of American outback," the "least-known and least-appreciated geographic province in the West." A land of "lonely desert basins" and windswept mountains, Jackson saw Nevada as "a hard country," challenging to all forms of life. In America's "Big Lonesome" only the tenacious and the rugged survived, and yet the remote and challenging aspect of the land possessed its own allure; this image of an unspoiled land's last refuge contained its own special enchantment.

While some observers were haunted by the harsh sterility of the Great Basin, others were entranced by its diversity. A March 1962 *Sunset* article on Nevada's Snake Range highlighted the beauty of its "alpine lakes, bubbling springs, and swift cold creeks." Underscoring the variety of plant life found in this "sky island," the article noted that in addition to its "stands of 2,500-year-old bristlecone pines" the range boasted "prickly pear blossoming alongside Douglas fir," and "mountain mahogany . . . standing 30 to 40 feet high in moist canyons." Like the other articles, this one was also haunted by the loneliness of the Nevada wilderness and remarked that the Snake mountains were "almost empty of humankind."

In some authors the nature enthusiast and the history buff were joined, and out of this wedding came some of the most striking images of the Nevada frontier. Nell Murbarger was such a writer. The author of *Ghosts of the Adobe Walls*, *Sovereigns of the Sage*, and *Ghosts of the Glory Trail*, Murbarger prowled through the American Southwest for over twenty years, talking to its people, recording its history, and photographing its deserts and its ghost towns. Armed with cameras and canteens, she explored Nevada's petrified forests, desert lakes, lost rivers, and deserted mining camps. Her photographs of these sites and her reactions to them were published in magazine articles entitled "Our Largest Petrified Tree," "Lost Rivers of Nevada," and "Birds of Anaho."

The image of Nevada that emerged from these pieces was of an immense, melancholy land, tinted in pastel hues; a "forbidding realm" composed of vast expanses of "sun-bleached wilderness," "wild" and "wind-swept" wastes, and improbable lakes "cradled in . . . color-splashed desert hills." In Murbarger's Nevada crystalline rivers vanished into "glaring white" sinks, "devoid of life and dry as mummy dust," and the fossilized remnants of ancient *Metasequoia* stood sentinel in the "terrible vastness" of the Black Rock Desert. Nevada was a bleak, barren, and uninhabited domain, dotted with the remains of ephemeral boom camps and filled with spectral memories.

Murbarger's visual images set the scene for her historical works. They are the stage upon which an epic struggle between man and the land he hoped to conquer unfolded. Typical of her reconstructions of Nevada's heroic past was an article she wrote for *Frontier Times* in May 1965. In this piece she focused on the nineteenth-century charcoal industry. Since charcoal was used as fuel in ore smelting, its production was a necessary adjunct to Western mining. The industry mercilessly exploited both the land and its people. Its workers, often drawn from newly arrived ethnic minorities, lived in hovels and were grossly underpaid, while its voracious appetite for wood decimated Nevada's timber resources. As the timber resources were depleted the cost of charcoal increased, and a conflict between the charcoal contractors and the smelters resulted in the infamous "Fish Creek War" which broke out near Eureka in 1879.

Murbarger described the charcoal industry as a "*mean* business" and a "*big* business," that swept "over the West like a pestilence,

leaving behind it tens of thousands of acres stripped of their timber" and "a black record of bloodshed, racial strife and corruption."
Changes in the mining industry, however, doomed this pariah of the
frontier to extinction. Although stone charcoal kilns shaped like bee-
hives still dotted the desert lands that Murbarger explored, nature
was then in the process of reclaiming its "denuded lands," even as
the desert winds erased "the black scars of the charcoal camps." In
the final conflict between man and nature in Murbarger's Nevada the
all-encompassing desert ultimately triumphed.

While writers like Murbarger developed a mythology of the state
that characterized its history as a relentless struggle between man
and nature, other writers employed Nevada's frontier heritage and its
wilderness environment as vehicles for explaining—and hence ex-
cusing—the foibles and eccentricities of its current residents. Pieces
bearing such titles as "High Old Times in Nevada," "Nevada: Heir to
the Wild West," "Clamor on the Comstock," and "Las Vegas, Home on
the Range" appeared in such journals as *Esquire*, *Collier's*, and *Holiday*
and stressed the continuity between past and present in Nevada.

Typical of these pieces was an article by Bill Barich, author of
the short story collection *Traveling Light* (1985). Written for the June
1985 issue of *Esquire*, and entitled "Desert Dreams," this article was
a delightful mix of snatches of Nevada's mining history, descriptions
of its deserts, and anecdotal characterizations of the state's current
inhabitants. The idea that united this pastiche was Barich's contention that "existence is random and tenuous" in Nevada's harsh desert
environment, and to survive one must develop a "bizarre" strategy
for life.

To prove this contention Barich described some of Nevada's
desert inhabitants. There was, for example, the "historian manqué"
who dwelt in the ghost town of Rhyolite. Descended from some of
America's most "prestigious colonial families and educated at Culver
Military Academy," at an early age he had fallen under the spell of
the American West. Possessing "Victorian" sensibilities, he perceived
himself as "something of a misfit, out of sync with the age." In short,
the image of the old curmudgeon surviving alone in some desolate
desert shanty and waiting for the world to reverse directions had for
a century persisted as part of the Nevada mystique.

Another writer who attributed Nevada's exotica to its "frontier mentality" was Tom Robbins. The author of such works as *Even Cowgirls Get the Blues* and *Another Roadside Attraction*, in the December 1988 issue of *Esquire* Robbins brought his "unique perspective on the American West" to Nevada. In "The Real Valley of the Dolls," Robbins suggested that "the trouble with Nevada is that it thinks . . . it's the last frontier, at a time when the last frontier has moved beyond . . . Jupiter."

Although these were brave words for a man who came to Nevada on a "pilgrimage to the Canyon of the Vaginas," Robbins nevertheless supported them through an insightful—if not entirely accurate—cultural analysis. The "state song," Robbins reported, was the "exaggerated belch"; the "state bird" was the "chicken-fried steak"; and Nevada was one of the few places left in America where ax murderers still used axes and not sushi knives. In addition, Nevadans were "rough ol' dudes" who never took off their hats; spent much of their time in barrooms complaining that "They didn't let us win in Vietnam"; and resided in double-wide trailers with nothing in their "grassless yard except a satellite dish as big as a moon." Robbins was, however, willing to "forgive" Nevadans for their eccentricities, since he noted that while citizens of other states were less inclined to shoot up their road signs than Nevadans, they were also less willing to share their "habitat with bombing ranges and plutonium dumps."

The most notable among these frontier apologists for the Silver State, however, and at first glance the most unlikely, was Lucius Beebe. An Eastern *litterateur* known for his baroque tastes, flamboyant life style, and scathing wit, Beebe's reputation as an author and a *bon vivant* was secure long before he graced Nevada with his presence. A descendant of Boston Brahmins, he passed his childhood years dynamiting vacant outhouses; for years he served on the editorial staff of the *New York Herald Tribune* where he applied his skill at pyrotechnics to New York's café society. Adhering to a personal philosophy which held that "nothing matters but the gallant gesture," Beebe was an anomaly even in New York.[5]

In 1948 Beebe and the photographer Charles Clegg, his associate and intellectual collaborator, descended upon Nevada to research the history of Wells, Fargo. Attracted, perhaps, to the state's tolerant attitudes and freewheeling ways—a theme Beebe continually explored in his work—the two soon ensconced themselves in Virginia City's

Piper's mansion and made Nevada their home. In short order they became two of its staunchest defenders.

In 1952 they revived the somnolent *Territorial Enterprise*, attracted such nationally known writers as Bernard De Voto, Walter Van Tilburg Clark, Roger Butterfield, Joseph Henry Jackson, Duncan Emrich, and Stewart Holbrook to its contributing staff, and sought to restore the paper's reputation as the West's most articulate newspaper. By 1953 its editorials were being quoted in both San Francisco and the Eastern press, and its proprietors' vision of Nevada's past was stamped indelibly upon the American mind.[6]

Centered as they were in Virginia City, perhaps it was inevitable that this vision would be dominated by the glory days of the Comstock lode, and Beebe and Clegg tended to highlight this aspect of Nevada's past in such works as *U.S. West: The Saga of Wells Fargo* (1949) and *Virginia & Truckee: A Story of Virginia City and Comstock Times* (1949). Beebe was a prolific writer, however, and his interest in the state was not limited solely to exploring its history. During the 1950s and the early 1960s he authored a series of articles on Nevada that were designed to promote the state's current image by embellishing it with a raucous mythology derived from its turbulent past. Nevada was "heir to the great tradition of the West," which he identified with the Comstock.

In a 1955 article written for *Holiday* Beebe developed the theme and employed it as a vehicle to justify Nevada's cavalier approach to divorce, gambling, and other practices. According to Beebe, the "consciousness of its Comstock beginnings has never entirely left Nevada." Its "folklore, mores, economic and social backgrounds . . . originated in the mining of precious metals," and mining was "an occupation whose morals [were] known for tolerance." This tolerant attitude associated with mining, and also, Beebe notes, with ranching—another important Nevada industry—had been common in the American West during the great days of the frontier. At that time broad-minded attitudes toward sex and "a willingness to wager anything and everything on the turn of a card was the hallmark of life beyond the Missouri."

With "the taming of the frontier," however, "the old uninhibited West" declined and along with it "open prostitution" and legalized gambling. This was true everywhere except in Nevada. The state's natural environment could support few industries other than mining, and this fact of nature, combined with a string of bonanzas that dotted the state's history in the early twentieth century, kept the tolerant attitudes of the old frontier alive. To anathematize Nevada, then, for its permissive values was to miss the fact that it "had more about it of the nineteenth century and less of the twentieth than any other part of the nation."

In 1962 Beebe returned to this theme in a *Saturday Review* article entitled "The Sincere Sinning of the One Sound State." In this article he synthesized his view of Nevada's frontier mentality with the highly successful image of Nevada's secure financial situation and lenient tax laws that had been trumpeted in the "One Sound State" campaign of the 1930s and the 1940s. In Beebe's hands these two facets of Nevada's character were joined in a raucous depiction of the state's emancipated ways.

The idea that unites Nevada's laissez-faire attitudes toward business and taxation with its tolerant approach to the foibles of the flesh is a conception of freedom that Beebe thought was bequeathed by its frontier heritage. If this was the case, then Nevada's current residents had come by their freewheeling, lax, and sinful ways honestly, and it was unfair to criticize their unique institutions as opportunistic. Although the gaming industry exploited Nevada's colorful past for its own benefit, the state's noted eccentricities were genuine, Beebe believed, and not a product of its tourist trade.

An example Beebe cited of Nevada's continuing eccentricities was the "Searchlight Plan." Searchlight, an old mining town near the Arizona border, was confronted with a crisis when it was discovered that the local brothel was operating within five hundred feet of the community's one-room school in violation of state law. Either the school or the brothel had to be moved. In typical Nevada fashion, the state's "most venerable newspaper"—Beebe's own *Territorial Enterprise*—suggested that it was the school that ought to be moved, not the brothel.

A second incident Beebe focused on was the "Contact project." This project was concocted by two California literati who, feeling their freedom of sexual expression was limited in their home state, were planning to take over the tiny Nevada community of Contact, over five hundred miles north of Searchlight on the Idaho border, and establish a literary colony there. The most distinguishing features of this colony were to be its literary bordellos and militant commitment to immorality.

These two highly publicized events and others of an equally bizarre nature, combined with the state's "easy divorces," "legal gambling," "multiplicity of saloons," and "wide-open red-light districts," revealed a continuation in the state's pioneer mentality. Its eccentricity was further confirmed by the fact that Nevada, contrary to all moral maxims, prospered from "the wages of sin." Its residents paid no state income or inheritance taxes, and in 1960 its per capita income was the highest in the nation. Nevada, for very concrete reasons, it appeared, was committed to its errant ways.

Beebe pictured a state where basic characteristics had not been altered since the era of the Comstock, and given its prevailing prosperity, it was unlikely that its character and image would change. The myths, the images of the nineteenth century, were all but patented and made available for the world to see and even admire. Only in Nevada did the true Old West still survive.

While worlds apart in their personal and literary philosophies, writers like Murbarger and Beebe celebrated, indeed mined, the Old West, and demonstrated the breadth, the diverse elements, the encompassing enchantment of an earlier age. They show how far the frontier tent can be stretched to cover disparate events and ideas. They and some of their fellow writers believed that many layers of time and experience were being woven into a contemporary image vital to an understanding of Nevada history, ecology, and modern society.

Although Beebe extended Nevada's frontier imagery to include the "neon-lit leprosaria" of twentieth-century Reno and Las Vegas, "where the walking dead never emerge to sunlight and the jungle night life is deadlier than in the Congo," many writers employed a different set of images when portraying the state's two urban centers. One of the most powerful of these motifs involved the specter of "mob" activity in Nevada's casinos, a popular subject in the nation's periodicals during the fifties and sixties. Employing the most sinister of images, these articles tapped the archetypal fear of the unknown. Receiving nourishment from the same paranoia that gave rise to McCarthyism, a generation of Americans believed that a series of unseen malevolent forces endangered their society. Among the demons that plagued the "haunted fifties" were communism and organized crime. Both were grounded in the same hysteria, and perhaps told as much about the saintly and their xenophobia as they did about the forces that tempted and threatened to engulf them.

That organized crime actually existed and made substantial inroads into Nevada gambling cannot be denied. But that reality had little bearing on the intensity of the imagery used to describe it. It is not the actuality of mob activity but the legends associated with it that are informative here. Since these legends were periodically rejuvenated by outbreaks of mob violence and the media exposés that followed in their wake, the saga of Nevada and organized crime assumed epic proportions.

The historic links between Nevada casinos and the mob were dramatized during the fifties and sixties by Estes Kefauver's Senate Committee on Organized Crime, the investigations and licensing activities of the Nevada Gaming Control Board, the crusading reporting of the *Las Vegas Sun*, and the publicity attending federal and local law enforcement efforts. The results of these investigatory efforts were publicized nationwide in such works as Lester Velie's October 1959 piece for *Reader's Digest*, "Las Vegas: The Underworld's Secret Jackpot"; Fred J. Cook's October 22, 1960, special issue for *The Nation*, "Gaming Inc. Treasure Chest of the Underworld"; and Edward F. Sherman's October 29, 1966, article for the *New Republic*, "Feds, Sharpers and Politics in Nevada." The tone of these articles was serious, critical, and objective. The narrative which unfolded in them, however, was so florid, so permeated with fraud, violence, and corruption that their mood of malevolence carried them beyond the realm of objective reporting and entered the realm of sensationalizing myth.

Few works in the popular media soiled Nevada's image as thoroughly as *The Nation*'s special issue on gambling in America written by Fred J. Cook. In this work Cook recounted the early history of mob activity in Nevada. In the early 1940s Benjamin (Bugsy) Siegel, formerly "of New York's infamous 'Bug and Meyer mob of executioners,' " and in the forties a Western agent for the New York and Chicago crime syndicates, recognized that legalized gambling in Nevada was "an untapped treasure chest" for the mob. Acting on his entrepreneurial instincts, he "bought into" two Las Vegas casinos and then, his appetite whetted, decided to construct "a fabulous hotel, dedicated to fabulous gambling" on the Strip: the Flamingo. Reputed to have been partially constructed with mob money, some of which Siegel carted across the country in satchels himself, the Flamingo opened for business in the mid-forties. Shortly thereafter the "Bug" and his mob partners failed to settle on an equitable distribution of the racket's Western revenues, and Siegel was executed gangland style on June 20, 1947, in a "Beverly Hills love nest." Such was the notorious beginning of mob involvement in Nevada.

The saga continued in the 1950s as the mob "moved into 'The Strip' in massive phalanx," and "Mert Wertheimer and his associates" extended "their grip on a whole string of hotels and gambling casinos in Reno." Humiliated by the nation's awareness of mob activity in the state, Nevada tightened its regulatory control over the gaming industry in the mid-fifties. The "indifferent success" of these measures was illustrated in "staccato" in May of 1957 when an attempted hit on Frank Costello, New York "czar" of the underworld, revealed he was toting accounts of the Tropicana's gambling returns around in his jacket pocket. The failure of efforts to clean up gambling in Nevada was further underscored in December 1958, when Gus Greenbaum (one of Siegel's Flamingo associates) and his wife were found "trussed up and butchered, their throats most efficiently slashed in their home in Phoenix, Arizona." Clearly, the mob had not been rooted out of Nevada gaming, and by 1960 Cook charged that Las Vegas was "virtually the capital of American crime" with "tentacles" that extended from it to New York City, Terre Haute, Biloxi, and Miami.

During the 1960s the by-now legendary association between Nevada and organized crime assumed a new twist when the attorney general of the United States, Robert Kennedy, joined the cast of characters. As laid out by Edward F. Sherman, one-time aide of Nevada governor Grant Sawyer, in a 1966 article for *The New Republic*, the stage for Kennedy's involvement in this drama was set by the fact that although Nevada had tried to purge itself of syndicate influence in the 1950s, "the gangsters had slipped into Nevada gambling before the door was closed, and . . . Nevada gambling never really did 'clean house.'" Responding to this situation in 1961 Kennedy sent a federal task force into the state charged with the responsibility of seeking out links with organized crime.

In violation of Nevada law the FBI installed over one hundred wiretaps in Las Vegas casinos. As news of the somewhat questionable activities of the "Feds" became known, Nevada's Democratic governor, Grant Sawyer (who had himself attempted to tighten Nevada's regulatory control over the gaming industry), was embroiled in a tough 1966 gubernatorial race with Paul Laxalt and sensed that political capital could be gained from this issue by adopting a "states' rights" stance toward the federal government. While Sawyer argued that the FBI was employing "Nazi-like tactics" and "running roughshod" over the state, Laxalt telegraphed apologies to J. Edgar Hoover for Sawyer's statements. For a time the nation was amused by the spectacle of a Kennedy Democrat attacking the federal government while a Goldwater Republican defended it. Although the 1966 gubernatorial campaign cannot be construed as a simple plebiscite on Nevadans' attitudes toward the federal government's crime-busting activities in their state, things did not work out as Sawyer had intended. Laxalt won the race and another colorful chapter was added to the saga of organized crime in Nevada.

Although Nevada's luster was tarnished by the problem of organized crime, mob-oriented articles did not monopolize the images associated with contemporary Nevada. Many authors wanted to discover the reality that lay behind Nevada's glittering mystique, and in pursuing this they probed Nevada's social, cultural, and economic life.

One of the more perceptive articles written on contemporary Nevada during the fifties was Daniel Lang's September 20, 1952, piece for the *New Yorker*. Entitled "Blackjack and Flashes," it delved into the process through which Las Vegans adjusted to the specter of nuclear testing in Nevada's southern deserts. Beginning with the initial apprehensions of the city's residents and moving to their cocky acceptance of "the bomb" (since it contributed to the wide-open character of their town, which was good for its tourist industry), Lang built a parable around Las Vegas's adjustment to the specter of nuclear annihilation. Las Vegans, he implied, learned to accept nuclear testing because they learned how to define it as not only harmless but beneficial. Lang's narrative revealed more, however, than the manner in which Las Vegans adjusted to the bomb. Anticipating by twelve years the spirit of the film *Dr. Strangelove: Or, How I Learned to Stop Worrying and Love the Bomb*, the Lang article exposed the process through which an entire generation adjusted to the specter of "the bomb" and revealed the absurdity of life in the nuclear age.

Another aspect of Nevada's contemporary life that contributed to its image was the economy of gambling itself. Articles focusing on the state's economic life grew in proportion to the proven success of the gaming industry. In 1952, despite its notoriety, gambling ranked behind retail sales, manufacturing, wholesale trade, railroads, and mining as "revenue-bearing enterprises" in the state.[7] It was obvious to some observers even then, however, that Nevada's economic future was tied to gambling. In "What Has Wide-Open Gambling Done to Nevada," a piece that appeared in the *Saturday Evening Post* in 1952, Robert Laxalt suggested that the legalization of gambling in 1931 and the arrival of mechanized tourism assured Nevada of "the biggest boom the state had known since the mining heyday of the Comstock lode."

In the long run Laxalt's observations proved correct. During the mid-fifties, however, Nevada's gaming industry experienced an economic crisis, some hotels in Las Vegas were forced to close, and articles on the recession in gambling appeared in *Time* and *Life*.[8] Due in part to these problems the economics of gaming was not a hot topic in the periodical literature of the 1950s. During the late 1960s, however, the nation's journalists discovered the economics of gambling in a major way. The ground for the bonanza was laid in Las Vegas during the 1950s when E. Parry Thomas assumed control of the Bank of Las Vegas and began to transform the structure of the Las Vegas gaming industry. Refusing to grant loans to Las Vegas casinos unless they agreed to modernize and expand, Thomas used the sluice gates of credit and finance to move the casino industry toward a sound corporate footing.

Then, during a financial crisis that swept the industry in the mid sixties, Thomas helped to alleviate the situation by facilitating Howard Hughes's investments in Las Vegas casinos. Hughes arrived in Las Vegas at a fortuitous moment. In 1966 the financial crisis in the gaming industry led Edward F. Sherman to predict that the Nevada casino era was coming to a close. One of the problems confronting the industry was that its underworld mystique barred many in the financial community from investing in gambling enterprises. In 1967 Hughes began buying casinos in Las Vegas, and by 1969 he had helped to transform the nation's image of Nevada gambling.

In 1969 Ovid Demaris, author and co-author of such dramatic exposés as *The Green Felt Jungle, America the Violent,* and *The Last Mafioso: The Treacherous World of Jimmy Fratianno,* journeyed to Las Vegas in quest of the elusive Howard Hughes. Although he failed to interview Hughes, he discovered the city's "obsession" with public relations and Hughes's place in its myth-making apparatus. As one Las Vegan informed Demaris, "Hughes has changed all this Mafia bullshit because The Man has a tremendous reputation for integrity! . . . I mean he is beautiful for the image of this town . . . Howard Hughes is the biggest thing that's happened to Las Vegas since, I'd say, Bugsy Siegel."

It would have been difficult for Las Vegans to discover a man better suited to repair their city's spoiled reputation. In the realm of myth making, Hughes was a master craftsman. As Demaris noted, over the years Hughes had fashioned for himself a number of romantic mystiques: "The Film Tycoon," "The Aviator," "The Playboy," "The Superpatriot," "The Industrialist," and "The Eccentric"—the greatest of all his roles; and now he was ready to lend his charisma to transforming the public image of gambling. Hughes's myth-making machine, we are told, wanted to portray Nevada gambling activities as "harmless pleasures" and "family fun." The success with which the Hughes organization pursued this goal was eloquently underscored for Demaris in an interview with the governor, Paul Laxalt. "Mr. Hughes's involvement here has absolutely done us wonders . . . I can see the change in the national press."

Hughes had made it acceptable for respectable business interests to invest in Nevada, and the money began to pour in. Corporations like Parvin/Dohrmann, Texas International Airlines, Levin-Townsend Computer Corp., and International Leisure invested in casinos. Articles in such reputable magazines as *Business Week* trumpeted these investments as sound and legitimate. Nevada gambling was on its way to becoming a respectable business enterprise.

It was not only Howard Hughes, however, that was working to make the pariah industry acceptable to American businessmen. During the 1960s the nation was undergoing a restructuring of its values, and its attitude toward gambling and other former vices was part of that change. An April 10, 1972, special report for *Newsweek* written by Pete Axthelm claimed gambling no longer existed on the edge of American society but had entered the mainstream. After noting that numerous states were attempting to legalize gambling so that they could tax its revenues and enhance their coffers, the report claimed that middle-class America now viewed gambling as an acceptable activity.

In 1976 a *Time* cover story echoed *Newsweek*'s earlier observations, as did a federal report released the same year. According to the federal Commission on the Review of the National Policy Toward Gambling, 80 percent of America's citizens now approved of gambling, and fully two-thirds had actually gambled.[9] By the mid-1970s it had become one of the nation's fastest growing commercial activities, with an estimated $75 billion a year being turned over in gaming activities. Further, during the early 1960s few states outside of Nevada had countenanced any form of gambling other than track betting, but by 1976 forty-four of the nation's states had legalized gambling activities of some kind.[10] While few commentators were certain why America's attitudes toward gambling had altered, Edward C. Devereux, Jr., a Cornell University sociologist, gave as good an interpretation as anyone when he suggested that it was due to the increased rationalization and secularization of American life. The nation's traditional commitment to public morality had collapsed and a Machiavellian rationale had taken its place; "anything goes if it works."[11] The nation, it would appear, was finally catching up with Nevada.

By 1980 the gambling industry in Nevada had become respectable. The president of Caesar's World, Inc., William H. McElnea, Jr., was even invited to discuss the new character of the industry at the Town Hall of California in Los Angeles. Making the most of this auspicious occasion, McElnea informed his audience that gaming—which he carefully distinguished from old-fashioned gambling—ought to be counted among America's preeminent industries. In effect, gambling, as gaming, had come of age. It was an industry of the eighties; it was an industry that even the yuppies could now enjoy.

Not everyone, however, was impressed with the meteoric ascent of Nevada's giant industry. During the 1950s one of the most penetrating critics of Nevada's gambling economy was Albert Deutsch. The author of such works as *The Mentally Ill in America: A History of Their Care and Treatment From Colonial Times, The Shame of the States,* and *Our Rejected Children,* Deutsch wanted to understand the impact of a gaming economy on the "common people" of the state. In an article he authored for *Collier's* in 1955 Deutsch took dead aim at those who praised Nevada for its low taxes and its fiscal responsibility by enumerating Nevada's social ills and the inequities of its welfare system.

Nevada, Deutsch noted, had the nation's highest crime and suicide rates, its infant death and tuberculosis rates were among the highest in the nation, and its health and welfare services were "on a primitive level." He also noted that the state's general relief standards were among the lowest in the nation and that the state's callous attitude toward its children was revealed in the fact that Nevada's schools "were suffering from acute financial malnutrition." Further, it was "the only state in the Union" that had no program for federally assisted Aid to Dependent Children. Nevertheless, the state received three times the national average "in federal grants for health, welfare and education," "more than half again as much as . . . that paid out to second-ranking Louisiana." All in all, Deutsch argued, Nevada did not tax its own citizens because it had "managed to work matters out so that it taxes the entire national population for many of its needs."

During the 1970s earlier reservations about Nevada's ability to control organized crime were resurrected. Sociologist Jerome H. Skolnick launched a three-year investigation of the regulatory problems associated with gaming. Although his investigation took him to both England and New Jersey, the primary focus of his study was Nevada. In 1978 he released the results of his study in *House of Cards: The Legalization and Control of Casino Gambling*. In this work Skolnick warned that "the control of legal casino gambling is an uncertain, even precarious, enterprise." He returned to the theme in an article for *Psychology Today* in July 1979. "Genuine control" of casino gaming, Skolnick warned, "often looks better on paper than in enforcement practice." Further, he cautioned, gambling not only "invites street crime" and prostitution, but also the "'dirty' money" of drug dealers and organized crime.

Tourism, closely allied with the gambling industry, had given rise to yet another group of images about contemporary Nevada. While Tahoe's Stateline was sometimes noted, the bulk of Nevada's big casinos were located in its two great gambling Meccas, Reno and Las Vegas, and the bulk of the literature revolved around these two cities. During the fifties and sixties such writers as *Saturday Review*'s travel aficionado Horace Sutton and *Collier's* John O'Hara visited Nevada's casinos, evaluated their entertainment potential, and shared their observations with their regular readers. In addition, such journals as *Holiday*, *Gambling Illustrated*, and *Ebony* ran pieces that were designed explicitly to attract customers to Nevada's casinos.

While Western imagery and references to Nevada's dude ranches sometimes surfaced in these pieces, their primary focus was upon Reno and Las Vegas. As such, they owed little to Nevada's nineteenth-century heritage and its frontier mystique. When they did borrow images from Nevada's past, these images were grounded either in the divorce colony and "Café society" mystique of Reno during the 1920s and 1930s or in the "fabulous oasis in the desert" thematic associated with Las Vegas in the 1940s.

Written to attract tourists to Nevada's casinos, superlatives were showered upon Reno and Las Vegas; "throbbing" hotels and "lavish" floor shows featured a "glittering array of performers" or "bigname talent." Terms like "glitter," "fabulous," and "phantasmagoria" were often applied, while hyperbolic expressions such as "gigantic, gargantuan, gracious, gay, gilded, gamblers' grotto" abounded. The two cities were also given high marks for their honest games, and during the 1960s they were congratulated for their enlightened attitudes toward race—a recent departure from an earlier Nevada tradition which often forbade blacks access to the big clubs. As *Ebony* somewhat sardonically put it, "the Negro's money is good anywhere for any purpose. Thus removed of any restrictions, he can enjoy himself—if it is his bent—all the way to the poorhouse."

While gaudy and overstated magazine articles continued to flourish in the seventies and eighties, descriptions of the glamour and excitement of Nevada's casinos increasingly were prepared by writers in the employ of Nevada interests. In the 1940s casino operators had learned the truth of the old maxim "It pays to advertise," and their publicity departments began to flood the known world with advertisements for the casinos' attractions. In addition, during the decade of the fifties Reno and Las Vegas, recognizing there was money to be made in catering to conventions, established convention centers in their communities. It was also during the 1950s that the state of Nevada got in the swing of things and established a Department of Economic Development with the promotion of tourism constituting one of its duties. In 1969 the department was reorganized, and—revealing the importance of tourism to the state—Travel and Tourism constituted one of its main divisions. Finally, in the 1980s a separate Commission on Tourism was established.

Typical of the professional presentations and image making pouring out of Las Vegas was the 1986 issue of *The Rotarian*. The Rotary Club planned to hold its international convention in the city in June, and most of the March issue of *The Rotarian* was dedicated to publicizing the upcoming convention. *The Rotarian* was assisted in its publicity efforts by a number of skilled Nevada image makers. A. D. Hopkins, editor of *The Nevadan*, for example, wrote a colorful overview of Las Vegas's history and ballyhooed its contemporary tourist appeal in an article entitled "Lively Las Vegas." John Reible, assistant manager of the News & Publicity Division of the Las Vegas News Bureau, wrote on the city's convention facilities. His piece, " 'The American Way to Play,' " borrowed its title from a highly successful ad campaign launched in the eighties by the Convention Center's sales staff. One of the most interesting articles was "Nevada's Business Frontier," written by David W. Toll, author of *The Compleat Nevada Traveler*. Toll emphasized Nevada's efforts to attract new industries into the state; and as he pointed out, American businessmen were "getting Nevada's Message."

Although articles like Toll's provided useful information about Nevada's economic life and business potential, others did little more than reiterate what was by 1986 a set of familiar clichés. The world of advertising had come of age in the last decades of the twentieth century, however, and the use of clichés was now guided by sophisticated semiotic analysis. The symbols employed in the articles were designed to stimulate interest in Las Vegas and to encourage participation in the June Rotary convention. The overall impact of *The Rotarian* pieces was both powerful and alluring. Few images of Nevada could have been more artfully prepared or more favorably presented.

A final constellation of images emerging out of the periodical literature revolved around the notion that Nevada, specifically Las Vegas, was *avant-garde*. This idea was first expressed in a February 1964 *Esquire* story entitled, "Las Vegas (What?). Las Vegas (Can't Hear You! Too Noisy). Las Vegas!!!!" written by Thomas K.

Wolfe. In the article Wolfe described the "sexually provocative dress" of the city's female inhabitants; the mind-warping, sense-dulling, "psychedelic" effect of its casino interiors; and the "Baroque Modern" architecture of its electric signs. The art forms Wolfe unearthed in Las Vegas defied traditional artistic categories, foretold things yet to come, and placed the city on the cutting edge of contemporary culture. Las Vegas's revolutionary "look," Wolfe believed, was an extension of the aesthetic sensibilities of its founding father: Bugsy Siegel. In the deserts of Nevada Siegel had fashioned a "Monte Carlo" for the "lumpen-bourgeoisie." Its artistic forms trumpeted a new age in the cultural history of man.

Wolfe used his Las Vegas piece to lead his collection of essays on contemporary culture: *The Kandy-Kolored Tangerine-Flake Streamline Baby* (1965). In the introduction to the work he returned to the idea that Las Vegas was *avant-garde*. Its culture was not a product of New York's "Café Society," and owed nothing, therefore, to the traditional artistic tastes of America's aristocratic elite. As such it was a genuine expression of the artistic sensibilities of the common man. Filled with their dreams and images, Las Vegas was a "super-hyper-version" of a whole "new style of life" in America. Las Vegas's artistic forms, Wolfe predicted, would shape American culture long after its "influence as a gambling heaven has gone."

Two architects who were at least partially inspired by Wolfe's insights were Robert Venturi and Denise Scott Brown. In a March 1968 article for *Architectural Forum*, they built upon Wolfe's contention that Las Vegas represented a new style in American life. The article, entitled "A Significance for A&P Parking Lots, or Learning from Las Vegas," suggested that architectural styles encountered in Las Vegas were characteristic of an entirely new urban form and were worthy, therefore, of serious study by architects.[12] In the fall of that same year, Venturi and Brown conducted a studio scrutinizing Las Vegas's urban forms at the Yale School of Art and Architecture. The findings of this research project supported the position they had put forth in their original Las Vegas article. Both were subsequently published in 1972 in *Learning from Las Vegas: The Forgotten Symbolism of Architectural Form*, which they wrote with Steven Izenour.

Learning from Las Vegas was one of the most controversial works on architecture published during the decade of the seventies. The authors argued that architects could learn from Las Vegas, that "Great Proletarian Cultural Locomotive."[13] Through the skillful manipulation of images drawn from pop culture, the architects and artists who designed Las Vegas's buildings and signs created structures that were inexpensive and yet appealed to the tastes of the common man. By treating Las Vegas as a subject worthy of serious scholarly concern, they elevated the study of its cultural designs into the realm of social and artistic criticism. In effect, "fun-loving" Las Vegas had become a subject worthy of serious scholarly analysis.

Robert Hughes, for example, the Australian-born art critic for *Time* magazine, wrote and narrated "The Shock of the New," an eight-part television series on the history of modern art. The 1979 BBC production included a discussion of Las Vegas. In 1980 Hughes transformed his work into a book bearing the same name. In Las Vegas, Hughes claimed, "the idea of art simply evaporates." It is overcome by "the stronger illusions with which this place is saturated: sudden wealth, endless orgasm, Dean Martin." Here "only the signs are real." The city itself "is a work of art: bad art, but art all the same." Following Venturi's lead, Hughes saw the "manic inclusiveness" of Las Vegas imagery as the "final refutation" of "high culture." Parodying "all cultures from Augustan Rome to Sinatra Shag," Las Vegas could only be "experienced in a mode of ironic removal." Modern art had lost its critical edge because it was overwhelmed by the "commercial extravaganzas" of real life. In effect, Hughes implied, modern art had been deprived of its critical function in Las Vegas, because the city itself was a metaphor of modern life.

Another contemporary critic who ventured to Las Vegas was the French sociologist Jean Baudrillard. Like explorers in times past, he recorded his impressions as a stranger in a strange land, and published them in *Amérique* in 1986. This work was translated two years later into English. The America that Baudrillard sought was "*astral* America . . . not the deep America of mores and mentalities, but the America of desert speed, of motels and mineral surfaces." What Baudrillard was seeking was Shangri-la: a land with "no origin or mythical authenticity," a nation with "no past and no founding truth." Like the children of Israel he wandered for a time in the meaningless deserts of America's cities and California, and then, with an unerring instinct, he pointed his car toward Las Vegas.

In Las Vegas Baudrillard found exactly what he had been looking for: an artificial paradise, a "hologram" of American life, a "mirage," a true cultural desert set in a natural desert. And gambling itself was a true "desert form." It was "inhuman, uncultured, initiatory . . . a crazed activity on the fringes of exchange." Las Vegas was the "hidden face" of the desert. The desert was the "acme of secrecy and silence," and Las Vegas was the "acme of prostitution and theatricality." The one mirrored the other.

Las Vegas possessed an irony and cunning of its own, however. Having been exposed as decadent by Baudrillard, it has metamorphosed and become a pilgrimage point for other intellectuals and social critics. Desiring to experience, firsthand, the malaise of modern life, they have merely added to the city's campy and kitsch mystique.

The meaning of Las Vegas for the average citizen was captured not by cultural critics, but by Mario Puzo. In a "coffee-table" book entitled *Inside Las Vegas*, published in 1976, Puzo, a self-confessed (but reformed) gambler, explained that there was no reason for Las Vegas to exist except for gambling.[14] Gambling, after all, was "one of the primary drives of mankind." The common man gambled because he was hoping for a miracle, and in Las Vegas a miracle could happen. Gambling was "an act of faith, possibly by the devil." People came to "Vegas to gamble and pray for miracles." They would probably lose, but even if they lost they would have escaped reality for a short time and in the process been surrounded by beautiful women and treated like royalty. This was what made it "perhaps the best-known city in the entire world."

Puzo had himself, of course, contributed to making Las Vegas one of the "best-known" cities in the world. His epic novel *The Godfather* (1969) used Las Vegas as one of the many sites in which its action unfolds. *The Godfather* told of the Corleone family's rise to power in the sinister New York underworld, and of its struggle to maintain itself in a hostile setting. By the time Puzo wrote *The Godfather* in the 1960s, the saga of Nevada and organized crime was well known. Bugsy Siegel and company had moved into Las Vegas's casinos during the 1940s, and this invasion of the state by the mob, and the violence that followed in its wake, had been duly noted in the press. The events associated with the Mafia takeover of Nevada's casinos were public knowledge, and numerous novelists were exploiting the city's tarnished image in adventure stories that highlighted Mafia themes. It was natural, then, for Puzo to employ Las Vegas imagery in his Mafia novel.

Part of *The Godfather*'s appeal was that it could be interpreted at many levels. At one level it was an exciting and glamorous portrayal of the inner workings of the Mafia, a subject that attracted many Americans precisely because it was veiled from their vision. At a second level it was the story of a family's struggle to perpetuate and preserve itself across generations, a recurrent theme and a problem in Western culture at least since the time of the Greeks. Finally, it touched on the immigrant experience in America. Displaying sound sociological instincts, Puzo revealed how some immigrants, when barred from advancing in American life through the socially acceptable channels, created their own illegitimate pathways to opportunity. This aspect of his book led John G. Cawelti to criticize Puzo for depicting the Corleone family "as basically good and decent people who have had to turn to crime in order to survive . . . in a corrupt and unjust society."[15]

Although the original novel did not center on Las Vegas, Puzo used the city as a stage for some of its most shocking—and therefore best remembered—chapters. He also included in his tale a description of the Mafia's early penetration into Nevada's casinos. Since 1969 over thirteen million copies of *The Godfather* have been sold. A best-selling novel of the 1970s, it generated three major films—the second of which included many scenes set in Nevada. Directed by Francis Ford Coppola, and featuring such actors as Marlon Brando, Al Pacino, James Caan, Talia Shire, Robert Duvall, and Diane Keaton, *The Godfather* trilogy constituted one of the great epics of American cinema. Through the artistry of Puzo and Coppola, the legend of Mafia activity in Nevada became a part of our nation's mythical heritage.

Puzo was not the only writer, however, to exploit Las Vegas's reputation as a "paradise" of the underworld. One of the most prolific fiction motifs associated with Nevada, in fact, was the saga of Las Vegas and organized crime. Such novels as Jack Waer's *Murder in Las Vegas* (1955), W. T. Ballard's *Chance Elson* (1958) and *Murder Las Vegas Style* (1970), Hal Kantor's *The Vegas Trap* (1970), and Don Pendleton's *The Executioner: Vegas Vendetta* (1971) employed Las Vegas imagery in their work, and contributed to the creation of an entire literary genre which could be entitled "Nevada and the Mob."

Although the literary quality of these novels varied, an analysis of the images displayed on their covers and the impact on readers reveals much about the general public's perception of Nevada. Companies marketing such texts employed what Stephen J. Gould recently called the "iconography of persuasion" in planning their sales efforts. Realizing that the images conveyed on a book's cover must "click" with a potential consumer in an instant, the ideal image for marketing was something "immediately grasped and viscerally understood by all." An analysis of the images employed to sell these novels reveals that those marketing them believed a well-worn Nevada trilogy—sex, gambling, and violence—appealed to the consuming public (not a particularly novel insight); and that it readily associated these themes with Nevada and the "Mafia."

The cover of *The Vegas Trap*, for example, displayed three figures: two men, both holding guns, and a blond woman in a tight dress. All were standing on an enormous green felt gambling table, stacked with gargantuan poker chips and dice. One of the men and the woman were hiding behind one stack of chips, while the other was shooting at them. In addition, a blurb on the cover told the potential consumer: "The chips are down and so are the chippies when a Mafia muscle-man gambles his life in the biggest 'scam' game ever to hit the Strip."

Although Las Vegas was invaded by the mob in the forties, it had to wait until the 1960s to be confronted with real decadence. This time the alien force intruding into the community was the drug culture. The saga of its penetration was recorded by Hunter S. Thompson in *Fear and Loathing in Las Vegas: A Savage Journey to the Heart of the American Dream* (1971). Thompson, the nation's best known "gonzo" journalist, originally published the work in two parts in *Rolling Stone* under the name "Raoul Duke," the persona, or at least the alias of the persona, that he assumed in the novel. Written in the first person, Duke told the story of a sex-crazed, brutish, and drug-driven sojourn that he and his Samoan attorney made into Nevada: "the last known home of the Manson family."

Although technically visiting Las Vegas "on assignment," Duke and his attorney were actually there to cover the "main story" of their "generation"; its flight from reality through drugs after the political collapse of the sixties. In flashes of insight—interspersed with drug-induced delusions and graphic descriptions of "carnivorous plants," "plastic palm trees," and the "caricatures of used-car dealers from Dallas" that populate Las Vegas's casinos—Thompson recounted the history of the sixties and analyzed the causes of the collapse.

In his hands Las Vegas was treated as a paranoiac metaphor, like drugs, for a flight from reality. It was the place where you went when "the weasels start[ed] closing in" during the "doomstruck era of Nixon." Las Vegas thus constituted a safe haven for disillusioned Love Children and acid freaks, because no one cared what they did there as long as they "tipped big." In Las Vegas a man could make himself a brute, and thus rid himself, as Dr. Johnson said, "of the pain of being a man." Thompson opened his work with this quote, and its end was contained in its beginning. Outdoing Tom Wolfe's foray into the Las Vegas of the 1960s in terms of sheer cynicism, Thompson closed out the decade with a despairing portrait of Nevada.

In truth, Las Vegas was a chameleon. In the last decades of the twentieth century the city of gaudy illusion came to represent many things to many people. Perhaps Baudrillard was at least partially right when he described it as a mirage. The city appeared a mirage; but only a mirage, as Puzo pointed out, because people live in a world that unceasingly craves illusions. Las Vegas seemed to be the fun-house mirror image of man's conscience, reflecting what he feared to be the truth about himself and his time.

While the contemporary images of Nevada contained in the nation's newspapers, periodicals, works of cultural criticism, and paperback novels are powerful and descriptive, they do not exhaust the literary attention Nevada received over the last forty years. The images associated with Nevada's frontier heritage and its wilderness environment were potent and, as in the past, some of the nation's best novelists were attracted to their siren call.

Nevada's wilderness environment and its frontier mystique have been popular subjects among American novelists at least since the days of the Comstock: J. Ross Browne, Mark Twain, and Dan De Quille all earned their reputations by first writing about their experiences in Nevada. In the early twentieth century such novelists as Bertha Muzzy Bower, Miriam Michelson, and Harry Sinclair Drago continued to explore wilderness themes and the frontier experience in their Nevada works. Despite their limited capacities as forms, these

motifs have remained a vital, expressive element in American literature.

Their continuing appeal in the last half of the twentieth century can be largely attributed to Walter Van Tilburg Clark, an eastern-
born, Nevada-reared author of three major novels and numerous short
stories. Perhaps no local writer has achieved the status of Clark. In
addition to publishing *The City of Trembling Leaves*, he wrote two
other novels during the 1940s that were so forceful they defined for a
generation the mythical contours of Nevada's wilderness and the epic
proportions of its inhabitants: *The Ox-Bow Incident* (1940) and *The
Track of the Cat* (1949).

In *The Ox-Bow Incident* it was the people, not the land, that was
emphasized. Using Nevada's mountains as a backdrop, and the ele-
mental forces of nature—wind, storm, and night—to set a foreboding
stage, Clark unfolded a narrative of outraged justice and human folly
on the Western frontier that transcended the confines of regional
themes and elevated his work to the status of timeless literature.
Employing the story of a Nevada lynching, Clark probed the ethical
demands that civilization imposed upon humanity and showed how
illusion and weakness could shatter those ethical imperatives. Clark
forcefully underscored the universal nature of this Nevada parable.
The human drama, he implied, was constant, whether it unfolded in
a borderland town or in the midst of a populous city. In Clark's hands
Nevada's inhabitants were neither diminished nor impugned by the
eccentric qualities of their character, but typified all of humankind.
The image that unfolded of Nevada's people negated the caricatures
and vacuous stereotypes so often employed in Western literature.

Clark returned to the theme in *The Track of the Cat*, except that
now he treated the land and its inhabitants as one. In a story of the
internal conflicts, intense passions, and broken dreams that haunted
and destroyed a Nevada ranch family, Clark used the ruination of his
characters to expose the tragedy of man's relentless struggle against
Nature. In this epic the wilderness was not merely a passive stage
upon which a human drama unfolded, but it was an active player in
the scenario. Employing the archetypical symbol of a black panther
to typify the forces of chaos in nature, and the mountains to represent
nature's awesome strength, Clark told a tale of two brothers' quest for
a mountain lion that was ravaging their cattle. In the process of this

hunt both brothers were slain by the black cat. Although the third brother finally triumphed over the cat the victory was hollow, for the family had itself already crumbled. The petty efforts of men to impose an alien order on nature, Clark implied, would always be doomed to destruction. Anticipating the works of Edward Abbey, Clark taught that humanity's salvation rests in a mystical and circumspect union of man and nature.

Few literary works have exerted as profound an influence over Nevada imagery as *The Ox-Bow Incident* and *The Track of the Cat.* Both received high literary acclaim, and both were hailed as either the best or among the best novels ever written in their genre.[16] Max Westbrook, underscoring Clark's use of archetypical images, believed Clark's novels transcended "mere regionalism," and asserted that Clark strove to create an "American sacrality": the unification of man's sacred self with the historical self that is the product of American democracy. Although Westbrook believed that Clark ultimately failed in his attempt, his career still represented "one of the boldest efforts in American literary history."[17]

The Track of the Cat and *The Ox-Bow Incident* were popular not only with literary critics. In 1943 *The Ox-Bow* was transformed into a major motion picture by Twentieth Century Fox. Directed by William Wellman, and starring such actors as Henry Fonda, Dana Andrews, Mary Beth Hughes, and Anthony Quinn, the film—like the book— was one of the classics of the 1940s. In 1954 *The Track of the Cat* was converted into a movie by Warner Brothers. It was also directed by William Wellman and featured Robert Mitchum, Tab Hunter, Teresa Wright, and William Hopper. Although not as successful as *The Ox-Bow*, it nevertheless helped to imprint Clark's image of Nevada upon the American mind. It was not only America, however, that was impressed with Clark's accomplishments. By the time of his death in 1971 Clark's works had "been translated into twenty languages, including Arabic, Urdu, Korean, and Japanese."[18]

Clark's work was significant in our study of Nevada imagery not only because of its international appeal but because he revealed how Nevada's frontier heritage and its wilderness environment could be employed in the creation of timeless literature. Serious literary investigations of the Nevada wilderness and its frontier experience would continue throughout the remaining years of the twentieth century.

Authors like George Stewart in *Sheep Rock* (1951), Joaquina Ballard Howles in *No More Giants* (1966), and Walter C. Wilson in *The Oneness Trail* (1956) would continue to explore the effects of Nevada's vast and brutal environment on the human character; authors like James M. Cain in *Past All Dishonor* (1946), Octavus Roy Cohen in *Borrasca* (1955), and Robert Laxalt probed the meaning of both the old and the new frontier experience.[19]

One of the most powerful interpretations of the modern frontier is found in the writings of Robert Laxalt. Laxalt, the son of a Basque sheepherder, was raised in Nevada and knows its land and people as only a Nevadan can. The author of such works as *Sweet Promised Land* (1957), *A Man in the Wheatfield* (1964), and *The Basque Hotel* (1990), Laxalt excelled at portraying the immigrant experience in the state. In Laxalt's works the common man held center stage, depicted with a Jeffersonian nobility and unsurpassed grandeur. Laxalt's narratives revealed the communion that existed between the land and the men who work it. He reminded his readers that heroism was most truly found in the simplicity and dignity of an honest man, and that it was the labor of common men and women that laid claim to Nevada's forbidding wilderness.

His most famous work, *Sweet Promised Land*, was a sympathetic and touching portrayal of his father, Dominique. A native of the French Pyrenees, Dominique had come to Nevada as a young man to earn his fortune. The descendant of generations of Basque sheepherders, he had learned this skill at an early age and had applied it in the lonely expanses of the Nevada wilderness. Although he had always intended to return to his native land, Dominique became deeply involved with the challenge of rearing sheep on the barren slopes of the Nevada hills. Forty-seven years later Dominique returned for a visit to his native France. Robert accompanied Dominique on the nostalgic return to his father's birthplace, and he recounts this experience and his father's reminiscences of his life in Nevada in *Sweet Promised Land*.

The scholar of Basque life, William A. Douglass, described the book as a "classic" and noted that it was "more than a simple literary triumph." Published in 1957, the book arrived on America's literary stage, Douglass believed, at the dawn of a new era. For years the nation had forgotten, perhaps even repressed, its immigrant heritage, and only in the sixties would it strive to recover this part of its past.

Although *Sweet Promised Land* recounted the struggle of only one man who sought to make America his home, the truth of his tale embodied the experiences of countless first-generation Americans. The work quickly received high critical acclaim. The National Book Society in England made it one of their first selections, and it was an alternate of the Literary Guild in the United States. Further, it was translated into both German and French and won praise from such American authors as William Saroyan and Tom Lea.

Few Nevada works captured the nation's imagination as did *Sweet Promised Land*. The *Miami Herald* proclaimed that Laxalt spoke "not only for the Basques but for the Italians and the Yugoslavs, for the Swedes and the Irish, the Portuguese and the Greeks—all our second-generation citizens. Rarely have they had a more eloquent spokesman." Henry Greene, writing for the *Chicago Sunday Tribune*, claimed "This is one to warm the cockles of your heart. . . . It has humor, tenderness, adventure." And Dan Wickenden in the *New York Herald Tribune Sunday Book Review* stated, "What makes [the book] so moving is its author's subtle perception and the skill with which he has expressed the curiously tangled emotions of a man who could not himself have found words for them."[20]

Another fine portrayal of the Nevada frontier was found in the writings of Edward Loomis. Loomis's image of Nevada unfolded in two short stories, "Heroic Love" and "Mustangs," and in a novel, *The Hunter Deep in Summer* (1961).[21] In these works he examined the painful process human beings must endure when they are deprived of their virtues, their heroes, and their innocence. "Heroic Love" recounted the sexual corruption and Samson-like fall of a young Nevada rancher; "Mustangs" focused on a young man's disenchantment when he discovered his cowboy hero had feet of clay; and *The Hunter Deep in Summer* narrated the final despair and disillusionment of an aging idealist.

In these tales Loomis revealed not only the fall of man, but also of the land. In each story Nevada's mountains and desert expanses served as the unspoiled counterpoint to a corrupt civilization. Civilization was represented by "Albo," the home of Loomis's characters. Albo was a mythical California border town, lying on the highway somewhere between Reno and Los Angeles. In the days of its youth it had been a cattle and mining town and had embodied the nobility and virtue of the frontier. During the forties, however, the automobile corrupted Albo and it was transformed into a glittering tourist town that had lost its innocence. It became California.

Just ten miles down the road, however, lay Nevada, the birth-place of heroes and the home of the last noble savage. Its majestic, "light-filled" desert mountains, its "desolate valleys," and its "forests of juniper and piñon pine" were beyond civilization and thus free of its evils. A stark, violent, pure wilderness, in Nevada man was still a hunter, unspoiled by civilized decay. It was the place to which disillusioned idealists fled in search of spiritual renewal.

Loomis's Nevada was a frontier land that had lost none of its virtue, a place where man and nature were still joined in a pristine embrace. This primal unity was haunted, however, by the specter of potential corruption and decay metaphorically lying across the bor-der in California. Loomis's image of Nevada was important because he underscored the recuperative power of its wilderness, a theme often overlooked in contemporary renderings. A stark departure from images that were so often preoccupied with its decay, in Loomis's hands Nevada emerged as pure and inviolate.

A peculiarly successful fictional interpretation of the frontier ex-perience was seen in the popular television series "Bonanza." This saga of a family dwelling on the beautiful Ponderosa Ranch near Lake Tahoe was one of America's longest-running television series, extending from 1959 until 1973. The popularity of the series and its longevity helped to define for a generation the meaning of Nevada's Western heritage. Although the program offered a highly idealized vision of the state's history, few Americans were untouched by the series, and most were overwhelmed by the spectacular views of the Sierra Nevada that opened its various segments.

Although novelists like Clark, *litterateurs* like Beebe, and his-tory buffs like Murbarger formulated their images of Nevada's mining heritage on the basis of their historical knowledge, John Seabrook, in a thirty-page piece for the *New Yorker* in 1989, entitled "Invisible Gold," did not have to turn to the past when he constructed his image of a Nevada gold rush. The gold rush Seabrook was covering was the one that is going on in the deserts of Nevada today.

During the 1970s the United States government abandoned its efforts to control the price of gold, and the market value of the pre-cious metal skyrocketed. As the price of gold soared, Nevada once again became a promised land. Deposits of gold previously defined as too expensive to mine suddenly became bonanzas.

One hundred and one major mines were operating in Nevada in 1990, and sixty-seven of those were mining gold, silver, or both metals. In 1987 Nevada mines produced 2.7 million ounces of gold, in 1988 3.7 million ounces, and in 1989 a record 5 million ounces. Nevada now produces more gold than any other state in the nation, and it ranks alongside "Canada and Australia for third place among top world gold producers. South Africa and the Soviet Union head the list."[22]

Once again there is gold in Nevada, once again miners pour into the state seeking their fortune, and once again desert towns boom with excitement. The glory days of the Comstock have returned, and along with them image makers like Seabrook are describing the state's "gritty, salt-flavored wind." Mining towns look like "desert mirages" in the day and like oases of neon at night. Historic yet current, wealthy yet hardscrabble, elusive yet tangible, Nevada images still roll across America; indeed they roll around the world and continue to defy predictions, expectations, and reality.

CHAPTER VII

Like a vine from a compost into images and words,

feeling their way into a culture.

—Gretel Ehrlich

Image, myth, mystique, nuance, and related expressive nouns have become everyday staples for business, for writers, and for Hollywood promotionals. Arnold Schwarzenegger consistently tells reporters that his "greatest creation is his image." The poet and western writer Gretel Ehrlich explains that our image of a cowboy riding alone into the sunset has evolved from myth organically grown "like a vine from a compost into images and words, feeling their way into a culture." The geographer-writers of *Western Images, Western Landscapes* (1989) suggest that new images may be needed to suit the complexity of the modern West. In the face of rapid change, perhaps only the essence of the West is to be maintained, and that through image.

Author-critic William Kittredge explains that the West "breaks our hearts" because of its beauty and promise, which has so often ended in a "cold and boring and lonesome and lost" human existence. "We have been taught to live in images" and to live for the "desire in the image." The French sociologist and observer of Nevada life, Jean Baudrillard, notes in *America* (1988) that images "are not something to dream about; they are the dream." Concocted out of concoctions, they blind and replace what might be true, or what might have been.

But in the traditional academic sense, Nevada floundered in evolving the more basic and formal images and myths. Differing from most regions of the country, the voice of the community did not appear in story after story, nor did the gossip, rumor, and innuendo blend into a repetitive and stubborn history. Nevada was much too

unstable to respond to the residue of its past. Although geographically isolated, the larger world with its affairs always seemed to attract
notice, and there was little opportunity for sensitive writers to witness studied lives or report on broken bodies and frustrated passions.
W. B. Yeats could brag that every river and mountain in Ireland was
associated with at least one deeply implanted legend. And T. S. Eliot
explained that tradition was something you had to work at, "you create it as time passes." But Nevadans had neither the time not the
permanence to reflect or to regret, to fear guilt, or to brood over
betrayal.

The hundreds of stories that might have flowed from the men
who built the railroads, founded the ranches, dug the ore, or raised
the dams never appeared. One is reminded of an Anatole France story.
A Roman asked Pontius Pilate late in life about Jesus, and Pilate responded, "I cannot call him to mind." Most Nevada transients easily
forgot their "drifting in the wilderness." Even Mark Twain, who spent
a few months in California as compared to a few years in Nevada,
often claimed "California blood" while remembering Nevada as "a
young man's joke," "a passing amusement," and "a mistake on the way
to California."

According to students of society the lack of roots has led to negative reactions in and negative images of the state. It created a Nevada
particularly vulnerable to confusion, depression, violence, and suicide. Deep mythical and spiritual forms grounded in tradition would
have provided greater cohesion and meaning for the ever-shifting
society. "A healthy society gives its members relief from neurotic guilt
and excessive anxiety through myth." In short, when historians rather
pompously declare that "Nothing is so unpredictable as the past," it
falls to myth and image to fill the vacuum, to provide the roots and
substance and hope. These same roots could have helped to foment
the great literature, popular belief, and other constructive cultural
manifestations upon which a healthy society rests.

Despite the modest and mixed collage of human reactions growing out of the nineteenth century, it was natural geography that
overshadowed all other images. The riveting and desolate landscape
was caught by many an anonymous bard and occasionally by one who
elevated it into an image of poetic delight. "Its mountains rise up like
waves from the pewter sagebrush sea and sail over the land in dusty

ranks, the grey-shawled granite of the Ruby Dome stretching up in the midst of them like wild horses breaking from the falcon-colored desert, wavering with the heat of the sun."

Soon after the turn of the century, however, the overwhelming desert motif gave way to human design based on technical idiom. The grand image came to be a refusal by the state to accept cautionary reality. Nevada refused to believe that there was no more gold or silver. It refused to believe that there was not enough water. It refused to accept established social norms. And as time passed, it refused to believe that revenues from tourists were reaching a plateau, but continued to demand that each annual income statement must surpass the last. In short, it refused to believe that there was no more and against all logic it came to believe that only growth could be tolerated. In Nevada the dominant image has been that the lights must never go out; the music must always play; the movie must never end. The state long ago adopted Buffalo Bill's theme, that past and present are just a form of entertainment. Therefore, Nevada created an uncompromising horizon, a land of immediate destiny. While always "colouring overmuch," often luminous and vulgar, and seldom translating myth or fostering historic change, nevertheless, Nevada has been provided with a unique image of perpetual movement and an indefinable spontaneity.

Perhaps the term "mirage" even more than "image" can telescope Nevada's last 150 years into a single progressive concept. The typical Western mirage of blue lakes and snowy mountains generally passed quickly and left the famished traveler with the grey desert and the burning sun. Unfortunately for hundreds of migrants to early Nevada, their hope was almost as short-lived as the mirage. But over the decades, man with new technology has reworked the human environment into a more pleasing and attractive reality. By late twentieth century, the mirage had come to represent a seemingly exaggerated expectation shaped into a practical everyday enterprise. For example, within one giant hotel complex, the Las Vegas Mirage provides waterfalls, a blue lake, and a humid green oasis stretching beneath luxuriant palms. Man has reshaped a frightening illusion into a pleasing and profitable concept. He has denied the logic of philosophers from Cicero to Daniel Boorstin. Cicero supported image and education because it rescued man from "the tyranny of the present," and Boorstin argues that myth, like history, "protects us from our own illusions." Contemporary Nevada, perhaps more than any other society in history, is the product of the present and a child of the grand illusion.

NOTES

Overview

1. Horace Greeley, *An Overland Journey, from New York to San Francisco, in the Summer of 1859* (New York: C. M. Saxton, Barker & Co., 1860), pp. 270–76.

2. Survey conducted by the authors.

3. Information supplied by Tara S. McCarty, director of the Cowboy Poetry Gathering in Elko, Nevada.

4. In the 1980s the Frenchman Jean Baudrillard in *America* reversed the scenario. He saw the desert as distinctly and uniquely American. Nevada deserts were not "theatrical like an Alpine landscape," not "eroded and monotonous like the sub-lunar Australian desert," not "mystical like the deserts of Islam." From *America*, trans. by Chris Turner (London: Verso, 1988), p. 69.

5. Idah Meacham Strobridge, *In Miners' Mirage-Land* (Los Angeles: Baumgardt Publishing, 1904), pp. 1, 26.

6. The articles were pulled together and published in 1918. John Muir, edited by William Frederic Badè, *Steep Trails* (Boston: Houghton Mifflin Co., 1918), p. 195.

7. Richard G. Lillard, *Desert Challenge: An Interpretation of Nevada* (New York: Alfred A. Knopf, 1942), p. 107.

8. Basil Woon, *Incredible Land* (New York: Liveright Publishing Corp., 1933). Also see *Nevada State Journal*, June 5, 1974.

9. *The Secret Diary of Harold L. Ickes. The Inside Struggle, 1936–1939*, vol. II (New York: Simon and Schuster, 1954), p. 581.

10. Robert D. Herman, editor, *Gambling* (New York: Harper & Row, 1967), p. 232.

11. Robert H. Ferrell, editor, *Off the Record: The Private Papers of Harry S Truman* (New York: Harper and Row Publishers, 1980), p. 317.

12. Robert D. Herman, *Gambling*, p. 232.

13. Tom Dunkel, "New Sources of Wealth Put Vegas in the Chips," *Insight*, March 5, 1990, p. 17.

14. Jean Baudrillard, *America*, pp. 2–3, 95, 123.

15. Ibid, p. 67.

16. Ibid, p. 128.

17. I am indebted to Professor John H. Irsfeld for assistance in evaluating and presenting the Las Vegas fiction. Also see John H. Irsfeld, "Las Vegas: West Egg?" in *Halcyon: A Journal of the Humanities* (Reno: University of Nevada Press, 1985), pp. 133–42.

18. Neil Postman, *Amusing Ourselves to Death: Public Discourse in the Age of Show Business* (New York: Viking, 1985), pp. 92–93.

19. I am indebted to Professor Charles R. Greenhaw for assistance with current literature on rural Nevada.

20. Tom Robbins, "The Real Valley of the Dolls," *Esquire*, December 1988, p. 205.

21. Bill Barich, "Desert Dreams," *Esquire*, June 1985, p. 320.

22. "Dropping on the Rubies," *Condé Nast—Travel Magazine*, January 1990, p. 90.

Chapter I

1. John C. Ewers, editor, *Adventures of Zenas Leonard, Fur Trader* (Norman: University of Oklahoma Press, 1959), p. 128.

2. *The Works of Hubert Howe Bancroft* (San Francisco: The History Company, Publishers, 1890), Vol. XXV, pp. 1–15.

3. James H. Simpson, *Report of Explorations Across the Great Basin of the Territory of Utah . . . in 1859* (Reno: University of Nevada Press, 1983), pp. 69, 91. James Hulse, "Captain Simpson of the United States Army," *Nevada Highways and Parks*, Special Centennial Issue, 1964, pp. 21–25.

4. For a moving account of the overland passage see Harold Curran, *Fearful Crossing: The Central Overland Trail Through Nevada* (Reno: Great Basin Press, 1982), pp. 29–32, 151.

5. John Mack Faragher, *Women and Men on the Overland Trail* (New Haven: Yale University Press, 1979), p. 195. John D. Unruh, Jr., *The Plains Across: The Overland Emigrants and the Trans-Mississippi West, 1840–60* (Urbana: University of Illinois Press, 1979).

6. For detailed coverage of the Mormon exodus from Western Nevada see Effie Mona Mack, *Nevada* (Glendale: Arthur H. Clark, 1936), pp. 143–72.

7. David Thompson, compiler, *The Tennessee Letters: From Carson Valley, 1857–1860.* (Reno: Grace Dangberg Foundation, 1983), p. 66.

8. Richard G. Lillard and Mary V. Hood, *Hank Monk and Horace Greeley: An Enduring Episode in Western History* (Georgetown, CA: Wilmac Press, 1973), pp. 7–8.

9. Horace Greeley, *An Overland Journey From New York to San Francisco in the Summer of 1859* (New York: Alfred A. Knopf, 1964), pp. 225–36.

10. Ibid.

Chapter II

1. J. Ross Browne, *A Peep at Washoe and Washoe Revisited* (Balboa Island, Calif.: Paisano Press, 1959), pp. 1–30, 57–64, 134–36, 178.

2. There is an extensive body of literature dealing with Mark Twain in Nevada. In particular see Paul Fatout, *Mark Twain in Virginia City* (Bloomington: Indiana University Press, 1964).

3. Patricia Nelson Limerick, *Desert Passages* (Albuquerque: University of New Mexico Press, 1985), pp. 61–76.

4. John J. Pullen, "Mark Twain and Artemus Ward: A Bittersweet Friendship is Born in Nevada," *Nevada Historical Society Quarterly*, Fall 1979, pp. 163–85; Richard G. Lillard, *Desert Challenge* (New York: Alfred A. Knopf, 1942), p. 35.

5. Dan De Quille, *Washoe Rambles*, with an introduction by Richard E. Lingenfelter (Los Angeles: Westernlore Press, 1963), Chapter XII.

6. Wilbur S. Shepperson, "Sir Charles Wentworth Dilke: A Republican Baronet in Nevada," *Nevada Historical Society Quarterly*, Fall–Winter 1960), pp. 13–29.

7. John Muir, *Steep Trails*, Chapter XII.

8. Ibid., Chapter XVI.

9. Robert Louis Stevenson, *From Scotland to Silverado*, edited by James D. Hart (Cambridge: The Belknap Press, 1916).

10. Richard C. Datin, "A Wilde Time in Nevada," *The Nevadian*, October 1980, pp. 5, 36.

11. Henry De Groot, "Mining on the Pacific Coast," *The Overland Monthly*, August 1871.

12. The author found almost a hundred articles, editorials, and photographs relating to Nevada while researching in Cornwall during the spring of 1968.

13. Wilbur S. Shepperson, *Restless Strangers: Nevada's Immigrants and Their Interpreters* (Reno: University of Nevada Press, 1970), pp. 178–81, 199–205, 224–27.

14. Henry T. Williams, *The Pacific Tourist* (New York: H. T. Williams, 1876), pp. 172–224.

15. Don D. Fowler, *The Western Photographs of John K. Hillers* (Washington, DC: Smithsonian Institution Press, 1989), pp. 50, 53–54.

16. Richard Reinhardt, *Out West on the Overland Train* (Palo Alto: American West Publishing Co., 1967), pp. 5–9, 111–62.

Chapter III

1. Earl Pomeroy, *In Search of the Golden West* (New York: Alfred A. Knopf, 1957), p. 63.

2. Israel Cook Russell, *Geological History of Lake Lahontan* (Washington, DC: Government Printing Office, 1885), pp. 7–9, 13.

3. Henry R. Mighels, *Sage Brush Leaves* (San Francisco: Edward Bosqui and Co., 1879).

4. Ibid., pp. 19–27, 172–73.

5. Dan De Quille, *A History of the Comstock Silver Lode and Mines* (Virginia City: F. Boegle, 1889), pp. 156–57.

6. Barbara Richnak, *A River Flows: The Life of Robert Lardin Fulton* (Incline Village, Nevada: Comstock-Nevada Publishing, 1983).

7. *Tuscarora Times-Review*, February 29, 1888.

8. Wilbur S. Shepperson, *Retreat to Nevada: A Socialist Colony of World War I* (Reno: University of Nevada Press, 1966), pp. 41–43.

9. William E. Smythe, *The Conquest of Arid America* (New York: Macmillan Co., 1905), Part 3, Chapter VII.

10. Lawrence B. Lee, *Reclaiming the American West* (Santa Barbara: Clio Press, 1980).

11. William E. Smythe, *The Conquest of Arid America*, Part 3, Chapter VII.

12. See the Nevada Historical Society folders on prizefights in Nevada and the personal materials of Phillip I. Earl, curator of history for the society.

Chapter IV

1. James T. Stensvaag, "The Life of My Child," *Nevada Historical Society Quarterly*, Spring 1980. Also see *First Biennial Report of the Nevada Historical Society, 1907–1908*.
2. Wilbur S. Shepperson, *Restless Strangers*, p. 33.
3. *The Pacific Reclamation Company: Farm Lands, Metropolis, Nevada* (Salt Lake City: The Pacific Reclamation Company, 1911). J. Carlos Lambert, *The Metropolis Reclamation Project* (Carson City: State Printing Office, 1925).
4. Wilbur S. Shepperson, *Retreat to Nevada: A Socialist Colony of World War I* (Reno: University of Nevada Press, 1966).
5. Sally Zanjani and Guy Louis Rocha, *The Ignoble Conspiracy* (Reno: University of Nevada Press, 1986). The figures above were compiled from citations listed in the *New York Times Index* under Nevada and related categories.
6. *New York Times*, February 3, 1909, pp. 1–2.
7. *New York Times*, July 3, 1910, p. 5.
8. Wilbur S. Shepperson, *Retreat to Nevada*, Chapter 2.
9. Phillip I. Earl, curator of history at the Nevada Historical Society, has written for local newspapers and has amassed extensive information and valuable materials on Nevada prizefights.
10. Paula Davis, "Crossing Nevada by Auto in 1914," *In Focus* (Annual Journal of the Churchill County Museum Association), 1988–89. Richard G. Lillard, *Desert Challenge* (New York: Alfred A. Knopf, 1949), p. 165. The Nevada Highway Department quickly grew into the largest and busiest agency within the state. The Arrowhead Trail crossing from Utah to Las Vegas to Los Angeles, the Roosevelt Highway from Ely to Tonopah to Mojave, the Victory Highway from Wendover to Elko to Winnemucca to Reno, and the Lincoln Highway from Ely to Carson City were highly advertised between the wars.

Chapter V

1. See "Reno Divorces, 1927 Model," *The Literary Digest*, April 9, 1927, for local and national reaction to the 1927 divorce law.
2. *Nevada State Journal*, May 11, 1931; and Richard G. Lillard, *Desert Challenge*, pp. 38–41.
3. *Congressional Record* (House of Representatives), February 24, 1949, p. 1500.
4. Joseph E. Stevens, *Hoover Dam: An American Adventure* (Norman: University of Oklahoma Press, 1988).
5. There is an extensive body of literature focusing on Hoover Dam. The *New York Times* statistics are based on a survey of the *New York Times Index*. Only articles clearly relating to Nevada were counted.
6. During academic year 1990–91 Tibor Frank visited the University of Nevada, Reno, as a Fulbright Professor. He had discovered the Mariette letters in the von Neumann collection at the Library of Congress and graciously translated them from the Hungarian into English. They were published in the *Nevada Historical Society Quarterly*, Summer 1991.

7. "Taking the Cure in Reno," *The Reno Divorce Racket*, 1931. The nondescript magazine of sixty-six pages contained eight highly sensational illustrated articles opposing the "Divorce Racket." Its flamboyance and many vulgarities seemed to defeat its declared religious sentiments.

8. Bernard Drew, "Nevada as the Pulps Saw Her." *Nevadan*, Sunday, July 23, 1978.

9. Ann Ronald, "Reno, Myth, Mystique, or Madness?" in *Halcyon: A Journal of the Humanities*, 1979; and "Why Don't They Write About Nevada?" *Western American Literature*, Fall 1989.

10. *Reno Evening Gazette*, October 16, 1937; and Phillip I. Earl, "This Was Nevada," *Nevada Appeal*, November 28, 1982.

11. Listed in chronological order, the forty articles are:

    Anne Martin, "Nevada: Beautiful Desert of Buried Hopes," *The Nation*, July 26, 1922.
    John L. Considine, "Primitive Tribunals of Early Nevada," *Sunset*, October 1922.
    John L. Considine, "Sack Senators of the Seventies," *Sunset*, July 1923.
    Katherine Fullerton Gerould, "Reno," *Harper's Magazine*, June 1925.
    Robert L. Duffus, "The Million-Dollar Bluff," *Collier's*, March 13, 1926.
    John L. Considine, "The Holdup at Verdi," *Sunset*, September 1926.
    The Editor, "Reno Divorces, 1927 Model," *The Literary Digest*, April 9, 1927.
    D. E. Cruzan, "The Gold Rush Puts on Dawg," *Collier's*, June 4, 1927.
    Idwal Jones, "A Town is Built," *American Mercury*, July 1927.
    John L. Considine, "Gridley's Wager," *Sunset*, April 1928.
    Grace Hegger Lewis, "Just What is Reno Like," *Scribner's Magazine*, January 1929.
    Genevieve Parkhurst, "In Reno—Where They Take the Cure," *Pictorial Review*, February 1929.
    Bernard De Voto, "Brave Days in Washoe," *The American Mercury*, June 1929.
    Swift Paine, "As We See It in Reno," *The North American Review*, June 1930.
    Judson King, "Open Shop at Boulder Dam," *The New Republic*, June 24, 1931.
    Henry F. Pringle, "Reno the Wicked," *The Outlook*, July 29, 1931.
    Paul Hutchinson, The Nevada Series, *The Christian Century*, November 25, December 2, 9, 16, 1931.
    Anthony M. Turano, "Nevada's Trial of Licensed Gambling," *The American Mercury*, February 1933.
    The Editor, "Passion in the Desert," *Fortune*, April 1934.
    Quentin Reynolds, "Relax in Reno," *Collier's*, December 28, 1935.
    Anthony M. Turano, "Reno the Naughty," *The American Mercury*, February 1936.
    Virginia Kellogg, "So You're Going to Reno," *Cosmopolitan*, December 1937.
    Frank J. Taylor, "Rich Man's Refuge," *Collier's*, February 19, 1938.
    J. B. Griswold, "Wild West," *American Magazine*, May 1938.
    Paul Dorsey, "Wild, Woolly and Wide Open," *Look*, August 13, 1940.
    Juanita Brooks, "The Water's In," *Harper's Magazine*, May 1941.
    Max Miller, "Reno: Honky-Tonk and Trading Post," *Reader's Digest*, August 1941.
    Roger Butterfield, "Harold's Club," *Life*, October 1945.
    W. Robert Moore, "Nevada, Desert Treasure House," *National Geographic Magazine*, January 1946.
    Cameron Shipp, "Blackjack Over Nevada," *Collier's*, September 21, 1946.

Meyer Berger, "The Gay Gamblers of Reno," *Post*, July 10, 1948.

Roger Butterfield, "Elko County," *Life*, April 18, 1949.

Roger Butterfield, "How Reno Lives," *Ladies' Home Journal*, November 1949.

Joseph F. McDonald, "Gambling in Nevada," *The Annals of the American Academy of Political and Social Science*, May 1950.

Robert Kahn, "A is for Atom," *Collier's*, June 21, 1952.

George Sessions Perry, "Cities of America: Reno," *Saturday Evening Post*, July 5, 1952.

Robert Laxalt, "What Has Wide-Open Gambling Done to Nevada," *Saturday Evening Post*, September 20, 1952.

A. J. Liebling, "Out Among the Lamisters," *New Yorker*, March 27, 1954.

A. J. Liebling, "The Mustang Buzzers," *New Yorker*, April 3, 10, 1954.

A. J. Liebling, "The Lake of the Cui-ui Eaters," *New Yorker*, January 1, 8, 15, 22, 1955.

Chapter VI

1. George Sessions Perry, "Cities of America: Reno," *Saturday Evening Post*, July 5, 1952, p. 72.

2. This article was reprinted in the July 15, 1990, Sunday edition of the *Sparks Tribune*. The quotes are taken from the *Sparks Tribune*.

3. Listed in chronological order, the eighty-two articles are:

   Joseph F. McDonald, "Gambling in Nevada," *The Annals of The American Academy of Political and Social Science*, May 1950.

   Robert Cahn, "A is for Atom," *Collier's*, June 21, 1952.

   George Sessions Perry, "Cities of America: Reno," *The Saturday Evening Post*, July 5, 1952.

   Daniel Lang, "Our Far-Flung Correspondents: Blackjack and Flashes," *New Yorker*, September 20, 1952.

   Robert Laxalt, "What Has Wide-Open Gambling Done to Nevada?" *The Saturday Evening Post*, September 20, 1952.

   Lucius Beebe, "Las Vegas," *Holiday*, December 1952.

   "Glittering Legends Surround the Swaggering Cosmopolis That Was Virginia City," *American Heritage*, Spring 1953.

   Lucius Beebe, "Territorial Enterprise and Virginia City News," *American Heritage*, Spring 1953.

   Charles Clegg, "Virginia & Truckee," *American Heritage*, Spring 1953.

   Richard Donovan and Douglass Cater, "Of Gamblers, a Senator, and a Sun That Wouldn't Set," *The Reporter*, June 9, 1953.

   William S. Fairfield, "Las Vegas: The Sucker and the Almost-Even Break," *The Reporter*, June 9, 1953.

   "Mr. Big," *Time*, June 15, 1953.

   "Nevada Fracas," *Newsweek*, June 22, 1953.

   Nell Murbarger, "Lost Rivers of Nevada," *Nature Magazine*, August–September 1953.

   Nell Murbarger, "Our Largest Petrified Tree," *Natural History*, December 1953.

   Freeman Lincoln, "Norman Biltz, Duke of Nevada," *Fortune*, September 1954.

   Ernest Havemann, "Gambler's Paradise Lost," *Life*, October 25, 1954.

John O'Hara, "Appointment with O'Hara," *Colliers*, January 21, 1955.

Lucius Beebe, "Nevada, Heir to the Wild West," *Holiday*, February 1955.

Albert Deutsch, "The Sorry State of Nevada," *Collier's*, March 18, 1955.

Robert O'Brien, "Clamor on the Comstock," *Collier's*, March 16, 1956.

"Fractured Crystal," *Time*, May 21, 1956.

Nell Murbarger, "The Birds of Anaho," *Natural History*, June 1956.

Walter Van Tilburg Clark, "Nevada's Fateful Desert," *Holiday*, November 1957.

Lucius Beebe, "Reno," *Holiday*, November 1958.

Lester Velie, "Las Vegas: The Underworld's Secret Jackpot," *Reader's Guide*, October 1959.

Horace Sutton, "Booked for Travel: A Brave in Squaw Valley," *Saturday Review*, February 6, 1960.

Horace Sutton, "Booked for Travel: Cowboys and Croupiers," *Saturday Review*, March 5, 1960.

"Las Vegas: Home on the Range," drawings by Ronald Searle, *Holiday*, June 1960.

Fred J. Cook, "Gambling, Inc. Treasure Chest of the Underworld," *The Nation*, October 22, 1960.

"They Are Almost Empty of Humankind," *Sunset*, March 1962.

Lucius Beebe, "The Sincere Sinning of the One Sound State," *Saturday Review*, October 20, 1962.

"Where's the Action," *Newsweek*, January 14, 1963.

Thomas K. Wolfe, "Las Vegas (What?). Las Vegas (Can't Hear You! Too Noisy). Las Vegas!!!!," *Esquire*, February 1964.

Nell Murbarger, "Forgotten Industry of the Frontier," *Frontier Times*, April-May 1965.

"Vacation in Las Vegas," *Ebony*, June 1965.

"I Would Like to Live There . . . Las Vegas," *Gambling Illustrated*, December 1965.

John Cronan, "Mr. Las Vegas Says . . . ," *Gambling Illustrated*, December 1965.

Gilman M. Ostrander, "Nevada: The Rotten Borough," *The Nation*, April 18, 1966.

Edward F. Sherman, "Feds, Sharpers and Politics in Nevada," *The New Republic*, October 29, 1966.

Edward F. Sherman, "Nevada: The End of the Casino Era," *Atlantic*, October 1966.

Horace Sutton, "Booked for Travel: Gamesmanship in Nevada," *Saturday Review*, November 4, 1967.

William Murray, "High Old Times in Nevada," *Holiday*, March 1968.

Mrs. Hugh Brown, "Railroad Days, A Memoir of Tonopah, 1904," *American West*, November 1968.

Dick Schaap, "Las Vegas: The Greatest Show-off on Earth," *Holiday*, December 1968.

Ovid Demaris, "You and I Are Very Different From Howard Hughes," *Esquire*, March 1969.

"Investors Take a Chance on Chance," *Business Week*, April 26, 1969.

"Duel of Aces in Las Vegas," *Business Week*, July 12, 1969.

Frank Trippett, "The Suckers," *Look*, May 19, 1970.

Laura Deni, "School for Gamblers," *Ebony*, December 1971.

Phyllis Zauner, "Finding the Real Reno," *Travel*, December 1971.

Pete Axthelm, "Everybody Wants a Piece of the Action," *Newsweek*, April 10, 1972.

"Raw Deal," *Newsweek*, September 17, 1973.

"Mrs. Harrell's Harem," *Newsweek*, October 1, 1973.

Roger M. Williams, "The Oldest Profession in Nevada—and Elsewhere," *Saturday Review/World*, September 7, 1974.

J. Robin Witt, "Compulsive Gamblers: Reno's Lost Souls," *The Christian Century*, October 30, 1974.

Barry Farrell, "The Killing at the Million-Dollar Brothel," *New West*, August 2, 1976.

"Gambling Goes Legit," *Time*, December 6, 1976.

"Taking the Risk Out of Gambling," *Time*, November 21, 1977.

Allen L. Otten, "States in the Gambling Business: It Doesn't Work," *Reader's Digest*, September 1978.

Carey McWilliams, "Second Thoughts," *The Nation*, April 21, 1979.

Heywood Hale Broun, "Gambling as Civic Virtue: Rendering Unto Caesar's World," *The Nation*, June 16, 1979.

Jerome H. Skolnick, "The Social Risks of Casino Gambling," *Psychology Today*, July 1979.

Jonathan Schwartz, "The Gospel According to Vegas," *Gentleman's Quarterly*, January 1980.

Elliot S. Krane, "Behind Closed Doors," *Casino and Cabaret*, May 1981.

Mark Tan, "Las Vegas: New Casinos, New Owners, New Shows," *Casino and Cabaret*, May 1981.

Barb Mulkin, "Only in Las Vegas," *Casino and Cabaret*, May 1981.

James G. McCue, "You Don't Have To Climb For Chukar," *Outdoor Life*, October 1983.

Bill Barich, "Desert Dreams," *Esquire*, June 1985.

John J. Glisch, "Gambling—Still the Number One Game in Town," *The Rotarian*, March 1986.

Richard Menzies, "Beyond the Glitter," *The Rotarian*, March 1986.

David W. Toll, "Nevada's Business Frontier," *The Rotarian*, March 1986.

A. D. Hopkins, "Lively Las Vegas," *The Rotarian*, March 1986.

John Reible, " 'The American Way to Play,' " *The Rotarian*, March 1986.

Rob Powers, "Las Vegas—An International Attraction," *The Rotarian*, March 1986.

Donald Dale Jackson, "The Great Basin Is a Lonely Place for a National Park," *Smithsonian*, November 1987.

G. S. Bush, "Our Youngest National Park," *Travel & Leisure*, March 1988.

Tom Robbins, "The Real Valley of the Dolls," *Esquire*, December 1988.

Douglas H. Chadwick, "Sagebrush Country: America's Outback," *National Geographic*, January 1989.

John Seabrook, "A Reporter At Large: Invisible Gold," *The New Yorker*, April 24, 1989.

Tom Dunkel, "New Sources of Wealth Put Vegas in the Chips," *Insight*, March 5, 1990.

Rich Landers, "Adults Only," *Field & Stream*, Western Edition, September 1990.

4. This expression was originally used by Bernard De Voto to describe San Francisco. Lucius Beebe, however, borrowed it to describe Nevada in "Nevada, Heir to the Wild West," *Holiday*, February 1955, p. 26.

5. "Lucius Beebe, Newspaper Columnist, Author and *Bon Vivant*, Dies at 63," *New York Times*, February 5, 1966, p. 26.

6. Lucius Beebe, "Territorial Enterprise," *American Heritage*, Spring 1953, pp. 67–68.

7. George Sessions Perry, "Reno," *Saturday Evening Post*, July 5, 1952, p. 70.

8. John M. Findlay, *People of Chance: Gambling in American Society from Jamestown to Las Vegas* (New York: Oxford University Press, 1986), p. 156.

9. Jerome H. Skolnick, "The Social Risks of Casino Gambling," *Psychology Today*, July 1979, p. 52.

10. "Gambling Goes Legit," *Time*, December 6, 1976, pp. 54–56.

11. Ibid., p. 56.

12. Robert Venturi, Denise Scott Brown, Steven Izenour, *Learning From Las Vegas: The Forgotten Symbolism of Architectural Form* (Cambridge: MIT Press, 1985), pp. xi–xii; xv–xvi.

13. This term for Las Vegas was coined by Venturi and Brown's students at Yale.

14. This work was described as a "coffee-table" book in "New Sources of Wealth Put Vegas in the Chips," *Insight*, March 5, 1990, p. 10.

15. Ann Evory, editor, *Contemporary Authors*, New Revision Series, Vol. 4 (Detroit: Gale Research Company, 1981), p. 492.

16. Max Westbrook, *Walter Van Tilburg Clark* (New York: Twayne Publishers, Inc., 1969), pp. 54, 93.

17. Ibid., pp. 11, 13, 14.

18. Clare D. Kingman and Mary Ann Tennenhouse, editors, *Contemporary Authors*, First Revision, Vol. 9–12, (Detroit: Gale Research Company, 1974), p. 171.

19. Wilbur S. Shepperson, *Restless Strangers* (Reno: University of Nevada Press, 1970), pp. 176–82, 191–92, 210–13, 242–43.

20. Quotes taken from jacket of Robert Laxalt, *A Man in the Wheatfield* (New York: Harper & Row, 1964).

21. Edward Loomis, "Heroic Love" and "Mustangs," *Heroic Love* (New York: Alfred A. Knopf, 1960).

22. Figures were taken from *Reno Gazette-Journal*, March 18, 1990.

INDEX